THE SIMPLE ANNALS

To past generations, and for those present and still to come.

Let not Ambition mock their useful toil,
Their homely joys and destiny obscure;
Nor Grandeur hear, with a disdainful smile,
The short and simple annals of the poor.

'Elegy Written in a Country Churchyard',
Thomas Gray

THE SIMPLE ANNALS

The History of an Essex and East End Family

Peter Sanders

ALAN SUTTON
1989

ALAN SUTTON PUBLISHING
BRUNSWICK ROAD · GLOUCESTER · UK

ALAN SUTTON PUBLISHING INC
WOLFEBORO · NEW HAMPSHIRE · USA

First published 1989

British Library Cataloguing in Publication Data

Sanders, Peter
The simple annals.
1. England. Social life, history
I. Title
942
ISBN 0-86299-559-0

Library of Congress Cataloging in Publication Data
Applied for

Cover design by Martin Latham
Cover picture: St. Mary's Church, Stansted Mountfichet, and Brick Lane Market, 1932. Tower Hamlets Local History Library

Typesetting and origination by
Alan Sutton Publishing Limited.
Printed in Great Britain.

Contents

Contents

Foreword

When Peter Sanders told members of his family that he was planning this history there were varying reactions. His Aunt Mary told him 'We all come from the gypsies'. She also told him 'I hope you finish this book before I conk out'.

For non-members of the family this is a superb book, the most impressive history of an 'ordinary family' that I have ever read. It has been well worth waiting for. As you read it, the book speaks for itself. The story unfolds in proper chronological order from the beginning to the end, and in every chapter there are new scenes and new relationships. It spans three centuries, and, like all histories, ends unfinished.

The author knows not only about his own family but about family history as a whole and the different approaches to it. He is fully aware, therefore, of the bearings of his subject and of the complex relationships between the history of one particular family and of local and national social history. For this reason, then, readers will turn to this book who are interested less in the details of the Sanders family than in the history of Essex and Bethnal Green and of class, of politics and of religion. They will learn much, for in dealing with all these topics it is wiser to begin from the ground and work upwards than to look down at the ground from above.

The author's own education at Oxford is a kind of indicative landmark in his family's history. When he won a place there to read Greats, his mother was overwhelmed with pride and his father told his friends 'I never thought that one of mine would ever go there'. For them education was 'a strange and unfamiliar land, full of signposts to places whose importance they had to take on trust', and when they talked of their own education it was 'as if they were relating their experiences in some remote foreign country which they had visited in their youth and which they had never seen again'. Clearly the experience of Peter Sanders himself has been quite different. If he had not followed the route he knows so well, this book would most likely never have appeared at all.

Throughout emphasis is placed on experience, and the experience encompassed in these pages is broad enough to suggest that although it is an 'ordinary family' which is under review there are several extraordinary features about it. The evidence is restricted, but it is adequate to open many doors that have long since been closed and many windows that for generations have been shuttered.

Family history has a future. It thrives on curiosity and it arouses great interest as the forgotten past is recovered. This book is more than a case study. It provides a model for any other family historian seeking to trace the intricate patterns of continuity and change.

Asa Briggs
Worcester College,
Oxford

Introduction

This is the history of an ordinary family.

With the achievement of full democracy the ordinary people have been given a voice in history to match their voice in the present, but they tend to have been given it en masse. We have histories of village labourers and the English working class, accounts of popular movements and struggles, analyses of population and poverty and studies of local communities. We also have biographies of outstanding individuals, of men and women who emerged from the mass and made themselves heard in the nation as a whole. But with few exceptions ordinary individuals and families have remained silent, or have spoken only because some selected comment or observation contributes to a theme of general significance.

Family history is about recovering the voices of those people who made up our history in its majority, and it is the claim of this book, and its aim to demonstrate, that to be aware of these voices is to add a new dimension to our understanding of the past.

In a very obvious way the more established approaches to the past can be informed and illuminated by family history. Both at the local and the national level, great tracts of economic, social and even political history are grounded in the actions of ordinary individuals, of men and women buying and selling, making goods and providing services, living out and experiencing the subtleties of class, going to church or chapel or nowhere at all, voting Labour or Liberal or Conservative. Underlying every theory and general statement is a rich and complex variety of individual experience.

But family history is much more than a quarry for broader enquiries. It deals, insofar as the evidence allows, with the total experience over time of particular groups of related individuals, and provides the historian with a

Introduction

unique opportunity to consider them in the round, not just as part of an aggregate or illustrations of a general pattern, but as worthy of understanding in their own right. The experiences of which they tell may be humdrum and parochial, but it is precisely such experiences that we want to know about. The validity of family history rests on the importance of the ordinary individual; or, to paraphrase the words of Stevie Smith, not on the totalities of the countless dead, but on the blessed significance of each precious one.

Every family, while part of a local community, has its own particular history. It does not necessarily rise or fall with the community, and it is more susceptible to sudden change. It can be ruined by a father's early death or raised up by the enterprise of a single individual. But it cannot be understood in isolation from the local community, any more than the history of that community can be understood in isolation from wider changes. Every event, every action has to be seen within its context. If Thomas Sanders in the seventeenth century was exempted from paying parish rates, we need to know how many others were exempted before we can assess the significance of this. If John Sanders in the eighteenth century declared in his will that he trusted assuredly through the merits of Jesus Christ to enjoy everlasting life, we have to examine the wills of his contemporaries to find out if this was merely a well–worn formula or an indication that he was a man of genuine faith. If Guiver Sanders in the election of 1830 voted for the Independent candidate, we have to find out who voted with him, and who voted for the Whig and the Tory. If Basil Sanders in the twentieth century left his wife and children at home and went to a public house on almost every night in the week, we need to know how common this was. Whatever the period, within the wider framework the individual voices take on a new resonance.

There are many ways of writing family histories, but the most common, and the way that is adopted here, is that of following the line of descent that is marked out by the family name.[1] Normally, of course, this means following the male line, but at one point in the Sanders' history, my grandfather's birth, it means going back through the female line, since he was illegitimate and had been given his mother's maiden name. Nobody now knows who his father was. His mother later married a man called Horace Galley, and was known to her son's children, not as their grandmother, since the story of his birth was kept a close secret, but as Aunt Galley. Such, it was felt, were the demands of respectability.

My parents both came from the East End of London. My mother was born in 1905, my father in 1906, and they met at the Nichol Street Mission in Bethnal Green. As I began talking to them, and to my aunts and uncles, about their past – about their parents and grandparents, about their home and their neighbours, about their school and their work, about the Nichol Street Mission and the local boys' clubs – I came to realise that I was being told of a world that was just as lost to us, in many ways, as the pre-industrial village. It was a world of crowded slums, with people packed in at more than two to a room, of street markets, pawnshops and soup kitchens, of cabinet makers and charwomen, rag and bone men and matchbox makers. Horses and carts clattered over the cobblestones, children played noisily in the narrow streets, husbands and wives fought each other outside the pubs on Saturday evenings, and the Nichol Street congregation sang their choruses on Sundays.

They also told me of annual visits to elderly relatives in Black Notley and Braintree, where Aunt Galley had been a millhand in a silk factory and her father a calf dealer, and where her grandfather, though no one remembered this, had kept The Falcon public house. He had not lived in Braintree all his life, but had been born in the Essex village of Stansted Mountfitchet, where the Sanders had prospered as carpenters for at least five generations. Thomas and Sarah, the first members of the family whom we can identify with certainty, had arrived in Stansted in or around 1658.

So the first part of this history is set in Essex. It begins with a family of village craftsmen in the seventeenth and eighteenth centuries, and goes on to a family in a small market town whose fortunes declined in the nineteenth century from those of a well-to-do innkeeper to those of a struggling millhand with an illegitimate child.

The second part is set in London. Aunt Galley spent the last thirty years of her life in Stratford, in what is now the borough of Newham. But the central experience lies in Bethnal Green, where my grandparents brought up nine children in a small terraced house in a turning off Brick Lane. The final chapter is set in New Southgate, where my parents came to live in 1937 and where they brought me up as a single child in comparative spaciousness and comfort. My father still lives there today.

'Everyman' is the creation of myth, and no family can claim to be representative of others. But at least in the geography of their history the Sanders are typical of countless families who moved from the Essex country-side to London in the nineteenth century and then back to one of the outer suburbs in the twentieth.

There are some family historians who pride themselves on particular family traits and traditions that have persisted over centuries, or so they believe. They define themselves, not only in terms of their appearance, but in terms of their character as well. It is possible, of course, for certain physical characteristics, like the Habsburg nose, to hold their own over several generations. It is also conceivable that in a few self-conscious elite families certain attitudes and postures are deliberately fostered, setting them apart from the crowd and even distinguishing them from other elite families. But in an ordinary family like the Sanders, if any physical traits have persisted we do not know about them, for the simple reason that we do not know what our ancestors looked like beyond the third generation back; and while some influences and interests may have held their own over a few generations it would be pointless to look for any that have endured over a period of more than three hundred years through village, town, city and suburb.

Yet there are two themes that are recurrent in this history and that are drawn from the nature of English society as a whole rather than from the family as such. The first is the dominance of individual over collective values. As master carpenters in Stansted and then as innkeepers and dealers in Braintree and Black Notley the Sanders were economically independent and self-reliant. Although they did well for themselves, they felt no obligation to share their wealth, except marginally, with less fortunate brothers, sisters and cousins, and still less with anyone else, except through the payment of their rates and taxes. Even when the Sanders formed part of the proletariat, when Aunt Galley was a millhand and my grandfather a printer, they were not conscious of themselves as members of a class that was locked in a struggle for its own collective interests. They did not join a trade union, they engaged in no form of conflict with their employers, and they continued to vote Liberal rather than Labour. In Marxist terms, they were members of a class in itself rather than a class for itself. My father, as an insurance agent, thought of himself as lower middle class, and even when he became a trade union official he was a man of compromise and accommodation rather than conflict and confrontation. He would never have dreamed of voting Labour. My mother once told me of a savings club which she ran in order to earn a little money on the side: 'I did my best to get on, you see.' Her words can stand, to a large extent, for the family into which she married.

The second theme is the tension between religion and respectability on the one hand and immorality and crime on the other. Though apparently independent of each other, in fact the two themes are closely linked, since it was those who 'got on' who tended to be respectable and those who did not who tended not to be. The pattern is far from invariable, but it is marked enough to be significant. There is a further refinement: that it was the eldest sons who were the most consistently prosperous and respectable (partly, I think, because they *were* eldest sons and might have had a greater sense of responsibility, but partly because, in Stansted at least, they probably inherited the family business), while the poverty, crime and illegitimacy were found mainly among the younger sons and daughters.

The extent to which a family history can be written depends, of course, on the evidence available, and for the Sanders, on the whole, we are lucky. For the period in Stansted several wills of the family survive, and there is a wide range of parish records, including the parish registers and the vestry minutes for the whole period, the vicar's tithe books from 1688, and the accounts of the overseers of the poor from 1744. There are also the records of the Independent Church, which tell of the dispute which split it apart in 1822, and which divided the family's loyalties too. At the county level there are extensive records, the most important being those of the quarter sessions, including court judgements, poll books, and hearth tax and land tax assessments. There is one serious gap. There were three manors in Stansted, of which the largest was Burnells. During the blitz in 1941 a bomb fell on Grays Inn, on the offices of Bird and Bird, the solicitors who kept all the records for Burnells, and these documents were completely destroyed. It was like a hole being blasted in Stansted's history and it is impossible to make good the loss. The records of the other two manors, Bentfieldbury and Thremhall Priory, are now safely housed, together with the other documents already mentioned, in the Essex Record Office in Chelmsford. There is further evidence for the Anglican Church in Stansted in the records of the Bishop of London in the Guildhall Library; some letters relating to the Independent Church have been preserved in Dr Williams's Library in London; and several families now living in Stansted hold deeds for property that was once owned by the Sanders. Also in private hands is a carpenter's notebook belonging to the Leveys, the Sanders' main competitors in the early nineteenth century.

Because of the nature of the records that survive we know more about the family's economic circumstances than we do about their characters or their beliefs. We can understand how carpenters earned a living at that time and what place they held in society, but we are told very little about the relations between husbands and wives, for example, and we have no idea of whether this man was kind or inconsiderate or that woman was quick-witted or slow. We also know more about the men than the women. Outside the parish registers and overseers' accounts (since more women than men received parish relief), they dominate the records as householders, ratepayers and parish officers. Even when the women appear they are often identified through their husbands or fathers, as in 'Tom Sanders widow' or even 'Tom Sanders daughter' at a time when Tom Sanders had been dead six years and the daughter was thirty-seven years old.

In Stansted the Sanders were a numerous family and played a leading part in the life of the parish. In the town of Braintree they were much less prominent. They rarely appear in the extensive records of the town, or in the records of Black Notley, where Charlie Sanders, Aunt Galley's father, went to live in or around 1874. Instead we learn more about them from the census returns, the certificates of the Registrar General at St Catherine's House, and the records of cases in the Petty and Quarter Sessions, where they appeared with a frequency that does not seem to have deterred them, and the corresponding reports in the local newspapers. Once again we know more about the men than the women, this time because they were more involved in criminal activity.

For the period in Bethnal Green we can draw on the memories of my parents, my aunts and uncles and their friends. At first we listened to them and made notes: later we used a tape-recorder. There are very few photographs, since my grandfather's album was thrown away. Of Aunt Galley and her husband only one photograph remains, and that is no studio portrait. It was taken by a street cameraman when they were on a day-trip to Southend. They pose with a solemn sense of occasion, the ladies' toilet set squarely in the background, and the mirror image of the word ladies shows that the photograph has been printed back to front. Of the surviving papers the most important are the diaries that my father has kept since 1929. For the most part they are merely records of his appointments. He was rarely stirred to record events, apart from the weather and the occasional bout of 'flu, and when he did he never went into detail or described his own reactions. On 12 April 1928, for example, when the woman he was hoping to marry told him that she had met someone else, he simply wrote: 'Began Sep. 5th 1924. Ended today.' And on Sunday 3 September 1939, he noted the outbreak of the Second World War with just two words, 'war started', and thought it equally important to record that he was 'at home' and 'dug up spuds'. Yet in spite of their limitations these diaries faithfully reflect the shifting patterns of his life and help him to remember many people and incidents that he might otherwise have forgotten.

Inevitably we know more about the recent past than we do about the seventeenth and eighteenth centuries. In Bethnal Green we have the rich volubility of people who are talking from living memory. In Stansted their voices are more faint and distant, and at times we lose them altogether. Mary, my father's elder sister, can tell us about every aspect of her life. Of Mary, the daughter of the first John in the family, all we know is that she lived to the age of seventy and that as an old woman she received relief from the parish and a weekly payment from her brother's estate. But at least some of these voices have now been recovered from the oblivion of historical silence. The annals of the poor need not be as short or as simple as Thomas Gray believed.

Acknowledgements

Collecting material for this history was sometimes like dismantling the proverbial haystacks in order to find a few needles. There were, literally, stacks of dusty volumes and rolls for the quarter sessions and petty sessions, and for newspapers and parochial records. In some cases there were indices and calendars to help us. In others we had to turn over page after page and open roll after roll in the hope of picking up the occasional reference. Without the help of my two sons, Richard and Philip, and for a shorter period my mother, this work would have taken even longer than it did.

My debt to my parents, my aunts and my uncles will be obvious to anyone who reads the chapters on Bethnal Green. Their words are quoted on almost every page. Other people have shared their memories with us, especially Bill Foster and Mercy Spearman, the Sanders' neighbours in Black Notley. Irving Sanders read through the chapters on Stansted and was generous with his comments and additional information. John Corley guided us around Braintree and pointed out places that we would never have found for ourselves. Dr and Mrs Robinson and Mr and Mrs Peck, the owners of two houses built by old Guiver Sanders, have shown us the deeds of their properties, and Aubrey Levey has entrusted us with his carpenter family's notebook that dates back to 1802. Raymond Joscelyne has allowed us to inspect Joscelyne's Depository, which was formerly one of the Independent chapels in Stansted. The New Cambridge Boys' Club in Bethnal Green has lent us its minute books and magazines. Joan Cole, another descendant of the Sanders, has confirmed our genealogical findings with her own.

The staff at the various libraries and record offices have all been most helpful and efficient, but I am especially grateful to the staff of the Essex Record

Acknowledgements

Office, who produced innumerable items and answered countless queries with unfailing patience and courtesy.

I am grateful to the following persons and institutions for their permission to reproduce the illustrations listed:

the Essex Record Office (1, 3, 4, 5, 10); the Museum of English Rural Life, Reading (2); the Braintree and Bocking Heritage Trust (12, 13, 14, 18, 19); Kenneth Scowen (7); Warner Fabrics Archive (16); the Greater London Photograph Library (21, 22, 27, 31, 64, 68, 69); Nicholas Breach (23); Tower Hamlets Local History Library (32, 48); St. Bride Printing Library (35); G.E. Jackson & Co. Ltd. (36); The Central Library, Islington (38, 39, 62); the New Cambridge Boys' Club (44, 45, 46, 47).

Finally, and above all, I thank Anita Jackson, who has helped me more than she knows.

PART I
ESSEX

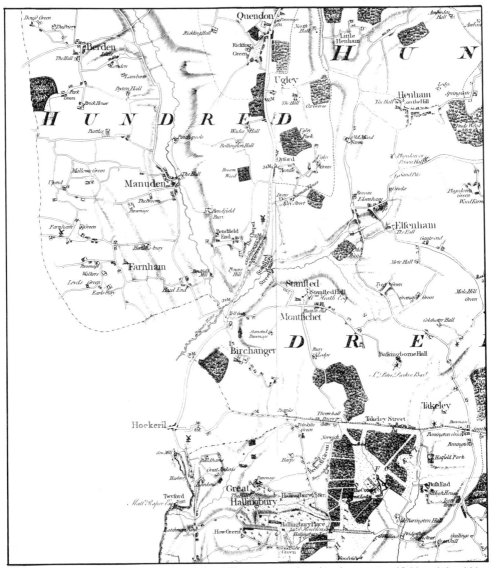

Stansted in 1777. In the east, Button End should be Burton End, and in the west Bendfield End should be Bentfield End. Bishop's Stortford, being in Hertfordshire, is not shown: it is to the west of Hockerill. The milestones on the turnpike road (the Great Newmarket Road) indicate the distance from London.

Stansted Mountfitchet: 1658–1834

TABLE 1:
THE FAMILY IN STANSTED

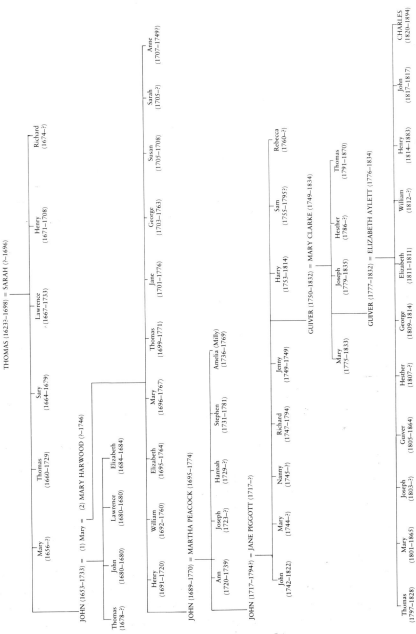

1

The Family in Stansted Mountfitchet

In 1658 or thereabouts Thomas and Sarah Sanders, with their two children, John and Mary, then aged about five and two, moved from the parish of Ugley to the neighbouring parish of Stansted. We know nothing for certain about their background, though Thomas may have been the Thomas Sanders, son of John and Susannah Sanders, who was born in Ware, about fourteen miles away, in 1623.[1] We do not know where they married. Perhaps it was in Ugley, but at that time, during the disturbances of the Civil War and the early years of Cromwell's Commonwealth, many marriages went unrecorded or were conducted by magistrates and the records have been lost.[2] We do not even know how Thomas earned his living, although there is good reason to believe that he was a carpenter. If so, he may well have moved to Stansted to find a wider market for his trade, since the population of Ugley was less than half of Stansted's. It was only a mile and a half for him to go and, being a poor man, as we shall see, he did not have much to take.

He and Sarah settled in the eastern part of the parish, and they then had five more children. By 1700, another 19 children had been baptized in the church with the name of Sanders; by 1750 a further 56; and by 1800 a further 42. All of them, except three who were illegitimate, were descended in the male lines from Thomas and Sarah, and there were just as many who were descended from the women. Several others, it seems, were baptized in the Independent Church, whose registers for this period no longer exist.

Our own particular line of descent is set out in the chart on page 4, and from this it can be seen that we come from Thomas's eldest son, John, who must have travelled from Ugley to Stansted with his parents as a little boy; from John's eldest surviving son, who was also John; and then from this John's eldest son, who was John again. At this point we depart from the senior line, being descended from John's third son, Guiver, and then from Guiver's eldest son, who was also Guiver. So we can think in terms of Thomas, three Johns and two Guivers, and it was the second of the Guivers who left Stansted in 1817 to become the licensee of The Falcon in Braintree.

As far as we can tell, their wives all came from Stansted or the nearby villages. In general couples would only marry in their late twenties, when they had saved enough money to set up home on their own.[3] The Sanders and their brides were comparatively young. The second Guiver, in fact, was only nineteen, and his wife twenty, and they were no doubt able to marry so young because Guiver's father, who was one of the wealthiest members of the family, was able to help them financially and provide them with a home.

We know very little about the relationships between these husbands and wives. In the only two wills which they have left, those of the first John and the elder Guiver, they both refer to 'my loving wife'. The phrase is common enough in this context, but it is not invariable, and it may well reflect a genuinely loving companionship. John had been married more than forty years and Guiver more than fifty when they wrote their wills, and they both made careful provision for their wives.

Five of the six men were exceptionally long-lived. During a period when the average expectation of life rarely, if ever, exceeded forty years, or for those who survived infancy the early fifties,[4] Thomas (if he was the same man as the Thomas born in Ware) was seventy-four when he died; the first John eighty; the second John eighty-one; the third John (probably) seventy-six ('Old Sanders' they called him when he paid his tithes); and the elder Guiver eighty-one – or eighty-one and a half if we are to do him full justice, since he or his children were so proud of his longevity that they had eighty-one and a half inscribed on his tombstone. With late marriages and early deaths only a minority of adults lived long enough to see their grandchildren.[5] Yet all these men saw theirs, and the second John and the elder Guiver saw their great-grandchildren too. It was only with the younger Guiver that the pattern was broken, since he was fifty-five when he died in 1832.

The women, on the whole, lived even longer. Mary, the first wife of the first John, died young, and Sarah died a year before Thomas. But all the other wives outlived their husbands, and Mary, the elder Guiver's wife, was eighty-five when she died.

Stansted Mountfitchet

The Sanders were prolific, even by the standards of the period, when the average completed family was made up of five children.[6] The first John, for example, had four children by his first wife and eleven by his second; the third John had nine and the second Guiver eleven. Not all these children survived, of course. This was a time when infant mortality was high, with only three in four reaching the age of ten.[7] And death was not even-handed. All four children of the first John's first marriage died young: all five of the elder Guiver survived.

It has been suggested that, because children's lives were so frail and uncertain, their parents did not make any substantial 'emotional investment' in them until they were past the dangers of their earliest years. This seems unlikely, if only because such 'investment' was necessary for survival. Even at the simplest level children in Stansted were baptized with names of familiar endearment, like Sary, the daughter of Thomas and Sarah in 1664, and Nanny, Jenny, Harry and Sam, four of the nine children of John and Jane in the 1740s and 1750s. By the early nineteenth century the sentimentality that we associate with the Victorians had already taken hold. When two of the children of the younger Guiver died, one aged five years and the other five months, he and his wife had a tombstone erected (a costly expense) with a consoling verse:

> Short was their stay,
> The longer is their rest.
> God took them away
> Because HE knew it best.

It seems much safer to assume that in general parents were as anxious, caring and loving as they are today.[8]

Most children left home in their early to mid teens to go into service or an apprenticeship. The Sanders girls were probably no exception. When Thomas, the brother of the second John, was unable to maintain his large family, his daughter Hannah was put out to service by the parish when she was only nine years old.[9] Many of the boys, however, were probably apprenticed to their fathers and so stayed at home until they married. For them patriarchy had a double hold, controlling them at work as well as in the home. Even when they were journeymen they might still be their fathers' employees, or they might enter into partnership with them.

Some children, of course, did not marry, while others married but had no children of their own. There were many branches of the family which literally died out. But, in addition to the men and women in our own direct line, there were several others who had large families, and the world in which all these children grew up was full of aunts and uncles and cousins and second cousins.

They could hardly have taken a walk to the shops or to the village pump in the Street without meeting one of their relatives on the way.

But the family we are describing was not, as historians used to believe, the extended family, with several generations living communally under the same roof. It was, more typically, the nuclear family, with just the parents and their children making up the household, in this respect like the family today, and the prevailing ethos was as individualist as our own.[10] Whenever possible, parents would pass on their property to their children, and to no one else besides; and if one member of the family did well he was under no obligation to share more than a fraction of his wealth with those who were less successful. In one particularly striking instance we find George, the youngest son of the first John, who had prospered and been chosen as an overseer of the poor, handing out weekly relief to his sister Mary, who remained unmarried to the end of her life.

Obligations between cousins were even more tenuous. In 1776, for example, the third John was prospering as a carpenter in the Street while his cousin, a poor labourer also called John, was dying only a few doors away and depending on the parish to supply him with firewood.[11] Not many years before the carpenter John had actually sold firewood to the parish for the poor.[12]

At the beginning of the nineteenth century, as social divisions became wider, each village, in the words of Eric Hobsbawm, 'increasingly hid two villages: the official parish, whose citizens the new County Directories recorded – the landowners, resident gentry, farmers, publicans, etc. – and the dark village, whose members they did not.'[13] We shall find the Sanders in both, with some being deacons of the Independent churches and some being imprisoned as petty criminals and lucky to escape transportation.

There is no evidence of bad relations between different branches of the family. Brothers and sisters attended each other's weddings and named their children after each other. Brothers might appoint each other as executors of their wills, and no doubt those who were most successful employed some of the others in their workshops. But with so many boys brought up in the same trade, relations must have been soured at times by economic competition, by the struggle for space in a narrow market. A son might have to wait for his father to die before he could take over the family business, and the success of one brother or cousin could easily lead to the ruin of another.

The most poignant story is that of Samuel, a cousin of the elder Guiver. Like so many of his relations he was brought up as a carpenter, but he was unable to establish himself. He tried to migrate to his wife's village of Great Hallingbury, but the churchwardens and overseers, worried that he and his family would become a burden on the rates, had them removed back to Stansted.[14] He struggled on, but in 1789 he had to turn to the parish for help. His wife was often ill, and by the early 1800s his own health had broken down. In December 1804, a few days before Christmas, he disappeared – perhaps, under the strain, he had been drinking too heavily – and search parties had to be sent out to find him. In February 1805 the Vestry baldly recorded the decision: 'Samuel Sanders Workhouse'.[15] Five months later he was dead.

It is probably still the popular view that our ancestors led stable and settled lives, rooted, generation after generation, in the same village or town, and the Sanders of our direct line would seem to bear this out. But in fact, as we now know, this popular view is wrong.[16] Our ancestors may have been less mobile than ourselves, but they were far from being tied to the place where they were born. Many children who left home to enter service or an apprenticeship went beyond Stansted and never returned. There were others who migrated later – men looking for work or trying to better themselves or women who married husbands from elsewhere. There was a constant shifting of population between Stansted, Bishop's Stortford and the nearby villages, and many must have been drawn to London, particularly towards the end of our period.[17]

So the fact that the Sanders of our direct line stayed in Stansted for five generations, so far from being normal, is something that needs to be explained. Studies in other villages have shown that those who migrated tended to be landless labourers, with little or nothing to hold them to the village, although prosperous farmers and others might also move to take advantage of opportunities elsewhere. Those who remained tended to be middling farmers, or well-to-do craftsmen and tradesmen who had set up their shops and workshops and built up their goodwill and a local reputation.[18] The Sanders were typical of such men. They did not rely on carpentry alone, but in the precarious, pre–industrial economy of the village they handed on their trade like a precious lifeline. And it was very important that they lived long enough to do this: their longevity helped to stabilise the family's prosperity. It was the younger Guiver, as we have seen, who broke the line by migrating to Braintree in 1817. His father, it seems, had given him funds to enable him to set himself up as a publican, but it is also possible that, with several of his relatives dominating the carpentry trade in Stansted, he felt the need to get away.

Until his departure, however, the Sanders of our direct line had lived long and prospered, and had stayed in Stansted for the better part of two centuries. Before we go on to consider them more closely, we must look around at the parish in which they lived, at the pattern of its roads and houses, and at the community of which they formed a part.

2

The Parish of Stansted Mountfitchet

The economy of the parish

With more than 4,000 acres Stansted Mountfitchet, or Stansted as it is more commonly known, is one of the largest parishes in Essex. At one point it touches the Hertfordshire boundary, and the Hertfordshire town of Bishop's Stortford lies three miles to the south. The river Stort, no more than a stream at this stage, forms part of the parish's south-western boundary. The landscape is quiet and varied, with little rises and falls on the chalk in the west and flat open land on the clay in the east. It is mainly rich agricultural land, but in the middle of the seventeenth century, when Thomas and Sarah first arrived from Ugley, the farming was more mixed than it is today.

The roads between Stansted and Ugley were then just rutted tracks, but during the reign of Charles II a new road was built, or an old road was improved, as part of the construction of one of the finest highways in the country, the road that was to take the king between his palaces in London and his stables at Newmarket. The Great Newmarket Road, as it came to be known, cut through the western part of the parish. Going north from Stansted it ran close to Saffron Walden, with a branch leading off to Cambridge on the way. Going south it ran through Hockerill, which has since become part of Bishop's Stortford. It was also one of the routes between London and Norwich, which was then the second largest city in the country. In 1744 it became a turnpike road, and thirty years later the diarist Parson Woodforde described it as 'the best of roads' he had ever travelled.[1]

Peter Muilman in 1772, writing under the name of 'A Gentleman', referred to 'the vast traffic of this much-frequented road'.[2] There were travellers on foot or on horseback, visiting friends or relatives or engaged in business. There were drovers with their dogs, from as far away as Northumberland and Scotland, pressing on with their herds and flocks to London. Increasingly there were the coaches and post–chaises, some of them stopping at Stansted for a change of horses and refreshment for their passengers. And there were the farmers, tradesmen and carriers, carting their goods to Bishop's Stortford, either to the weekly market or, after 1769, to the head of the Stort Navigation.

For the people of Stansted and the nearby villages the town of Stortford, as they called it, had always been the hub of the economy, but it became even more important after the Navigation to London had been opened. Their farmers sold grain in its market and grew barley for its flourishing maltsters. By 1800 Stortford was sending more malt to the London brewers than any other town in England.

In Stansted the traffic of the Newmarket Road was catered for by at least four inns and alehouses, and large fields were provided where the drovers could leave their stock overnight.[3] There were also several houses and 'a few neat shops, but not', wrote Muilman, 'of any considerable trade'.[4] Sixty years later, in 1836, the historian Thomas Wright found Stansted to be a large and populous village, and referred to the 'numerous capital houses' on 'the great road from London to Cambridge and Newmarket'.[5] An old chapel stood at the crossroads in this part of the village, and so the whole of this settlement was known as the Chapel.

A few hundred yards to the east, at the bottom of Chapel Hill, was the Street, the oldest settlement in the parish. It was still overlooked by a few flinty walls on a grassy mound, which was all that remained of the old Norman castle. The street itself was broad and spacious, and was lined by more inns and shops. The road from Elsenham and Thaxted joined it from the north, and the road from Takeley and Dunmow from the south. It was close to Stansted stream and liable to flooding and, considering its low-lying situation, Muilman said, it was 'in a better condition than could be expected'.[6]

There were two other hamlets in the parish – Bentfield End in the west and Burton End in the east. Stansted Hall, the home of Sir Thomas Myddleton, stood in proud isolation in its park on a hill by the road between the Street and Burton End. And close to the house, and just as far from any settlement, was the church of St Mary the Virgin.

There was no local stone for building and, though brick could be made from the local clay, it was so expensive that until the eighteenth century its use was confined mainly to chimneys. So most houses were timber-framed, with lath and white-painted plaster between the struts, and for this reason it was particularly easy for village carpenters, like the Sanders, to develop into general builders. The roofs were covered with tiles or thatch, and only later, after the opening of the canal, with slate.

In the 1660s and early '70s, as we know from the returns of the Hearth Tax, there were about 120 households in Stansted.[7] If we allow between four and five people to each household we get an overall population of between 480 and 600.[8] An increase in the numbers in the parish registers suggests that by 1700 the population had risen to well over 600, possibly more than 700. It remained steady at this level until 1750, and then rose rapidly to 1,285 in 1801, the date of the first census, and 1,560 in 1831.[9]

Of the 120 households in the 1660s and '70s at least a half had only one hearth, and about a quarter had two. Of the rest, taking the 1662 returns, seven had three, 13 had between four and seven, two had nine, and one, the household of Sir Thomas Myddleton, had no fewer than 31. About 40, or a third, were too poor to pay rates and were therefore exempted from the Hearth Tax, and nearly all of these had only one hearth. Using these returns as a rough guide to principal occupation, we can say that about 70 of Stansted's 120 households were headed by labourers or cottagers, about 30 by craftsmen, shopkeepers or small farmers, about 20 by well-to-do yeomen, and at least three by members of the gentry, who by definition did not have to work for a living. There must have been servants, mainly young, unmarried people, in about a quarter of these households, ranging from the occasional farm servant to the troop of retainers maintained by the Myddletons.[10]

Agriculture, of course, was the mainstay of the economy, and continued to be so throughout our period. According to the 1801 census four out of every five adults worked mainly on the land. And those who did not, like the craftsmen and the shopkeepers, made most of their money by serving those who did.

In Stansted, which was typical of this area, enclosure was a long and gradual process and so the parish was spared the upheaval of the comprehensive parliamentary enclosure that caused so much hardship elsewhere.[11] But in other ways there were far-reaching changes. With the price of corn rising in the late eighteenth century and reaching new heights during the wars against France, many fields were turned over from pasture to arable. In 1844, when a detailed and comprehensive survey was carried out, there were more than three acres of arable land for every acre of meadow and pasture.[12] And there is evidence that as the profits from farming increased so the woods were steadily cut back.[13]

There was also a continuing tendency for the smaller farmers to be bought out. At the beginning of our period, in the 1660s, they were still present in significant numbers. Towards the end, in 1831, they had almost disappeared. There were then only 16 occupiers of agricultural land: two of them worked their own farms without help, and the rest employed 183 labourers between them.[14] As early as 1759 about half of the parish was in the hands of one man, the lord of the manor.[15] The familiar pattern of a few large landowners, a middling number of prosperous tenants, and a crowd of landless and impoverished labourers had become increasingly established.

With their new-found wealth from dearer corn the larger farmers could now afford to imitate the gentry, at least in their more attainable comforts and refinements. Previously they had hired their labourers by the year and provided them with board and lodging. Now they hired them by the week or the day and they were unwilling to share their homes with men whom they regarded as their social inferiors.[16] The old bonds of familiarity and friendship were snapped. Class divisions became sharper and more embittered. The word 'respectable' entered the fashionable vocabulary, and the unrespectable and at times disrespectful poor were feared as a threat to the existing order.

The labourers had always struggled for a living, but until the 1790s they and their families at least had enough to eat. On the farms, in addition to the men's employment, there was casual labour for their wives and children, like weeding, stone-picking and bird-scaring. And with the wool trade in worsteds and fustians still flourishing, the spinning wheel was a fixture in almost every common home. Gradually, however, the woollen industry in Essex was stifled by competition from the north, and even before mechanisation had set in spinning became hard to come by.[17] The steep rise in prices in the 1790s was not matched by rising wages, and more and more men had to turn to the parish for support. Poaching became more widespread and desperate, and the Game Laws were enforced with increasing brutality.

In the Swing Riots of 1830 and 1831 labourers throughout the southern counties protested against low wages and unemployment by going on strike, burning hayricks, breaking up threshing machines and maiming animals. There were so-called riots in several villages nearby, but not in Stansted itself, though two men were accused of maiming a lamb, and one was convicted and transported for seven years.[18] In 1834, however, the leading farmers reduced the wages of their common labourers from nine shillings a week with beer to eight shillings a week with beer. More than a hundred men gathered together, refused to work at the new rates, and stopped at least one of their colleagues from working. There was no violence, but two of their leaders were taken before the Quarter Sessions in Chelmsford, convicted of conspiracy, riot and assault, and sentenced to a year's hard labour.[19]

The craftsmen were generally better off, and throughout our period the average wage of a carpenter was about half as much again as a common labourer's.[20] Like the farmers, they benefited from the quickening of the local economy. After the opening of the Stort Navigation foreign deal could be obtained more readily and roofing slate from Wales became available. Customers and clients were more numerous and affluent, and a comparison of the maps made in 1777 and 1843 shows the large number of buildings put up during this time.[21] But competition was fierce. The successful might invest in the property market and follow the farmers up the dizzy heights of gentrification. Those who could not hold their own might sink to the level of common labourers. The Sanders, as we shall see, provide examples of both.

The government of the parish

When Thomas and Sarah arrived in Stansted they would have known at once that the most powerful man in the parish was Sir Thomas Myddleton at Stansted Hall. He was the lord of the two largest manors in Stansted, Burnells in the east and Bentfieldbury in the west.

The Myddletons were typical of those families who had made their money in trade and invested it in land. In 1613 Sir Thomas's grandfather had been elected as Lord Mayor of London, and two years later he had bought his estate in Stansted to add to the lands which he already held at Chirk Castle in Denbighshire. After his death his property was divided among his sons, and in the Civil War the Myddleton who had inherited Chirk Castle was given command of the Parliamentary forces in North Wales. Stansted, like most of Essex, supported the Parliamentary cause, and it was no doubt because of the family connection that the parishioners contributed £21 to a fund 'to reduce North Wales to the obedience of Parliament'.[22] The Myddletons held Stansted for five generations. Another Sir Thomas, in the last generation but one, was a Member of Parliament for Harwich, a Whig, and a supporter of the Glorious Revolution. His son, the last Sir Thomas, also a Whig, represented the county from 1708 onwards. He had no male heir, and shortly before his death in 1715 his estate in Stansted was purchased by Thomas Heath.[23]

The Heaths, like the Myddletons, had made their money in trade, and they were the lords of the manors of Burnells and Bentfieldbury until 1808 when, again like the Myddletons, they had no male heir.[24] The estate was then split.

Burnells passed to Ebenezer Fuller-Maitland, who was already a major landowner in Essex, and Bentfieldbury to the Goslings, who had estates in the adjoining parish of Farnham and elsewhere.

There was a third manor in Stansted, Thremhall Priory, which held land in several parishes. In Stansted it was confined to a few hundred acres around Bentfield End and around what had once been the Priory itself in the south-east corner of the parish. At the time of Thomas and Sarah's arrival it was owned by the Rays, but in or around 1770 it was acquired by Jacob Houblon, the descendant of a family of eminent merchant bankers, whose home was in Great Hallingbury to the south.[25]

The squires of Stansted, particularly the Myddletons, were leading members of the county gentry. They had a powerful say in choosing the two knights of the shire who would represent Essex in the House of Commons, and one of them, as we have seen, was chosen himself. Because of the expense involved, most elections went uncontested. The gentlemen of the county simply met beforehand and decided who they wanted to represent them. It was only if they could not resolve their differences that 'the peace of the county' was disturbed and a contest had to take place.

The qualification for the franchise was the possession of freehold property worth at least forty shillings a year, and most men in Stansted were excluded by this. In theory the electors were the independent gentlemen of England, able to choose their representatives freely. In practice many of them were tenants of the great landowners or could be influenced by them for other reasons. In 1710, for example, forty-seven electors from Stansted voted, and all but four of them supported Myddleton.[26] In 1830 and 1831, however, when the issue of parliamentary reform split the country, the electors of Stansted were divided too.

More important for the parish were the gentry's activities as Justices of the Peace – not just the squires, but the leading landowners and the clergy as well. Sitting in Petty and Quarter Sessions they exercised a daunting array of administrative and judicial powers. They could act as a check on parish government, approving the parish rates, for example, and they also appointed the parish constables. In their criminal jurisdiction they were supported, when necessary, by jurors who had to be owners of freehold or copyhold land worth at least ten pounds a year – a qualification more demanding than that for the franchise, and in Stansted there were rarely more than ten men who could satisfy it. With* these allies the magistrates dispensed justice, defended the interests and rights of all property owners and stamped down on any popular discontent. They enforced the Game Laws in their own class interest and imposed heavy punishments on labourers who tried to combine against their employers. If their authority was threatened they could call on the military.

Penal administration was not strongly developed, and prison sentences were rarely for more than one year, but whipping, hanging and, later, transportation were commonly meted out. The fate of William Wybrow, a Stansted labourer, was not unusual. When he was found guilty in 1829 of stealing a new pair of shoes, two handkerchiefs and a gold ring, to the total value of five shillings, he was sentenced to be transported beyond the seas for seven years.[27] The more serious cases were heard at the Assize Court. In 1786, when Thomas Brett was found guilty of burglary in Stansted, he was hanged.[28]

The manorial courts retained only the vestiges of the powers they had exercised in the Middle Ages. They elected the parish constables and dealt with territorial infringements, like unauthorised encroachments on the waste, but for the most part they were concerned with transfers of copyhold land, and their rolls were little more than registers of ownership.

For day to day parochial administration it was the vestry and its officers that mattered. Its meetings were open to all adult ratepayers, but in practice they were dominated by the gentry and the wealthier farmers and tradesmen. Throughout our period the minutes were signed or marked by a small group of men, usually about seven or eight, who included, in addition to the parish officers, a nucleus of four or five who tended to go on from year to year and who were normally qualified jurors as well. The vicar, if he attended, was chairman.[29]

The vestry met every Easter to elect one of the two churchwardens, the other being nominated by the vicar. These officers were responsible for maintaining the fabric and property of the church and for providing bread and wine for communion. In most years they spent very little and so the rate they levied was not a heavy imposition. They also made reports to the Bishop of London on the spiritual state of the parish, and presented to him any serious 'crimes' that were committed, like incest, adultery, fornication and heresy.

The vestry also elected the two overseers of the poor, whose main duty was to relieve those who were unable to support themselves because of age, illness or infirmity. They had to provide the children of the poor with training to do a particular job, and they were supposed to find work for the able-bodied unemployed, which they were rarely able to do. Their expenditure was heavier than the churchwardens', and their rate was nearly always much higher. The administration of poor relief was flexible and adaptable. For those who needed regular financial help there were weekly payments, 'the weekly collection', and for the 'casual' poor there were occasional payments as the need arose. For the homeless there was accommodation in the poorhouse, or they were looked after by friends and the parish paid the rent.

Women were more likely than men to be poor, especially those who had been widowed or abandoned with children by their husbands. The old were badly at risk too, for there was no old age pension, no subsidised retirement. The longer a man lived and the less he could work, the more he had to eat into any savings that he might have made. Even those who were comfortably off might have to turn to the parish at the last.

In 1730, a typical year in the first half of the eighteenth century, the weekly collection was given to twenty-four people, sixteen of them widows and only four of them men.[30] But inflation brought widespread poverty, and in the closing years of the century scores of able-bodied men were driven to the parish to supplement their wages. From just over £100 in the early 1700s the poor rate went up to more than £700 in the 1770s, and as the price of bread soared during the crisis years of the French wars it went well beyond £2,000.[31]

To deal with this torrent of claims and expenses the parish had to improve and enlarge its administration. In 1764 the number of overseers was increased from two to four, and eventually a committee of overseers was set up which met once a week. In 1773 the parish purchased a workhouse, which was later reported to contain sixteen people, most of them elderly or children.[32]

The constables, whose duty was to keep the peace, and the surveyors of the highways, who maintained the roads with obligatory help from their fellow parishioners, were the other main parish officers. The constables, though chosen by the manorial courts, were sworn in by the magistrates and presented their accounts to the vestry, while the surveyors were appointed at first by the vestry but later by the magistrates.

In any list of parish officers the churchwardens always came first. They were men of substance and standing, and since their duties were not very heavy some of them were willing to be re-elected for several years. The overseers were drawn from the same class as the churchwardens – they had to be 'substantial householders' by law – but their work was so demanding that, until their number was increased to four, very few served for more than two years.[33] The constables were usually more humble men, and some of them seem to have enjoyed the job since they carried it out for long periods. The office of surveyor was generally avoided.[34] None of these offices was paid, and the poor never held office of any sort.

The nature of parish government must naturally have varied from time to time and from officer to officer. Towards the end, when poverty was endemic, it may well have been harsh and unfeeling. But even then, and certainly in earlier periods, many of those who were receiving relief would have been related to those who were dispensing it and at the very least would have been known to them personally. The parish was a close-knit community, and its administration must often have been tempered by ties of familiarity and personal concern.

Every parish office was filled at one time or another by a member of the Sanders family, and friends and relations were also appointed. Connections of this sort were important when decisions were being made about who should receive relief and who should be given contracts for parish work, like making coffins for pauper burials and providing beer for parish labourers. It was always helpful to have someone in the vestry who could put in a good word for you or put business your way.

Organised religion and education in the parish

The very words parish, churchwarden and vestry reflect the Church's long involvement in local administration, and the Church was normally a powerful force for local order and stability. At the time of the Restoration, however, it was badly divided within itself. Robert Abbot, the vicar of Stansted, had been a committed Parliamentarian and was implacably opposed to the High Church doctrines imposed by the Cavalier Parliament. Defying the Act of Uniformity of 1662, he refused to declare his unfeigned assent to the revised Prayer Book, and he was therefore ejected from his living.[35] Seventy other ministers of religion in Essex chose the same course, and so did the minister at Bishop's Stortford.

After this upheaval the Anglican Church gradually settled down as the comparatively quiet and undemanding institution that is familiar to us from contemporary writings. The closeness of St Mary's Church and Stansted Hall, set apart from the four main hamlets, was significant at several levels. The lord of the manor was the patron of the living, and the vicar was normally a Justice of the Peace. Between them they collected all the tithes in the parish, with the squire taking the great tithes on arable crops and hay (until 1710, when the tithe on hay was bequeathed to the vicar)[36] and the vicar the small tithes on livestock, vegetables, fruit and wood.

At the beginning of the eighteenth century, when the Sanders were most closely connected with the Church – the first John, as we shall see, was a churchwarden for some time – the vicar was John Reynolds, a Cambridge graduate. He emerges from the careful records that he kept as a man who was acutely sensitive and vigilant about everything that touched on his income, his rights and his relations with the gentry. But he was also conscientious in carrying out his duties. He conducted divine service and preached twice every Sunday, he catechized the young during Lent, and he built a new rectory, mainly at his own expense. The churchwardens, in their reports to the Bishop, invariably spoke well of him. He 'endeavours to reclaim all profane Persons and Schismaticks', they said; 'He visits the sick and afflicted'; and, according to John Sanders and his colleague, he 'behaves himself peaceably and gravely'.[37]

There is very little evidence about the religious experience of the ordinary churchgoers in Stansted at this time. In their wills most of them entrusted their souls to Almighty God and expressed the hope of everlasting life through the merits of Jesus Christ, though some said more and others nothing at all. But it is impossible to say how far these pieties were inspired by any deep religious faith.

Although it was the duty of the churchwardens to present to the Bishop any cases that arose of heresy, fornication and so on, in practice they were reluctant to lay information against their fellow parishioners. In 1719 Reynolds was called upon to marry a couple who, according to him, 'to their Eternal Shame', had been 'guilty of Fornication before Marriage'. There was not any dispute about this, since they were bringing their illegitimate child to be baptized on the same day as their wedding. In spite of Reynolds' demands, however, 'The Church Wardens would not present them'. All he could do was to add a thick black cross against their names in the marriage register as a 'Marke' of what they had done.[38] He was more successful in 1724. After the churchwardens had reported that 'We have none in our Parish who lie under a fame or suspicion of Adultery, Fornication or Incest', he was able to persuade them to insert between the lines 'except Hannah Griggs and Elizabeth Layman Guilty of Fornication'. On lesser crimes the churchwardens were more resolute: 'We cannot present any Persons as Common Swearers or Drunkards', they wrote, 'tho' doubtless there are some, but we know not who they are'.[39] Reynolds was fighting a losing battle. From the 1730s onwards it was the common practice throughout the diocese to report 'omnia bene', 'all well'.

John Allen, who succeeded Reynolds, was vicar for more than forty years, and like Reynolds seems to have been a diligent pastor. But towards the end of the eighteenth century the church apparently entered a gradual decline. The parish registers were poorly kept, the vicar no longer attended the vestry, and the church buildings fell into disrepair. By that time the Sanders had left the Anglican Church and transferred their allegiance to the Independents.

While reporting that there were no 'Papists, Jews or Hereticks' in the parish, the vicars and their churchwardens had to acknowledge the presence of numerous 'Schismaticks', as they called them at first, or 'Dissenters' as they called them later. After the Act of Uniformity the Church of England officially embraced the whole community, and no other form of worship was allowed until William and Mary came to the throne and the Toleration Act was passed in 1689. But there were some, like Robert Abbot, who could not come to terms with the Anglican Church.

As well as a small but determined group of Quakers, there was a much larger community of Independents, or Congregationalists,[40] a community that was particularly strong in Essex, and indeed in the whole of East Anglia. They had to meet in secret at first, but in 1698, after the passing of the Toleration Act, they established their first meeting house in Stansted towards the bottom of Chapel Hill. According to a return made in 1716 there were 350 'hearers' in the congregation, many of whom came from other villages, and they were proud to record that thirty-five of them were men with county votes, including eleven who were 'gentlemen'.[41] The rest would have been mainly shopkeepers and craftsmen and their families, with very few labourers among them. During the Civil War and the Commonwealth there had been many free-spirited Christians who had threatened to turn the world upside down, but by the eighteenth century the Independents had lost this revolutionary zeal. They were respectable men and women of God, with more interest in preserving the social order than in overthrowing it.

Although they were now 'tolerated', they were still second-class citizens. Like all Dissenters, they could not become Members of Parliament, for example, or study at the universities of Oxford and Cambridge. And there was the usual animosity between them and the Anglicans, with disputes over the distribution of charity and the provision of elementary schooling, and later with differences in political support.

Apart from the Dissenters, Reynolds and his churchwardens also had to report that there were 'Severall' persons 'who, we believe, frequent not any Place' but 'keep at home'. How many we do not know, but by 1707 they were so little condemned by public opinion that the churchwardens had to admit that 'it would be endless to present them'.[42] And there were many who fell short in other ways. There was a steady increase, for example, in the proportion of children born out of wedlock. From less than 1 per cent in 1650–99 it steadily went up to more than 5 per cent in 1800–49. The reasons for this are not fully understood. Sexual relations before marriage were common, as we can tell from the number of couples who had children less than eight months after their wedding. Many women who had illegitimate children were simply those who had agreed to intercourse but whose expectations of marriage had then been disappointed. It is possible that with increasing poverty and mobility more men, unable or unwilling to face up to their obligations, slipped away from the parish and disappeared. But illegitimacy was more common in some families than in others, and perhaps for some reason this group was increasing.[43]

For all the beauty and elegance of its art and architecture, the eighteenth century, as we are often reminded, was a period of great coarseness and brutality, even among the gentry. Stansted Fair, for cattle and toys, was held on May Day and the following day every year, and was probably no different from the rowdy gatherings which drew down the condemnation of the respectable elsewhere.[44] Towards the end of the century, however, those movements for the reform of manners began which were to develop into the full-blown moral consciousness of the Victorians, and in 1848 the Essex Independents congratulated themselves on the marked softening of manners that had taken place in the previous fifty years.[45]

The experience of the ordinary people of Stansted, though narrow and limited, was not literally parochial. They had many contacts with people from the nearby villages and Bishop's Stortford and, with the traffic of the Great Newmarket Road passing through and with London only thirty-three miles away, their horizons were wider than those of many others. There was also a well-nigh universal patriotism, a pride in being free-born Englishmen, and for some, particularly the Independents and Quakers, there was the added dimension of the religious experience.

Education, however, had little broadening effect. The famous grammar school at Bishop's Stortford, where Dr Johnson's black servant, Francis Barber, was educated, was far beyond the reach of most parishioners. For the earlier period there were only dame schools in the parish.[46] It would seem from the records of the churchwardens and overseers that they gave their pupils a good grasp of figures, but little command of the written word. The Independents had established a school by 1776,[47] and Mordaunt White, who was a man of some standing and ability, was running a school in the early 1800s. In 1812 a charity school was set up, and by the 1830s there were 'three free schools, chiefly supported by voluntary subscriptions'.[48] Yet most children were untouched by formal education. Of the bridegrooms who married in St Mary's Church between 1776 and 1812 only 42 per cent could sign their names, and of the brides a mere 33 per cent – figures that are about 20 per cent below the average for the country as a whole.[49] Most of the Sanders could sign, but for some it was an obvious effort. Others could only scrawl their marks.

3

Poverty and Prosperity

At the Easter vestry in 1712, when he was approaching the age of sixty, John Sanders was elected by his fellow parishioners as their churchwarden. It was the greatest honour they could pay him, and he held the post for five years. In the vestry minutes his signature appeared alongside those of Sir Thomas Myddleton, the squire, John Reynolds, the vicar, and the other dignitaries who made up the small and privileged circle of Stansted's vestry. Each Easter he and his colleague presented their accounts, which usually covered such inexpensive items as paying the bell-ringers, oiling the bells, washing the surplice, and purchasing bread and wine for the sacraments.[1] But in 1716 they had to buy a new bell, which cost the parish more than £50, and for the rest of the century, and well into Victoria's reign, the tenor that rang out over Stansted's fields and hamlets bore the names of John Sanders and his colleague, Thomas Stock.[2]

Other members of the family, at different times, became overseers, constables and surveyors of the highways, but John was the only one to be elected as churchwarden. It was an achievement all the more striking when we consider the poverty of his background. In the 1670s his father, Thomas, had been listed in the Hearth Tax returns as a householder with only one hearth and too poor to pay parish rates. And in 1676 his mother, Sarah, had been a recipient of charity. At the Easter vestry in that year 'Goodwife Sanders', with two other 'poor' women and three 'poor' men, all of them 'of honest name and fame', had been 'cloathed' by Sir Thomas Myddleton.[3] This meant, if the terms of the original charity had been observed, that she would have been given enough cloth to make up a suit of clothes, together with a hat, shoes and stockings, and she would have been obliged to wear her new suit to church on the following three Sundays to satisfy the churchwardens that she had used the cloth for the purpose intended.[4] After that, as she went round the village, her charity clothes would have been a constant and visible reminder of her need.

Thomas and Sarah were not unusual in their poverty. As we have seen, one householder in three was exempt from paying rates, and over a period of ten years the men and women who were clothed by charity must have made up about a fifth of the adult population. But it was difficult for their children to shake off its grip, and John's younger brothers never succeeded. In the 1720s, for example, two of them were included among 'the Poor of Stansted', 135 individuals in all, who were given shares of a benefactor's legacy.[5]

For the first fifty years of his life there was nothing to suggest that John would be any different. We have already alluded to the grim tragedy of his first marriage, with his wife and their four children all dying within the space of ten years; and his second wife, Mary Harwood, from a poor family herself, would not have brought him any great wealth. But his father died in 1698 and, if he was a carpenter, which seems most likely, then John, as the eldest son, would have taken over the family business.

He was also helped by what on the face of it seems a stroke of good fortune. At the turn of the century he was living in Bentfield End and renting a house with one and a half acres from Matthias Palmer, a prosperous yeoman. Matthias was a widower with no children. When he died in 1704 he left most of his property to his brothers and their families, but the house and the land he left to John.[6] Why he did this we do not know but, whatever else was involved, he seems to have taken a liking to John, and John's later election as churchwarden shows that he was able to win the approval of other leading men in the parish.

He was evidently a man of some character and ability, and he made a success of his carpenter's business. But like many other craftsmen at the time he also branched out into small-scale farming, and his growing income from this is partly reflected in the tithes which he paid to the vicar on his livestock, vegetables, fruit and wood. Before 1700 he had never paid more than 6d. a year, and only once had he made the traditional 4d. Easter offering. By 1707 his tithe and offering had risen to 3s. 4d. and by 1729 to 18s. Apart from working his own one and a half acres, he was hiring other land as well. He kept cattle and pigs, and probably horses too, and he had an orchard and grew hay as winter fodder for his animals. We know that he was growing crops as well (though the tithe books for these no longer survive), since in 1718 he sold the vicar oats to the value of £3.[7]

He was eighty when he died in 1733, and he had been unwell for at least two years. In his will, made in 1731, he described himself as 'somewhat infirm in

Body' ('but of sound and perfect mind and memory, thanks be therefore given to Almighty God'); and most men did not make their wills until they believed that death was near. In his old age he had probably used up any savings that he had been able to set aside, for he merely left his house and his one and a half acres to his loving wife, Mary, and after her death it was to go to their youngest son, George, who had not yet married and was still living at home.[8]

Mary was well provided for. She lived on for another thirteen years and, in spite of being an elderly widow, there was no need for her to turn to the parish.

By the time of John's death the Sanders were firmly established among the leading carpenters in the parish. In the records of the overseers of the poor, which date from 1744, there are literally scores of entries for the payment of their bills, mainly for providing coffins for the poor. They always had competition from outside the family – from the Champneys in particular in the early years and from the Leveys later – but the men in our own direct line, and several others too, were more than able to hold their own. Two of them at least, the second and third Johns, received more than the usual support from their wives.

The second John established his workshop in the Street. His wife, Martha Peacock, was the only surviving daughter of a yeoman who died young, and it was probably with the land that he acquired through her (and through his devoted mother-in-law, who described him in her will as her 'beloved son' and left him her remaining twenty acres)[9] that he qualified as a county elector.[10] In Philip Morant's *History of Essex*, published in 1768, he was listed as one of the eight major landowners in Stansted (in addition to the lord of the manor).[11] He had no interest in farming himself, and sold or let most of his inheritance. His tithes and his Easter offering seldom came to more than two shillings, and the only animals recorded were his pigs.[12]

The third John too carried on his business in the Street. He did not own enough land to qualify as a county elector, and he paid very little in tithes. His wife, Jane Piggott, was the daughter of a well-to-do innkeeper, but she had several brothers and sisters and when her father died in 1760 her share of the inheritance was only £10.[13] She was the first of the Sanders' wives, however, to appear in the records in an active economic role. Though there is no direct evidence of it, all the women in the family would have earned a few extra shillings by spinning wool, but Jane also helped her husband in the business, selling firewood on occasion to the overseers of the poor. She was also the village midwife, and when a mother was too poor to pay for her services the parish would meet the bill. At various times in the late 1770s and early '80s, for example, she was paid 5s. 'for delivering two women', and 3s. on each occasion 'for laying Thos. Savil's wife' and 'for laying of a Travling woman'.[14] Just as important, when her own family had left home, she sometimes fostered children for the parish or provided board and lodging for people who were homeless. At one time she looked after 'the child of Osborne Ware', a 'negro', no doubt a servant, who had been baptized in the parish church at the age of fifteen but who had evidently fathered an illegitimate child on one of the village girls and then disappeared. For seven or eight months in 1771 this child was looked after by Jane at the rate of a shilling a week.[15]

We know very little about the property owned by the second and third Johns, partly because they lived in the manor of Burnells, the records of which no longer survive, and partly because they did not leave any wills. We know much more about Guiver Sanders,[16] whose home was in the manor of Bentfieldbury and who left a will of considerable length.[17]

As the third son in the family he was perhaps less sought after than his two elder brothers, John and Richard, who both married well. His wife, Mary Clarke, had been born in Manuden, less than a couple of miles away, and had probably come to Stansted in service. Her mother had died in childbirth, and her father, who had been poor enough to receive charity, had died when she was only eight years old.[18]

In 1782 Guiver set up his workshop in the Chapel, while two of his brothers, John and Henry, had their workshops in the Street. It was a good time to be an established craftsman in Stansted. The turnpiking of the Great Newmarket Road and the opening of the Stort Navigation had given a new stimulus to traffic and trade. And it was a particularly good time to be in one of the building trades. The population was growing fast, and the rocketing price of corn during the French Wars was filling the farmers' pockets. Guiver took advantage of his opportunities, and he was not always scrupulous in the way he did so. He branched out into speculative building and steadily built up his property, and on one occasion his angry neighbours presented him to the manorial court for 'digging Turf and Soil on the Waste', perhaps to get clay for his bricks. On another occasion he agreed to put an extra room on a house but built it slightly smaller than the stipulated size, for which 30s. was deducted from the price.[19]

By 1815 he owned forty acres of land and was qualified as a juror as well as a county elector,[20] and by the end of his life in 1832 he had amassed more wealth than any other member of the family. He had property in the Street and Bentfield End, and also in Hockerill, near Bishop's Stortford.[21] But his main profits, it seems, came from the Newmarket Road. Over a period of more than forty years, starting with his own house and workshop in 1782, he gradually bought up and developed the land on the right hand side of the road going down from the crossroads towards Bishop's Stortford. In order to purchase some of this land he borrowed £400 on the security of some of his cottages elsewhere. Just two of the houses that he built on the land, now known as The Old Manse and Roycot, he sold for £400 and £200 respectively.[22]

In 1835 the house where he and Mary had lived was put up for auction after Mary's death in the previous year. It was sold for £350, and was described by the auctioneers as 'a truly valuable estate, comprising a substantial Sash fronted dwelling house divided into 2 tenements, containing 3 comfortable sitting rooms, 6 airy bedrooms and convenient Closets, Kitchen, Dairy, Ale & Wine cellars, detached Brewhouse, Coal House, spacious CARPENTER'S WORK-SHOP & STOREHOUSE, Large productive Garden, Yard & other appurtenances ...'[23] So for the first time we get a direct glimpse into the domestic arrangements of our ancestors. Guiver and Mary lived spaciously in comfortable sitting rooms where they were warmed by coal fires in the winter.[24] They slept in airy bedrooms and made use of convenient closets. They brewed their own beer, kept their own wine cellar, and grew their own fruit and vegetables. Guiver's will adds further but not very informative details, for it mentions their furniture, linen, plate, china and glass. There was also a well in the garden. They would naturally have kept servants, and in 1818 the overseers' records make mention of their maid. Rather surprisingly, they did not occupy the whole house, for it was divided into two tenements, and we know from the census of 1811 that the second tenement was occupied by a certain Tom Howlett.[25]

Mary had not kept a strict account of her age, and on her tombstone it was given as eighty-three when in fact it was eighty-five. Guiver, as we have seen, was meticulous, and his age was given as eighty-one and a half, the only adult's age to be given as a fraction on all the tombstones in the churchyard. Some faint echo of his spirit seems to hover around this extra half, for even if it was recorded by his children the awareness of it must have been his. It reveals a grim determination, perhaps, not to be done out of anything to which he was entitled, like putting down every halfpenny on his bills. And we are reminded that he was a man who had encroached on the common land and had had to be pulled back by his neighbours, and who had built a room smaller than the size he had agreed and had then been cut down on his price. Old Guiver had been an ambitious, acquisitive man, and he had been loathe to let anything slip.

In 1817, at the age of forty, Guiver's and Mary's oldest son, who was also called Guiver, had moved with his wife and children to Braintree and become the licensee of The Falcon public house. He had been brought up as a carpenter, and until his move he seems to have worked in his father's shop and lived in one of his properties.[26] His change of trade was relatively easy: no apprenticeship was needed, only capital, and this it seems was provided by his father, who referred in his will to a 'substantial sum' that he had given him some time before.

He and his wife Elizabeth may well have left Stansted because the competition in carpentry was too fierce there and because Braintree, which was developing as a silk-manufacturing centre, could offer them greater opportunities. There is no sign of any estrangement in the family. They named four of their first five children after Guiver's brothers and sisters. They witnessed several weddings together, and more than fifty years later the Stansted and Braintree branches of the family were still in touch.[27] But whatever the reasons for the move, they must have been very powerful to have taken Guiver from the place where he had been born and grown up, and where the family was still so rooted and established.

Of the five men in our direct line who were brought up in Stansted, four – the three Johns and the younger Guiver – were the eldest surviving sons in the family. This gave them a marked advantage, particularly if they took over the family business. The younger children did not necessarily suffer – a few, like the elder Guiver, were very successful – but there was much more of an element of risk. So while some of them flourished, or at least did reasonably well, others sank into abject penury.[28]

All the boys in the family would have been brought up as carpenters, and of those for whom we have any evidence more than half tried to earn their main living from the trade. The contrasting fortunes of two pairs of brothers can stand for the rest.

In the generation of the second John there was George, his youngest brother, who married a widow when he was thirty-six, inherited the family home, acquired several more properties, paid more than £2 a year for his small tithes, was a surveyor of the highways and an overseer of the poor, became a bricklayer and an innkeeper as well as a carpenter and builder, and, like Guiver two generations later, was presented to the manorial court by his neighbours for 'digging up a parcel of waste', this time at Bentfield End Green, and also for erecting a brick kiln at the same place.[29] He was the only member of the family to establish a regular presence in the vestry regardless of any offices that he held. By contrast Thomas, the third son in the family, had eleven children, refused on one occasion to pay his tithes in full, and was convicted of taking part in a riot when he and some of his neighbours destroyed a house that had just been built, apparently in violation of some common right.[30] We have already mentioned how his daughter Hannah was put out to service by the parish when she was nine because he and his wife were too poor to look after her, and how Samuel, his youngest son, tried to leave Stansted but was sent back and eventually died in the workhouse. His eldest son, George, ran away, abandoning his wife and children, who had to be supported by the parish.[31] When he himself died in 1771 his widow became dependent on parish relief.

In the generation of the elder Guiver social divisions, as we have seen, were widening, and we have already referred to Hobsbawm's distinction between 'the official parish' of the respectable citizens and 'the dark village' of the labourers and poachers. John, who was Guiver's eldest brother, was very much a man of the official parish. Although his main trade was carpentry, it seems that for several years he served as a gamekeeper and tithe collector for the lord of the manor,[32] and for ten years, from 1803 to 1813, he was one of the parish constables. He and his family were strongly attached to the Independent Church. His eldest son, who was also John, was elected as a deacon and played a leading part in the events that will be described in a later chapter.

Henry, who was younger than John and Guiver, also belonged to the official parish, but only just, and several of his children slipped into the dark village, which was a much more dangerous world. He ran his own carpentry business, living in one of Guiver's houses,[33] and he seems to have been mainly responsible for the undertaking side of the trade. He married twice and had eleven children, but before their marriage both he and his first wife had illegitimate children by other partners.[34] When some of his children died young they were given a pauper's burial. His eldest son, also called Henry, was convicted of grand larceny in 1815 for stealing a few rabbits, fowls and ducks from the village doctor and was sentenced to a year's hard labour,[35] and later he was convicted of petty larceny and was bound over to keep the peace.[36] Three other sons also appeared in court, though nothing serious was proved against them.[37] In the parish registers these sons of Henry described themselves as carpenters. In the court records they were described as labourers. It was common for men to claim the dignity of a craft and for magistrates and officials to ignore them, but these four may well have been driven by competition from their cousins to do more casual labouring than carpentry.

There were other men in the family who tried their hands at other trades, once again with mixed success. Thomas, for example, the brother of the first John, and William, a brother of the second John, both set themselves up as butchers. Whereas Thomas, as we have seen, ended his days among 'the poor of Stansted', William prospered, and so did his children. Others became licensed victuallers, in the same way as the younger Guiver. His uncle Richard, for example, became the landlord at The White Bear, and his brother Joseph was the landlord of The Three Colts from 1809 until his death in 1835.[38] It is possible, though, that several of these men continued to practise as carpenters as well. Joseph certainly did so, and his most valued possessions, as listed in his will, included not only the violins which he played to entertain his customers but also his carpenter's tools.[39] Even the younger Guiver, at The Falcon in Braintree, continued to describe himself as a carpenter.

The fortunes of the women were as mixed as the men's, but since none of them inherited the family business there was little or no difference between the eldest daughters and the rest. Some married men who became county electors. Others married men who became dependent on the parish. Mary, a sister of the second John, did not marry at all, and probably worked as a servant. As an old woman she relied on parish relief, which she received at first from her brother, George, who happened to be an overseer at the time. And Rebecca, a sister of the elder Guiver, had an illegitimate daughter when she was twenty and then, presumably, left Stansted, since she does not appear again in the records.

It was only with the five children of the elder Guiver and Mary that the risk of poverty was removed, for their parents were so wealthy that they were all well provided for. Apart from the younger Guiver and Joseph, who both became innkeepers, the youngest son, Thomas, took over the family business, and the two daughters, Mary and Hetty, both married men of considerable substance.

The Sanders had come a very long way since the 1670s, when Sarah had been 'cloathed' by Sir Thomas Myddleton and she and Thomas had brought up their seven children in a little cottage with only one hearth and had been too poor to pay parish rates.

4

The Carpenter's Shop

In 1717 the vicar, John Reynolds, neatly recorded in his small tithe book that Mr John Eden of Bollington Hall had paid £1 5s. for his tithe and that 'John Sanders received it'.[1] He was referring to the first John Sanders. Bollington Hall was a mile north of Bentfield End, and what seems to have happened is that John was doing some work at the Hall, or on the farm, and that Mr Eden, instead of riding to the village himself, asked John to take the money for him. John occasionally did work for the vicar too. In 1729 Reynolds' successor, John Allen, noted that he had paid him 12s. 6d. for 'wood, for work & a saw'.[2]

John worked as a carpenter for more than sixty years, but these are the only fragments of evidence about what he actually did. More details are available for those who followed him, especially in the overseers' records. The churchwardens' accounts include two bills from the elder Guiver, and there are also two bills from John Sanders and Son, Guiver's eldest brother and his nephew, one for mending the village pump and the other for mending the fire engine.[3] By piecing together all these details, and by filling in the background from other sources — from advertisements in contemporary newspapers, for example; from a small leather-bound book in which the Leveys, the Sanders' competitors, jotted down a few random notes from 1802 onwards and which the Levey family has carefully preserved; from the manuals for country builders written by William Salmon of Colchester and his son (one of which, *The Builder's Companion*, was used by the Leveys at least); and above all from Walter Rose's book, *The Village Carpenter*[4] (in which the author, a Buckinghamshire carpenter, draws on the memories of his grandfather, who was born around 1805) — we can form some idea of what was involved in running a carpentry business in Stansted, at least in the eighteenth and early nineteenth centuries.

Guiver's 'spacious carpenter's workshop' stood on the same site as his house, and all the Sanders who headed their own firms would probably have had the same arrangement. Walter Rose's description of the workshop he knew as a child would no doubt have fitted Guiver's just as well: 'Large heavy benches lined the walls, their tops dented and crevassed with age and the wear of many tools. . . . On the walls were fitted racks for the smaller tools – chisels, gouges, bradawls, etc. – and each saw hung on its own special nail. . . . A strong odour of wood pervaded the place, a mingled scent of newly cut pine, oak and elm. . . .' Each man had his own regular bench and his own set of tools, 'jealousy prized, cared for and guarded'.[5] Guiver himself made special mention of his tools when disposing of his property, leaving them to his son Thomas, who was to carry on the business. So too, as we have seen, did his brother Joseph, the landlord of The Three Colts, who passed on his tools to two of his sons.

The Sanders would have employed several men in addition to their own sons and brothers. We know of two apprentices, employed by the second and third Johns, and if the apprenticeship records were more accessible we would no doubt know of several more.[6] When they mended the village pump in 1810 John Sanders and Son were employing at least three men from outside the family. Each man would have worked about ten hours a day, six days a week.

Close to the workshop, as we know from Guiver's will, was the sawpit, where the logs would be sawn into planks by the sawyers. The top sawyer, the senior man, would stand on the trunk, holding his end of the saw, while the bottom sawyer, the junior man, would stand in the pit, holding the other end of the saw, and wearing a wide-brimmed hat to keep off the sawdust. Guiver would have told them how many planks he wanted and of what size. They were probably not his employees, but would work for all the carpenters in the area. When the planks were cut they would be stacked in the yard and left to season.

The Sanders would have bought most of their wood locally, and many of the trees that were felled in Stansted must have finished up in their workshops. Sometimes the butts were auctioned at local inns: sometimes there was a direct sale. Page after page of the Leveys' notebook sets out the length, the girth and the cost per foot of the oaks and elms that they bought from the local landowners. Most of the Sanders' transactions went unrecorded, but when the wood belonged to the church or the parish its sale was sometimes noted in the tithe book or the overseers' accounts. At various times in the 1730s and 1740s John Allen, the vicar, sold more than a dozen 'ringes' of wood to George Sanders, the first John's youngest son, usually at 10s. 6d. a ringe;[7] and in 1826 the parish sold some trees and pollards to John Sanders, Guiver's nephew, for £9 10s. 6d.[8]

At first very little of the Sanders' wood came from abroad, perhaps just the occasional load of deal that a carter might bring up from London. But with the opening of the Stort Navigation they no doubt bought the deal that they needed for their joinery from the head of the canal in Bishop's Stortford.

An advertisement in 1807 for the sale of a carpenter's shop in the Essex village of Stebbing gives a detailed account of a carpenter's stock at this time: 'a quantity of oak and elm timber, dry oak, elm, and walnut-tree board and plank, white and yellow deals, splint, lath, oak and elm scantlings; a general assortment of nails, locks, bolts, screws, joints, coffin furniture, and under-taker's stock; several work benches, turning lathe, complete chest with tools, and many other implements in the business'.[9] Guiver's stock would have been much the same.

As Rose describes, there was continual going and coming between the workshop and the places for which the work was intended: 'a few days' work in the shop, making doors, windows, or other fitments for a house or farm, then a period at the place fixing the work, and doing what else was required there'. Nearly everyone needed the carpenter at one time or another: 'no farmer who did not need his new cow-cribs, sheep-troughs, or ladders. No house, from the vicarage to the labourer's cottage, but had at some time or other a defect in its woodwork for which the services of our men would be required.'[10] The carpenter with his bag of tools, walking along the lanes and footpaths, was a common sight. Years later, when John Wilkins, the Stansted gamekeeper, wanted to take poachers by surprise, he would sometimes disguise himself as a carpenter, wearing a white apron and a blue jacket and carrying a carpenter's tools.[11] The goods that were made in the workshop were either carried or, more commonly, carted to the place where they were needed. But often the work was done on the spot, especially on the farms, when a suitable tree growing in a hedgerow would be cut down for the purpose.

We do not know how far the Sanders' business extended. In the 1820s 'Mr Sanders' (probably John Sanders, Guiver's nephew) carried out some work for the parish of Farnham,[12] and it is possible that if the records of other nearby parishes had survived there would have been references to the Sanders in them as well. The Leveys, we know, did work in Ugley, but apparently not beyond. In Stansted itself the Sanders had countless dealings with the parish and the church. For the most part, except for the coffins they made, the accounts merely record that their bills were paid. But even the few details that are given show the wide range of work which they carried out – making a table, mending a bed, repairing the stocks, the pump and the fire engine, several jobs at the workhouse and the poorhouse, making and fitting a stable door, repairing the church roof, fixing a flagpole to the tower, 'flooring a pew', making 'a frame for the Kings's arms', and altering the singing gallery.[13]

For their other customers they would have carried out the whole range of carpentry and joinery, from mending furniture to the erection of timber-framed cottages and houses and black-tarred, weather-boarded barns. These buildings are their most lasting memorials. As carpenters they would have been responsible for all the woodwork, and some of them became involved in the rest of the construction too. George, the first John's youngest son, became a bricklayer as well as a carpenter, and the elder Guiver, as we have seen, was a speculative builder. While carrying out the carpentry himself, however, he probably contracted out the rest to other craftsmen.

For many carpenters, including the Sanders, the undertaker's trade was an important part of their work. It was a common pattern throughout the country: the carpenter made the coffin and so came to take on the rest of the business – fitting the lining and the brass plate on the coffin, and sometimes supplying the shroud for the body; organising the bearers and providing refreshment for them; paying the vicar, the clerk and the grave-diggers.

The funeral was normally held within two or three days of death, and making the coffin was always a job that was given the highest priority. At harvest time, when everyone in the parish turned out in the fields and the village streets were deserted, the only reason for excusing the carpenter would be the need to prepare a coffin. On the day of the funeral the undertaker, the bearers and the mourners would gather at the home of the deceased, and would then go in procession to the church. The undertaker led the way, followed by the bearers, with the black pall falling down from the coffin over their shoulders, and then by the straggling line of mourners. Since the church was so far from the village, it was often a long journey and heavy work for the bearers, especially if they had to come from Bentfield End. They always needed refreshment. In June 1747 Will Sanders, a nephew of the second John, who was then licensee of The Bell, provided 'bred Cheas and Bear' for the funeral of Daniel Larn. Six months later, in January 1748, it was his own turn to be buried, and '2 Gallens of Beer' were provided by the parish.[14]

Some funerals were highly elaborate. The bodies were richly clothed, the coffins ornate with gilt fittings, and the palls made from crimson velvet. When John Edridge, an Independent grocer and clearly a man in the Puritan tradition, made his will in 1725, he stipulated that his body should be 'decently buried not after the Pompous Modes and fashions now too much followed but in a plain Coffin of Ten Shillings Value and with something that may be a refreshment to my loving friends accompanying me to the Ground'.[15] But the only funerals of which we have any record are those paid for by the parish, and these were of the cheapest kind. The coffin would have been made of elm, not oak, there was no question of erecting a headstone, and the unmarked graves frequently overlapped. Sometimes the parish paid only for the coffin. For example:

18 July 1750	'Paid J^no Sanders for the coffin'	6s.
5 August 1809	'Henry Sanders for Amey's Childs Coffin'	13s. 3d.

More often it paid all the funeral expenses:

24 June 1760	'Paid John Sanders bill for bestowin of Mary Plum'	£1 2s. 6d.
25 April 1791	'Paid Guiver Sanders for 2 Burials'	£2 4s.

The overseers' accounts contain scores of such entries, and the Sanders' income from the undertaker's trade must have been considerable.

Like other village craftsmen, the blacksmith, the bootmaker and the tailor, for example, the carpenter received his customers at his shop and carried out work for them there. Unlike them, he often had to go into their homes and onto their farms, either to fit the work into place or to carry it out on the spot. It was not always work that followed a set pattern. Some jobs might be done only once in a lifetime, like mending the stocks or making the frame for the King's coat of arms in the church. Even common items, like doors, windows and gates, varied in size and design. The carpenter had to find out, and then carry out, exactly what his customers wanted. Walter Rose claimed that he and his father's men knew the run of every house in the village, 'the condition of its structure and the peculiar mentality of the folk that inhabited it'.[16] Moreover, as undertakers, they had to serve their neighbours at the most painful and distressing moments of their lives.

The carpenter worked for the whole community, from the lord of the manor to the poorest labourer, and his relations with his customers were as important as his skills. He would pass on to his sons not only his trade, but also his knowledge of the parish and its past. As they walked around to different jobs he would always be pointing out work that he had done, or work that his father or even his grandfather had done, and he would talk about the people whom they met in the street or who lived in the houses that they passed. To an extent perhaps greater than any other craftsman, the carpenter was closely and intimately involved in the life of the entire parish, and this would have been especially true of the Sanders in Stansted, with their long family tradition and extensive connections. Few men would have known more about their fellow parishioners than old Guiver Sanders in his workshop in the Newmarket Road.

5

Status and Belief

Carpenters earning their living by trade could never be regarded as gentlemen. Although they had done well for themselves the Sanders could never be on terms of social equality with the leading families of the parish.

Even if we had not known about them already, the social assumptions of the times seep through the language of the written records. Whenever the first John was elected a churchwarden the vestry minutes referred to him as plain John Sanders, but his colleague appointed in 1712 was 'Mr. John Hutley' and in 1713 'Mr. Stock'. It was the same when he died. Though all men were equal in the eyes of God, and though death was acknowledged as a mighty leveller, the burial registers of the eighteenth century church implacably reflected the social order. So he was recorded again as John Sanders, unlike, for example, Edward Nourse Esqr., who was buried just five days later.

The second John Sanders was also plain John, and his brother George, though an established member of the vestry, was recorded in exactly the same way as his father. On the two occasions when he was elected as an overseer he appeared in the minutes simply as George Sanders while his colleagues were named as Mr Judd and Mr Bones. He had loftier pretensions than other members of the family, and in his will he described himself as a yeoman. But no one else ever gave him this rank.

So it went on. The use of the title Mister became more general, but in any list or account where a distinction was drawn between those who were given it and those who were not the Sanders, almost invariably, were among those who were not. The third John, for example, was given no title when he was mentioned in his father-in-law's will, but another son-in-law was called Mr Clement Philip.[1] The elder Guiver was sometimes called Mister, but only in documents in which everyone else was too.

They were not well educated either. The elder Guiver, in fact, was completely illiterate. In the deeds recording the sale of The Old Manse sixteen men added their signs and seals. Guiver, who had actually built the house, was the only one who made a mark, and even that was a straggly, untidy cross.[2] The three Johns and the younger Guiver could all sign their own names, but there is no evidence that their command of the written word opened up great vistas of knowledge and understanding. Apart, perhaps, from reading the Bible, it was probably no more than a functional tool, useful when drawing up bills for their customers. At times their signatures were wavering and uncertain, and when the title of churchwarden had to be added to a document the first John found it safer to hand his pen to the vicar.[3] They certainly placed no great value on the wider benefits of literacy. Three of them at least – the second John and the two Guivers – married women who were unable to sign their names, and not all of them made sure that all their children could write – though the eldest sons in the family invariably could.

The full measure of their skill with the pen can probably be seen in the bills drawn up by John, the brother of the elder Guiver. In his constable's bill for 1810[4] he recorded his expenditure in a fairly neat hand, but his spelling, like that of most parish officers, was wayward and variable. Perhaps in parts it allows us to hear the echoes of a broad Essex accent, with 'Walding' for Walden, 'Waltomstoe' for Walthamstow, 'shurdels' for schedules and 'sarving surmuns' for serving summons. In the next generation, however, his son John, the deacon of the Independent Church, wrote letters with immaculate spelling and grammar, acquired several religious books as well as his Bible, and was probably the best educated man in the family.[5]

Except for the elder Guiver, we know very little about the Sanders' religious convictions, if indeed they had any at all. As a churchwarden the first John Sanders would have been a practising Anglican, and the opening formula of his will, which we have quoted already, displays at least the conventional piety: 'First and principally I commend my Soul into the Hands of Almighty God, my most merciful Creator, trusting assuredly through the Merits of Jesus Christ my most gracious Redeemer to enjoy everlasting Life'.[6] But it would be dangerous to go beyond this and to describe him as a man of deep Christian faith.

Of his son, the second John, all we can say is that he paid his Easter offering throughout his life, but so irregularly as to suggest a lack of commitment. It was probably in the generation of the third John that the Sanders moved across to the Independent Church, though the only evidence that we have for this is that Jane, his wife, was not buried at the parish church, or at any of the parish churches around, and so might well have been buried by the Independents, whose records no longer survive; that the same might be true of John himself (a John Sanders was buried at the parish church in 1794, but there were several Johns in the family at that time and we cannot tell for sure which one it was); and that several of their children became Independents.

For the elder Guiver and his contemporaries, however, there is such a wealth of detail that their religious experience is given a chapter to itself.

Again with the exception of the elder Guiver, we know very little about their political views. We can be fairly sure, however, that the first John and his wife, like their squire, Thomas Myddleton, were in sympathy with the Glorious Revolution that brought William and Mary to the throne in 1688. The son who was born to them in 1692 was the first member of the family to be christened William, and he was obviously named after the king. Their youngest son, George, born in 1703, may well have been named after Queen Anne's husband, and their youngest daughter, Anne, born in 1707, was almost certainly named after the queen herself.

The second John, as a county elector, rode to the county town of Chelmsford to vote in four elections, but the way he voted is not very revealing. In 1722 and 1734 he supported the Whig candidate, who was heavily defeated on both occasions. In 1763 and 1768 he supported the Tory candidates, and all these were defeated too. His votes in the first three elections tell us nothing except that, like most electors in Stansted, he was prepared to follow the lead of the local gentry. In the fourth, however, Stansted's electors seem to have been relatively independent, with 30 of their votes going to the Whigs and 18 to the Tories. One of the Tories was Jacob Houblon, who lived close by at Great Hallingbury and who was purchasing the manor of Thremhall Priory in Stansted at this time. John's votes for them suggest that he had Tory sympathies, or that for some reason he was susceptible to Houblon's influence.[7]

The third John was not qualified to vote, but in his son, the elder Guiver, we can see the emergence of a well defined political consciousness, set very firmly in the culture of Dissent. He voted in three elections, in 1810, 1830 and 1831, and in all three there were two main causes before the voters – the reform of parliament and, to a lesser extent, the abolition of slavery. In 1810 these causes were still weak, and they were easily defeated. In 1830 and 1831 they were finally triumphant, and the support of the Dissenters was a major factor.

In 1810 Guiver followed the majority in voting to maintain the status quo, perhaps because of local pressure. For almost fifty years the county had been represented by a comfortable and unchallenged coalition of one Whig and one

Tory MP. But when the Whig member died in 1810 the squirearchy decided to replace him with a second Tory, John Archer Houblon, a descendant of the man for whom Guiver's grandfather had voted. The election was contested by Montagu Burgoyne, who campaigned as a 'radical and unofficial Whig', and who argued passionately for both reform and abolition. Guiver, like all except two in Stansted, voted for Houblon, who was an easy winner. The two who voted for Burgoyne were the doctor and the schoolteacher, who as professional men probably enjoyed more independence than the rest.[8]

In the general election of 1812 the Whig/Tory pact was re-established – Guiver did not vote on that occasion, perhaps because the proceedings were brought to a close after five of the fifteen days allowed[9] – and it went on untroubled until the general election of 1830. The Whig candidate then was Charles Callis Western, Colonel John Tyrell stood for the Tories, and they were challenged by William Wellesley, a nephew of the Duke of Wellington, who stood as an Independent. Wellesley had hoped for Western's support, since they both advocated the reform of parliament and the immediate abolition of slavery, but it soon became clear that Western and Tyrell were fighting as a coalition in the traditional way. Wellesley complained of this 'unprincipled' alliance, but, as one of Tyrell's supporters observed, 'the voice of the gentlemen of the county' was against him. The Anglicans in particular were opposed to him, and afterwards he complained of 'the Blue Clerical Gentry on their sporting nags, scampering from hamlet to village . . . to solicit votes for Tyrell and Western'. Most Dissenters, however, supported his two main causes, reform and abolition, and he had not alienated them.

At the end of the first two days of voting Wellesley was slightly in the lead, but gradually Western and Tyrell pulled ahead. The crowd around the hustings were mainly Wellesley's supporters, and in the speeches at the end of each day Western, especially, was regularly shouted down. There was continual scuffling and uproar. On the third day a small riot broke out, and on the fourteenth Wellesley, now desperate, challenged Tyrell's agent to a duel, offering him 'the satisfaction of a gentleman', and both men were bound over to keep the peace. At the end of the poll, on the fifteenth day, Tyrell had received 2,638 votes, Western 2,556 and Wellesley 2,301.

Nineteen electors from Stansted voted, and there was no question this time of their following the line laid down by the great landowners. The pattern of voting was not straightforward, but in general the Anglicans supported Tyrell alone or Tyrell and Western, while the Independents supported Wellesley alone or Wellesley and Western. In fact, of the five who voted for Wellesley alone four were Independents, and among them was Guiver Sanders, who had cast his vote on the fourteenth day, the day of the threatened duel. He was almost eighty, and we can imagine that he would have preferred to stay quietly at home, and that he decided to go to Chelmsford only because the contest was so close and he cared about the issues.[10]

A year later, in 1831, another general election had to be held. The Reform Bill of the Whig Government of Earl Grey passed the first reading in the House of Commons, but only by a single vote, and William IV promptly dissolved parliament. Tyrell, Western and Wellesley again stood for the county of Essex, but this time the issues were more important than the family compact. Tyrell's support for reform was lukewarm and limited, and Western had to join forces with Wellesley. At the end of the poll Western had received 2,367 votes, Wellesley 2,250 and Tyrell 1,707. The issues were clear cut and so was the voting. Fourteen electors from Stansted took part. Six supported Tyrell alone. Eight voted for Western and Wellesley. Seven of the eight, including Guiver, were adherents of the Independent Church.[11]

It was the last election in which Guiver took part. He died in May 1832, a month before the Reform Bill finally became law.

6

The Independent Church

In the old Newmarket Road, in the middle of the property developed by Guiver, is a large, rather ugly, red-brick building standing back a few yards from the pavement. A large sign across its pedimented top tells you that it is JOSCELYNE'S DEPOSITORY, but the style and grim ornament of the front – the arching pattern of the brickwork over the wooden doors with their Gothic hinges, and the small stained-glass squares in the lower windows – tell you unmistakeably that it was once a Dissenting chapel.

It was built by the Independents in 1822 and, according to the minister, Josiah Redford, old Guiver had been 'prompted' by Providence to offer the land for this purpose.[1] The first brick was laid at six in the morning on the first of May, and the building was completed within three months. The cost was £550, and most of this was raised by local subscription within a year. 'This was the Lord's doing', Redford wrote, 'and it was marvellous in all our eyes. Hallelujah! Praise the Lord.' But it was not marvellous in everyone's eyes, and there were others in Stansted who looked upon this new meeting house, not as the Lord's doing, but, in the words of William Chaplin, the minister at Bishop's Stortford, as 'a public monument of disgrace brought upon the dissenting cause'.[2] For Redford was not founding a completely new community, but leading a breakaway from the existing church, the Old Meeting as it was called from then on, which had gathered in its meeting house towards the bottom of Chapel Hill for more than a hundred years.

We do not know how long the Sanders had been connected with the Independent Church. The membership lists of the Old Meeting go back to people who joined in 1766, and before the split in 1822 the only Sanders to appear were Hannah, the wife of Guiver's brother John, and her son John, who was later one of the staunchest supporters of the Old Meeting, standing firm when others seceded and eventually being elected as a deacon. But the lists are far from complete, and in any event the members, 'the church', were only a minority of those who assembled at the meeting house every Sunday. The rest, 'the congregation', were 'hearers' or 'subscribers', and it is clear from various records, mainly lists of contributors,[3] that they included several other members of the family. There were Guiver and Mary, who were generous in their contributions, and three of their children, Joseph, Hetty and Thomas. There was 'John Sanders Senior', who was probably Hannah's husband, and William Sanders, a watchmaker, who we believe was their grandson[4] and who was evidently a close friend of old Guiver. He rented a house from him in the Newmarket Road and was later to witness the making of his will.

The Independents, or Congregationalists, were so called because each congregation was independent and not subject to any overall control. They appointed their own ministers, which made them more powerful than the Anglican laity, and they elected their own deacons, who normally represented them in matters of discipline and administration. For seventeen years, however, from 1807 to 1824, the Old Meeting in Stansted was without any deacons.

Since the chapel used by the Old Meeting was replaced by a new building in 1878, and since the chapel of the New Meeting is now a warehouse, it is impossible to recreate their appearance inside. But the arrangement, at least of the Old Meeting, is perhaps best recaptured by Mark Rutherford's description in his *Autobiography* of the 'large, old-fashioned' chapel in the eastern counties where he worshipped as a boy in the 1840s. 'The floor was covered with high pews. The roof was supported by three or four tall wooden pillars which ran from the ground to the ceiling, and the galleries by shorter pillars. There was a large oak pulpit on one side against the wall, and down below, immediately under the minister, was the "singing pew", where the singers and musicians sat, the musicians being performers on the clarionet, flute, violin and violincello. . . . The chapel was lighted in winter by immense chandeliers with tiers of candles all round.[5]

The church books of both Meetings give a detailed account of the organised religious life of Stansted's Independents, and in the collected sermons of *The Essex Remembrancer* we can listen again to the Reverend Robert May, among others, the first minister to be appointed by the Old Meeting after the split.

There were two services each Sunday, in the morning and in the evening, and then, as now, the centrepiece was the sermon. The very titles listed in *The Essex Remembrancer* are enough to convey the full weight and import of the Independents' spiritual concerns. May preached on 'Mourners Comforted', for example, 'Divine Forgiveness' and 'The Burdened Sinner Directed to Christ', while the subjects chosen by his colleagues included 'Justification by Faith', 'Satan's Malice defeated by Christ's Intercession', 'Continuance on Earth not desired by the Believer', and 'Memory the Source of the Sinner's Torment in Hell'.

Their prayer meetings, which they held in the vestry between services or on weekday evenings, were generally described as interesting, serious, solemn, delightful, encouraging (if well attended) or refreshing (as in 'a time of refreshing in the Lord'); and we are told on occasion that 'Many found it good to be there'. They prayed for the divine blessing on their services, that 'backsliders' might be reclaimed, and that the Spirit of the Lord might be poured upon them from on high. They deplored the general desecration of the Lord's day, the spread of infidelity and, in 1831, the incendiarism of the Swing Riots.

Their county electors, as we have already seen, voted for those candidates who supported the abolition of slavery, as well as the reform of parliament, and this is reflected in their church activities. They had a missionary society, set up in 1812, and on 1 August 1834 the whole day was given over to 'Thanksgiving to God on a/c of the emancipation of the Negro slaves in our Brit. Colonies'.

A Church Meeting was held once a month, attended only by the members, and among other things they dealt with applications for membership. Entering the church was no formality. Normally the deacons would 'wait upon' the candidates and question them closely on their religious experience. In most cases they were satisfied and recommended acceptance, but in 1824, at a time when the Old Meeting was still without deacons, one candidate was examined by the whole church, which rejected him, 'finding him ignorant of the great principles of salvation'.

The Church Meeting also dealt with cases of discipline, and again it was normally the deacons who made the necessary enquiries. In 1813 Robert Tyler was 'suspended from the Lord's Table' for three months for 'cruelly beating his father'. In 1823, shortly after the split, Mrs Gaffee was dismissed from membership after admitting to Messrs Reed and Sanders (this was John Sanders, Guiver's nephew) that she had been guilty of the sin of fornication. This was a particularly painful 'wound' because Mrs Gaffee was the widow of a former minister. In 1833 Samuel Gilbey was suspended from the church after it had been proved 'that he had for a long time been contracting various debts without having the least prospect of paying them'. And in 1834 John Munchall was 'solemnly excommunicated' for 'profanely violating the Lord's day' by selling goods 'secretly' and 'by artifice'. All these cases are taken from the church book of the Old Meeting, but there were similar cases at the New Meeting. In 1834, for example, Hetty Tripp, Guiver's daughter, was excommunicated for 'continued absence . . . from public ordinances' and failing to respond to a request for an interview.

The other great duty which the members normally had to carry out was that of appointing the minister, but in Stansted this seems to have been shared with the congregation. When the Reverend Benjamin Gaffee died in October 1818 the church had to find a replacement, and the members and hearers were each asked to set aside one hour in private 'for the purpose of imploring . . . the direction & blessing of the Most High'. At another level they directed their enquiries, as on similar occasions in the past, to the Evangelical Academy at Hoxton, which could provide them with a supply of students eager to begin their ministerial careers or put them in touch with other ministers who might want to move and take up a new appointment. It took them three years of argument and wrangling before they could make their decision. In August 1821, however, they were all agreed that Josiah Redford, a student from the Academy, should be invited to become their minister, and two months later he was duly ordained. At last the church's difficulties seemed resolved, and when, in January 1822, Redford went away for a few weeks to fulfil a previous engagement in Bristol, he believed that he was leaving his charge 'in Unity and prosperity'.

What happened after this is disputed, and there are two main accounts, one written by Redford later the same year, and the other by Robert May, Redford's successor at the Old Meeting, who must have relied on the testimony of others, including John Sanders, Guiver's nephew, and who only put pen to paper in 1833. Redford says that 'On his departure, it transpired, that he had privately entered into a matrimonial engagement and connection with the younger daughter of Mr. John Tyler of Bentfield End'. This caused 'much dissatisfaction' among the members. On 24 January, while still in Bristol, he received a 'very condemnatory letter' from William Chaplin, the Independent minister at Bishop's Stortford, and on 30 January the church met and passed a vote of suspension. May, professing extreme reluctance, only tells us what he thinks we need to know. He would gladly, he says, draw a veil over Redford's 'most gross and scandalous behaviour'. 'This much however is due to the cause of Truth and good morals . . . that he was found to have been living in fornication *at the very time of his Ordination*'. This must obviously have been the charge, and in fact when he married Amy Tyler of Bentfield End, as we know from the baptism of their son in May, she was already several months pregnant. The great cause of offence, sex before marriage, was the same as that which had shocked John Reynolds a century before, but this time it was the minister himself who was the offender.

Redford hurried back from Bristol, and on 3 February, a Sunday, assuming that the majority were against him, he publicly tendered his resignation. According to his own account, however, this turned out 'to be both premature, and quite contrary to the feelings of a large majority'. During the next week a member of the church, Joseph Blackaby, and a member of the congregation, William Sanders, went round the village to whip up support, and on the following Saturday, 9 February, they submitted a letter to their 'beloved, & highly esteem'd Minister', condemning the severe measures that had been adopted and asking him to continue among them, if necessary, 'in some more humble spot'. This letter was signed by 27 of the 31 members, John Sanders being one of the four exceptions, and by 194 'attendants'. It no longer survives, but in the light of subsequent events we can be sure that Guiver and Mary added their marks.

May's account is again different. After Redford had admitted his 'criminality', he says, 'It was deemed prudent, by neighbouring Ministers, and pious people in general, that he should be advised to leave the village'. But Redford would not listen: 'he . . . was destitute of any personal property, & finding himself wrecked as to all prospect of rising in the esteem of the Religious public, he appears to have determined upon making one grand & powerful struggle for the possession of the Meeting House where he should continue to exercise his ministry'. And May accuses him of drumming up support by enlisting new subscribers who would vote for him at a 'decisive meeting' which was about to be convened.

The meeting to which May refers was announced at the church service on the morning of Sunday, 10 February. It was to be a meeting of the church and congregation held on the evening of the following Tuesday, and two ministers from London were invited, Thomas Wilson, the treasurer of the Evangelical Academy, and John Clayton, who had been Redford's pastor in London. (Redford was convinced that John Sanders, with Isaac Hodges, was responsible for these invitations.) On one issue May was right: the Independent establishment was united against Redford. But he was probably wrong when he accused Redford of enrolling new subscribers to tip the vote. Redford was taking his stand upon the strict principles of Independency, and was arguing that only church members could exercise discipline over the minister. His supporters did not want any outsiders at all. On the Sunday afternoon Joseph Blackaby[6] publicly protested that the members had not invited Wilson and Clayton to the meeting, and that the church was being deprived of its rights.

On the Tuesday evening the meeting house was packed. According to May, Redford had been 'mustering his newly enlisted forces in a neighbouring barn' beforehand, and when Clayton and Wilson arrived 'Nothing could exceed the vexation and dismay which the hostile party displayed . . .; a mob in the galleries shouted out "Redford for ever!" and heaped upon those who were opposed in sentiment to themselves, and especially the Visitors, the most opprobrious epithets. In vain did Mr. Clayton remind them of the awful impropriety of their behaviour; his voice was drowned by the scorning of the rabble. . . . At length, however, . . . Mr. Redford came forward and finding that his plans were frustrated he made a long harangue to the audience, occasionally cheered by the shouts of his party, and surrendered his pastoral office, together with the keys of the meeting house. . . . At the breaking up of the assembly nothing could exceed the riot & disorder that prevailed. Not content with abuse, the *lives* of many were threatened; stones, & other missiles were hurled against Mr. Redford's opponents, and one of the members of the Church . . . was severely wounded in the face, others owing their escape to the protection of peace officers or to flight!!! Such alas! was the unhappy termination of Mr. Redford's ministry at the Old Meeting'.

But May's account, though detailed and lurid, does not explain how it was that Redford's plans were frustrated and why he gave up the keys of the meeting house when the majority so clearly wanted him to stay. For this we have to turn to Redford's account, which shows that at the very beginning of the meeting his opponents produced their trump card – the original trust deed of the church. This, apparently, had been mislaid for some time, but was now brought forward and read out. In Redford's words, it showed that 'the power . . . as to all final decisions' was vested 'not, as in strictly Independent Churches it ought to be, in the votes of the majority of the Church members, but in the Trustees', several of whom lived outside the parish and were evidently opposed to Redford. Because of this Clayton and Wilson suggested that Redford should then and there sign a paper relinquishing all his rights as pastor of the Old Meeting. According to Redford, 'the multitude' pleaded and begged him to refuse. But his hand was forced, he signed the paper, and in this way the 'painful contention' was terminated.[7]

But, so far from being the end of the affair, this was only the beginning. Redford's supporters had already suggested that, if he could not hold on to his position, he should continue among them in some more humble spot. That was what he did, preaching in cottages and then in barns, which were always full to overflowing. It was at this point that old Guiver made his providential offer of land, and the New Meeting was established in the Newmarket Road. 'The mischief', wrote Chaplin, 'is now in full force'.[8]

Seventeen of the thirty-one members went with Redford, and many of the congregation. The Old Meeting was left crippled, with no minister, and its attendance sometimes reduced to a mere handful. As far as we know, the only Sanders to remain there were Guiver's nephew, John, and his family. All the rest threw in their lot with Redford.

It was a profitable development for Guiver. Although Redford referred to his 'offer' of land, in fact he charged nine guineas for the freehold. More important, he installed all the woodwork, and his bill for this came to £163, though he allowed a discount of £12. For his nephew, John, the affair was a disaster. He was persuaded to bring a charge of libel against one of Redford's supporters, and when he was unsuccessful he was left with a lawyer's bill of £103. Nine years later he was still trying to pay it off.[9]

Under May, who was appointed a year later, the Old Meeting gradually recovered, and by 1829, according to Redford, it had about 300 'hearers'. But the New Meeting held its own, and its hearers numbered about 100 more.[10] Redford continued to be ostracized by the neighbouring ministers, but May in turn had reason to complain of Redford's 'malevolence and repeated annoyances'.[11]

John Sanders was elected a deacon at the Old Meeting, and William Sanders a deacon at the New. Occasionally the New Meeting put out feelers for reconciliation, and there were elaborately worded exchanges between the deacons. But as long as Redford remained pastor of the New Meeting there was no real possibility of a reunion.

So the Independents of Stansted remained divided. Disagreements were common in Dissenting Churches, and John Binfield, in his study of Victorian Nonconformity in East Anglia, concludes that 'The Dissenting Congregation, autonomous, consciously seeking the influence of the Spirit vouchsafed to the Church meeting to do His will, . . . was peculiarly liable to internal conflicts'. There were many causes — 'distrust of an energetic youngster replacing the well-tried methods of a long-loved minister, disagreement with the leading family, accusations of immorality or dishonesty, mingled with doctrinal fears or accusations of ritualism'.[12] In this case the main issue that split the church was obviously Redford's 'immorality'. But there may have been more to it than that. Those, like John Sanders, who condemned Redford were not merely taking a stand against his conduct. They were also maintaining their links with the Independent establishment and mainstream respectability, and they looked for leadership to William Chaplin from Bishop's Stortford and to Thomas Wilson and John Clayton from London. Those, like Guiver and William Sanders, who supported Redford, resented and resisted this outside interference. They were not going to be told what to do by anyone who did not belong to the church. And Redford, with his insistence on the strict principles of Independency, was able to exploit this local feeling.

John Sanders, the deacon at the Old Meeting, died in 1842, leaving his Bible to his eldest son and his other religious books to be divided among his other children. 'I desire to commit my immortal soul', he wrote, 'into the hands of a covenant God in Christ Jesus to be washed in the precious blood of Christ the eternal son of God to be made meet to be a partaker of the Saints in light'.[13]

William Sanders, the deacon at the New Meeting, fell out with Redford and left the Meeting for a while, but when Redford departed he was welcomed back and resumed his office. The church was still wracked with dissension and conflict, and its support dwindled over the years. In 1875 it was reformed as a Union Church of Baptists and Independents. There were only four members, and William Sanders, now 73 years old, was elected as their only deacon. He died five years later, and was commemorated by a marble plaque on the walls of the building that is now Joscelyne's Depository on the land that had been 'offered' by old Guiver Sanders.[14]

7

Postscript to Stansted

The census returns in the nineteenth century show that most of the Sanders who were born in Stansted did not stay there, and many of them must have formed part of the great drift of population from rural Essex to London. The returns for 1881, the last which are open for inspection, show 44 Sanders still living in the village. A few of them were carpenters, and one was a builder with 26 employees. But they were soon to be eclipsed by more successful rivals, and the builder went bankrupt around the turn of the century.

When I was beginning work on this book, and had just discovered that the Sanders came from Stansted, I asked the vicar if there was anyone who was particularly knowledgeable in the history of the village. He gave me the name of Irving Sanders; and Irving and his family, as I found when I met them a few weeks later, were the only Sanders left in the village descended from Thomas and Sarah. All the rest had died or moved away.

In 1982 I made the journey in reverse, moving from London to live in Stansted, or more precisely in Bentfield End, about two hundred yards from the site of the house which the first John Sanders had inherited from Matthias Palmer in 1704. When she heard where I was going Mary, my father's sister, who was then 79 years old, commented that when she was a little girl her father had taken her to Stansted Fair. Her great-uncles from Braintree went there too, one of them, Alf, to sell his song-birds. It seems more than a coincidence that, of all the fairs in Essex and London, this was the one to which her father had taken her. Alf at least had business to do, but even so it is possible that the Sanders who had originally moved to Braintree, the younger Guiver, Elizabeth and their children, had chosen the occasion of the annual fair to visit the relatives they had left behind, and that their descendants had kept up the tradition even though the family links had been broken. Mary cannot remember visiting any relatives. And before I began research for this book there was no one in the family who had any idea that the Sanders had ever lived in Stansted.

1. The Street in Stansted, now called Lower Street, *c.* 1910.

2. 'The Carpenter'. An illustration from *The Book of English Trades and Library of the Useful Arts* (London, 1824).

3.   Stansted Hall, the home of the Myddletons, then the Heaths, from an engraving of *c.*1770.

4.   St Mary's Church, Stansted, 1756.

5. The Old Workhouse. A sketch made by the local historian, Joseph Green, in 1890.

6. The Three Colts public house in the Great Newmarket Road (now the Cambridge Road). Joseph Sanders, brother of the younger Guiver, was the landlord here from 1809 until his death in 1835. It remained in the hands of the family for a further forty years.

7. A view of the Great Newmarket Road (now Silver Street), taken in 1957 from the site of the old chapel (now replaced by a cast-iron fountain). The house where Guiver and Mary lived was the white-fronted house on the left, set back a little from the road.

8 (above) and 9 (below).   Two of the houses built by the elder Guiver in the Great Newmarket Road. Above, the house now known as The Old Manse, which he sold to the Independent Church in 1821 for £400. Below, the house now known as Roycot, which he sold in 1823 for £200 to John Atkin, 'Tailor and Draper' and a fellow adherent of the Independent Church. The Old Manse is still timber-framed. Roycot now has a brick frontage.

10. The Old Meeting House of the Independent Church on Chapel Hill. A sketch made by the local historian, Joseph Green, shortly before the building was replaced in 1864.

11. The New Meeting House, built on the land in the Great Newmarket Road (now Silver Street) which the elder Guiver was 'prompted' by Providence to offer to Josiah Redford's Independent Church in 1822. For many years it was a furniture warehouse, Joscelyne's Depository, but shortly before this book went to print it was taken over as a leisure centre.

Braintree and Black Notley: 1817–1894

A sketch map of Braintree based on the Ordnance Survey Map of 1875. Pound End was in the southern part of the town, round Walters' silk mills. Hoppit Hill has been renamed as the Notley Road, and Notley Hill as Rifle Hill. Charlie and Jessamy's house is circled.

TABLE 2:

THE FAMILY IN BRAINTREE AND BLACK NOTLEY

GULVER (1777–1832) = ELIZABETH AYLETT (1776–1834)

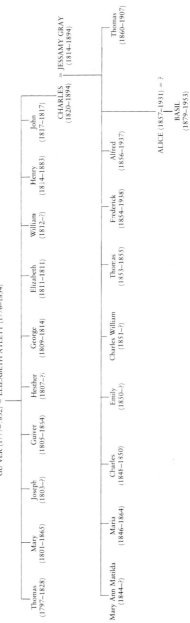

Thomas
(1797–1828)

Mary
(1801–1865)

Joseph
(1803–?)

Gulver
(1805–1854)

Hesther
(1807–?)

George
(1809–1814)

Elizabeth
(1811–1811)

William
(1812–?)

Henry
(1814–1883)

John
(1817–1817)

CHARLES = JESSAMY GRAY
(1820–1894)   (1814–1894)

Mary Ann Matilda
(1844–?)

Maria
(1846–1864)

Charles
(1848–1850)

Emily
(1850–?)

Charles William
(1851–?)

Thomas
(1853–1855)

Frederick
(1854–1938)

Alfred
(1856–1937)

ALICE (1857–1931) = ?

BASIL
(1879–1953)

Thomas
(1860–1907)

8

A Leather Purse and Twelve Gold Sovereigns

On the afternoon of Tuesday 7 June 1836, Thomas Andrews, a lead-smelter from Lambeth, stood talking with some friends in the street outside The Spotted Dog public house in Chelmsford. A bye-election was being held for the newly formed constituency of South Essex, and the two candidates, who had been nominated that morning, were the Tory, George Palmer, and the Whig, Champion Edward Branfill. Andrews, who had been brought up in Bocking and was qualified to vote, had come to give his support to Branfill. The election proceedings had been characteristically rowdy, and Andrews had been drinking freely. He had bought some cigars, and had sent them to The Queen's Head, where the coach would leave for Bocking later in the day. A friend, however, now offered to take him, and Andrews agreed.

It was a warm day, and the window of The Spotted Dog was wide open. A young man sitting inside with two friends had caught sight of Andrews, noticed that he had been drinking, and was listening carefully to every word he said. When Andrews remarked that he would have to get his cigars back from The Queen's Head, the young man leaned out of the window and offered to fetch them for him. Although Andrews came from Bocking, and the young man from Braintree, and although Bocking and Braintree formed a single town, the young man, according to Andrews' later account, was 'quite a stranger' to him. He accepted the offer but, probably because he did not trust the young man entirely, he followed him to The Queen's Head, where he saw him collect the cigars.

At this point the Whig band marched by, and Andrews joined it, with the young man keeping close to his side. The two friends of the young man, it seems, were not far behind, although they would later deny being anywhere near. The bandsmen went into the yard of The Saracen's Head, the inn overlooking the hustings, and Andrews, flushed with drink and excitement, drew out his purse and ordered ten gallons of beer for them. He remembered later that, after paying for the beer, he had put his purse back into his left-hand coat pocket. He also remembered that it had contained about twelve gold sovereigns. As Andrews stood in the midst of the bandsmen, Edward Church, who carried the banner for the band, noticed the young man holding his arm. He also noticed one of the young man's friends walk by and 'wink his Eye at him', to which the young man 'nodded his head'. 'It struck me', he said later, 'there was an understanding between them beyond accidentally seeing each other.'

When the bandsmen had drunk their beer Andrews went into the parlour of The Saracen's Head, with the young man holding him by his left arm; and when he sat down the young man sat down, again keeping to his left. George Lake, the innkeeper, claimed later that the young man's two friends were with him as well, but he could not swear to this. He noticed them, he said, 'because they were of a different class of persons to those he was accustomed to have there, and he was rather surprised to see Mr. Andrews in their company.' Andrews and the young man stayed in the parlour for about a quarter of an hour while Andrews drank brandy and water. The young man then got up and said he would go and fetch the band back. Andrews waited for him for about five or ten minutes, but he did not return. Then Andrews found that his purse was missing. He looked for the young man and made enquiries throughout the town, but with no success. He then reported his loss to the authorities, and the search for the young man and his two friends began in earnest.

The first to be caught was Frank Motier, aged 22, a jobber from Bocking. It was Motier who, according to Edward Church, had winked at the young man in The Saracen's Head yard, and Andrews claimed to have seen him there too. But Motier, while admitting that he had been at The Spotted Dog earlier, denied that he had ever been at The Saracen's Head.

Jonathan May, the other friend, aged 22, a cap-maker from Cambridge, was followed to The Mason's Arms, but then gave his followers the slip. Later he was seen at Moulsham by Richard Gosling, a tailor. When May noticed Gosling coming towards him, he ran away over the fields. Gosling chased after him. May pretended to throw something into a hedge as he ran, but Gosling pressed on and caught him. Gosling asked May why he was running away, and May asked Gosling why he was chasing him. Gosling asked May what he had thrown away, and May said that he did not know. Gosling then said that he understood that May had been involved with two others in robbing a gentleman. 'I'm buggered if I've got any of his money,' May replied.

The young man himself could not be found, but people knew that he was Charlie Sanders, the youngest son of Guiver and Elizabeth, and that he lived in Braintree, and two or three days later he was arrested there and brought before Bernard Scalé, the vicar and magistrate. In a statement made before Scalé he said that he knew nothing about the gentleman's purse. He had not left Chelmsford 'till late on Tuesday' (the day when he had been with Andrews), and he had then gone to London 'by a Colchester van'. Whose van was it? 'I do not know whose it was.' He had slept in the van, and had reached London at 4 or 5 a.m. on the Wednesday. Why had he gone to London? 'To get work if I could.' Yet he had left London on the afternoon of that same Wednesday. He had travelled back 'by Fakes's van', slept in it overnight, and reached home, at his sister's in Braintree, by 9 a.m. on the Thursday. Why had he come back? Because 'Fakes's man asked me to come down with him by his van he being alone.' After taking his statement Scalé committed him to Springfield Gaol to await trial by jury at the Quarter Sessions in Chelmsford.

The charge was stealing a leather purse and twelve gold sovereigns, and the case was heard in the first week of July. It was quickly decided that there was no evidence against Motier, and he was acquitted at once. As for May and Sanders, 'The proof was not sufficiently clear against the prisoners, and the Jury returned a verdict of not guilty.' But although Andrews had been drinking he was probably right in believing that Charlie had stolen his purse. Why otherwise had he attached himself to Andrews in the first place? Why had he stuck so close to his left side? Why had he not come back to The Saracen's Head after saying that he was going to fetch the band? Had he really gone to London to find work? If so, why had he come back within the day? There was not enough evidence for a conscientious jury to be satisfied beyond all reasonable doubt, but there is enough for anyone else weighing up the balance of probabilities.[1]

Six months later Charlie almost had to stand trial again, this time at the Assize Court on an even more serious charge. Together with another man, he was accused of stealing lead from St Michael's, the Anglican church in Braintree. We do not know the details, only that there was insufficient evidence to justify a prosecution, though statements were taken from eleven witnesses.[2]

The family's standing had fallen dramatically. In June 1831 old Guiver Sanders had travelled from Stansted to Chelmsford to cast his vote in the great struggle for the passage of the Reform Bill. In June 1836 Charlie, his grandson, had taken advantage of the excitement of the election to steal a leather purse with twelve gold sovereigns from a half-intoxicated voter. Guiver had been a generous adherent of the Independent Church. Charlie did not belong to any church and had been accused of stealing lead from St Michael's.

Charlie went on to have four illegitimate children by a gypsy woman before marrying her and having six more children. His four daughters became silk weavers, and three of them had illegitimate children themselves. All of his four surviving sons were in trouble with the law in one way or another. Charlie eventually became a calf dealer and by the end of his life had built up a small but successful business. But the Sanders never regained in Braintree the position and respect which they had enjoyed in Stansted.

9

The Falcon and the Town of Braintree

Charlie was born and brought up at The Falcon, his father's public house, and he was the eleventh and youngest child in the family. He was only twelve years old when his father died in 1832, and his mother, who then moved to London, died just two years later. His eldest sister, Mary, and her husband, William Cook, took over The Falcon. They were old enough to be Charlie's parents, and it seems that they continued to look after him there. When he came back to Braintree from London after the theft of Thomas Andrews' purse he went home, he said, to his sister's, and Mary was almost certainly the sister he meant. Although he claimed that he had gone to London to find work, he also gave his occupation as an ostler. It is possible that he was employed by William and Mary to look after their customers' horses.

The Falcon stood in the High Street, at the very heart of the old town of Braintree. This part, as Thomas Wright described it in 1836, was a tangled complex of streets, 'irregularly formed' and 'inconveniently narrow', with many 'ancient' timber-framed houses.[1] Charlie said later that his father was an innkeeper but the Falcon was not so much an inn as a public house.[2] It was not very large, and most if not all of the living accommodation must have been taken up by the family.[3] By the 1820s more than half of the public houses in the country had fallen into the hands of the large brewers, but Guiver was the owner as well as the landlord of The Falcon, and he probably brewed his own beer on the premises.[4]

No one could run a public house or an inn unless they were granted an alehouse licence at the general Brewster Sessions which were held each year in September, and in order to obtain a licence they had to guarantee their good behaviour and provide the names of two sureties. In Braintree, as a regular business arrangement, the publicans formed groups of three and stood sureties for each other.[5] In 1830, however, as part of the movement towards free trade, the Beer Act allowed anyone to sell beer on payment of a fee of £2. The result was a proliferation of beershops and, it was said, a wave of drunkenness throughout the country. Many publicans, faced with this new competition, concentrated more on the sale of spirits, while others joined the increasing number who were selling out to the large brewers. Guiver held out, but at some time before 1840 his son-in-law William Cook, while remaining the licensee, made over The Falcon to Hawkes and Company, a brewery which has since been taken over by Benskins.[6]

In geography, though not in government or sentiment, Braintree and Bocking formed a single town.[7] Their combined population was about four times as large as Stansted's, and at the time when Guiver set himself up in the High Street it was increasing rapidly. From 4,842 in 1811 it went up to 8,186 in 1851. Then it remained relatively stable, rising gradually to 8,829 in 1891. By that time it had also spread southwards into the northern tip of the parish of Black Notley. There was a rapid turnover too. In 1821 only a quarter of the population of Braintree had been born there.

Since Roman times the town had stood at the crossroads formed originally by the road from Colchester in the east to St Albans in the west and the road from London and Chelmsford in the south to Gosfield and Brancaster in the north. In 1848 the railway was opened and linked Braintree through Witham to London and Ipswich. And in 1869 a second line was opened, running through Dunmow to Bishop's Stortford in the west, a development which would have made it easier for the Sanders to keep in touch with their relatives in Stansted.

The town was an important centre for the local farmers. A market was held in Braintree every Wednesday and, as Cunnington, a contemporary local historian, points out, it was 'much frequented' because 'we have a large scope of country at the back of us, in which there are no markets of any consequence'.[8] On market days the old streets in the centre were 'blocked up ... with droves of cattle, loose horses, and implements'.[9] It was often dangerous to be walking about, and throughout the century there were accidents as horses bolted or cattle stampeded. The great event of the year was the Braintree Fair for cattle and hops in October. This, says Cunnington, was 'much resorted to', and cattle were sent from as far away as Scotland and Wales.[10] A Corn Exchange was built in 1839, another clear sign of civic pride and the importance of the agricultural interest. With the depression later in the century, however, there were many complaints of sluggish trade in the market and a falling away of business at the October Fair.

One of the main reasons for the growth in population was the establishment of the silk industry. In the country as a whole it never attained the importance of the woollen and cotton industries, and it was always under threat from French competition. In the south it was concentrated in Spitalfields in East London, but the wages of the Spitalfields weavers were legally protected at a comparatively high level, and so several manufacturers moved to Essex. Braintree and Bocking became their leading centre, and by 1833, according to Cunnington, the silk firms already employed 'many hundreds of workers', women and children as well as men.[11] In the long run Courtaulds and Walters were the most successful companies. Samuel Courtauld set up his main mill in Bocking, while Daniel Walters established his business at Pound End, in the south of Braintree. Charlie Sanders, as we shall see, lived in this part of the town for about twenty years. His daughter Alice worked for Walters and so, almost certainly, did her sisters.

While Courtaulds, with more than 1,000 workers, eventually specialized in black crape, which became popular after Queen Victoria went into mourning, Walters concentrated on fine figured silks and velvets. In 1861 D.W. Collier, in *The People's History of Essex*, reported that the firm employed nearly 300 workers and that it was 'one of the foremost in the kingdom for superiority of design and beauty of workmanship. . . . The house has a good foreign trade, and the very richest brocatelles, damasks, tissued satins, etc., which adorn the palaces of our Queen are produced in these works at Braintree'. In 1860 the import duties on silks were removed as part of a free trade treaty with France. Most firms in the town could no longer compete, but Courtaulds and Walters were at least able to hold their own. In 1894, however, Walters closed down, and a year later they sold out to Warner and Sons.

At first male silk weavers earned more than farm labourers, but by the 1830s they were down to the same level. They seem to have done slightly better later, at least at Courtaulds, where in the 1860s the weekly wage for male weavers was 15s. a week, with women earning a few shillings less and young girls about 4s. to 5s.[12] The hours were long: even after the legislation of 1847 women and children had to work 60 hours a week. This did not compare badly with the carpenters at Stansted, but much of the work was grindingly repetitive.

Both Samuel Courtauld and Daniel Walters were authoritarian and paternalist. They refused to allow any trade union activity, but took pride in acting as benefactors to their workers. Though wages were poor and hours were long, the weavers were spared the worst conditions of the northern mills. At first most of them were outworkers. They collected skeins of silk from the company, wove it on handlooms in their homes, and then returned the finished article. It was often a family affair, with the women and children doing the preparatory work, the winding and the warping, and the men carrying out the weaving. With the development of the mills, however, most employees became factory workers. Walters enlarged their premises at Pound End and in their 'New Mills' they introduced looms that were too wide for the home and others that were driven by steam power and not hand. By 1893 they had thirty-three power looms operated by seventy to eighty workers.[13]

Several of the mills are still standing. They were simple, functional buildings, with red brick walls at the base surmounted by white weather-boarding and long continuous stretches of windows to let in as much light as possible. A visitor to Walters' in 1874 found them 'large, lightsome and perfectly ventilated', and claimed that every visitor was struck by 'the healthiness of the workpeople', which was 'a perfect contrast to the yellow visages and dull eyes of Northern factory hands'.[14] This observation was repeated thirty years later by a visitor who, after being directed to the factory by 'a rosy-cheeked girl', 'could not but compare the good appearance of these girls with the factory "hands" one sees thronging the cotton mills in the North, with shawls tied over their heads'.[15] Another visitor in 1880 was impressed by the cleanliness of the mills and their employees, which was necessary, he was told, since even the slightest dirt would leave an indelible stain in the silk. But the noise in the weaving rooms was deafening, especially where the looms were driven by steam, and some of the jobs which he saw must have been tedious and unremittingly demanding, like that of the girls who had to watch the silk passing from one process to another to check that none of the threads was broken. About half the millhands were women.[16]

The annual outings of Courtaulds and Walters were regularly reported in *The Braintree and Bocking Advertiser*, and the writer always went out of his way to emphasise the workers' enjoyment and appreciation. A typical Walters outing would begin with two or three hundred workers, together with their children, gathering outside the factory at six in the morning and being led in procession by a band to Braintree station. Their destination was nearly always an east coast resort, like Yarmouth or Walton-on-the-Naze. They would arrive by eight, march with their band to a hotel, eat a 'hearty' and 'substantial' breakfast, and then, if the weather was good enough, set off for the cliffs or the beaches, led once again by the band. Then there would be organised games — cricket, football, archery and boating. On some outings the band stayed with them through the day, playing a 'choice selection of airs'. On others it played in front of the hotel where the company's management was passing the day. After tea at the hotel the excursionists would return to Braintree, where they would arrive at about ten in the evening. They would escort their 'esteemed manager' to his home amid 'ringing cheers' and displays of fireworks; and at the end they would gather outside the factory, the band would play the national anthem, and they would all disperse to their homes. The expenses of these outings were all met by the firm, and the *Advertiser* had no doubt that in the 'increased zeal' of their employees they would 'receive the reward to which such liberality entitles them'.[17]

Braintree, it was said, was as famous for its silk as Epsom for its salts and Chelsea for its buns: 'men, women, and children seem all to be engaged in weaving silk'.[18] But there were other trades as well. In addition to those which were common to most towns, there was a brush-making company, West's, which in 1851 employed more than seventy people, and towards the end of the century engineering began to replace silk manufacture as the chief industry of the town.

Braintree was governed by a select vestry, but many of its functions were taken over in due course by new and more powerful authorities – the Board of Guardians for the poor in 1835, the Local Board of Health in 1850, and finally, in our period, the Urban District Council in 1894. The most obvious improvement was in the cleanliness of the town. By 1833, according to Cunnington, most of the inhabitants of the principal streets had paved the footpaths in front of their houses, but the drainage was primitive and there was no underground sewerage. In 1848 an Inspector of the Board of Health reported that the town was 'in a most wretched condition' and that he had 'never yet seen its equal for filthiness'. Typhus, he said, was 'raging', and six years later there was an outbreak of cholera. After the appointment of the Local Board in 1850 the work of improvement began in earnest. By 1874 the town could be described as 'a clean and eminently salubrious place', and in 1881, according to Kelly's Directory, it was 'clean, well-paved, lighted with gas, and supplied with water from an artesian well'.

Though the spire of St Michael's, the Anglican church, rose high above the buildings in the centre of Braintree, the religious life of the town was dominated by the Nonconformists, who in 1851 made up three-quarters of its churchgoing population. At first, however, it was the Anglicans who provided the town's main schooling, and it was only in 1862 that the Nonconformists, led by George Courtauld, set up schools of their own in Manor Street. After the passing of the 1870 Education Act control of the Manor Street Schools was transferred to the Braintree School Board, but the Anglicans maintained their independence. Throughout this period there were several small private schools in the town.

In addition to the churches and the schools, there were many organisations which aimed, as they saw it, to raise the level of the working class, particularly towards the end of the century. Among others, there were the Literary and Mechanics' Institution, the Workmen's Club, the Total Abstinence Society, and local branches of the Band of Hope and the British Women's Temperance Society. Chartism was strong in the 1840s, and in 1890 the Socialists set up a local branch in the town.

Those who aspired after respectability in Braintree were always worried by the town's 'immorality' and crime. The illegitimacy rate was certainly high. In the 1840s, when Charlie's illegitimate children were born, it was 8 per cent among the children baptized at St Michael's. There were the usual complaints about debauchery at the fair, and as late as 1893 one of the local clergy condemned it as an occasion of quarrelling, fighting and drunken 'orgies', when many young people 'lost their moral balance' and fell into 'irretrievable sin and moral ruin'.[19]

More seriously, there were many who put the blame on the mills. 'I have often heard it complained that the morality of Braintree . . . is getting worse and worse', wrote a correspondent to the *Advertiser* in 1869, 'and the reason I have always heard assigned is "the factories".' The conversation there, he had been told, was 'something awful'. A few months earlier, in an article which provoked this correspondence, the editor of the *Braintree Parish Magazine* warned parents against exposing their children to 'the fierce temptations of factory life'. When this was drawn to George Courtauld's attention, he protested that he was at a loss to understand what was meant. And 'Veritas', one of his supporters in this newspaper debate, said that he knew every aspect of factory life, that any immodest or disorderly behaviour was suppressed, and that the behaviour of the children 'savours more of boisterous mirth than of "something awful".'[20] Walters were very careful to enforce proper behaviour on their premises. Their visitor in 1880 noticed that, while both men and women were employed, 'whatever the system adopted to ensure it, regularity, order and cleanliness, are particularly noticeable in every department'.[21]

There was little that the manufacturers could do about what went on outside the factories. In 1846 Samuel Courtauld had complained to the magistrates about the young men who gathered at his factory gates and made obscene remarks and advances to the girls as they came out. And Courtauld's critic in the *Advertiser* complained: 'One can scarcely walk down the streets of Braintree at night without seeing knots of factory girls and young lads standing about laughing and talking in a very loud and immodest manner'.

This argument is of particular interest to us because three of Charlie's daughters, including Alice, my great-grandmother, worked in the mills and had illegitimate children. It was not confined to Braintree, but was part of a much wider debate about the effects of industrialisation on morality. It was generally believed that factory work, by taking women away from the home and putting them alongside men in the workplace, broke down the moral framework of the working class family and encouraged illicit relations. But in fact illegitimacy was just as high, if not higher, in the rural areas, and the close supervision in the silk factories in Braintree could hardly have been conducive to any sexual promiscuity. Whatever the underlying reasons for the rise in illegitimacy, factory life does not seem to have been one of them.[22]

More research is needed on levels of crime, but Braintree, it was thought, suffered more than most, and the public houses in particular were widely regarded as sources of disorder and violence. They had to be closed by 9 p.m. in winter and 10 p.m. in summer, and great efforts were made to enforce this. The local papers frequently record cases of publicans being brought before the bench for keeping open after hours, allowing disorderly conduct on the premises, or trading on Sunday. Guiver Sanders was twice fined for offences 'against the condition of his alehouse recognizance', £1 in 1824 and £3 in 1828, but we do not know what exactly he had done wrong.[23]

His son-in-law, William Cook, almost lost his licence. Some of the more respectable citizens of Braintree, mainly tradesmen and Dissenters, with John Cunnington, the local historian at their head, were worried by the rowdiness at certain public houses which kept open long after hours. In the year ending September 1834 they and the night watchmen of the town recorded thirty-three offences involving five licensees, including William Cook. In the ensuing court proceedings Cunnington alleged that, in spite of repeated warnings, several of the publicans had persisted in keeping late hours, sometimes as late as three in the morning. He mentioned three instances when, as a result, riots had taken place and one man had lost his life. Braintree, he argued, suffered badly from crime, and he attributed this to 'the disorderly state of the public houses in the town, and the inducements which were held out by allowing music and dancing'.

The publicans were indignant, they said, at this system of espionage, and wanted to know who was controlling the town, the magistrates or a few 'menial individuals'. And they protested about this 'union of different religious sects to overturn the bulwarks of the constitution'. They argued that their offences were trivial, and that 'in a general way', considering that Braintree was a 'manufacturing town', the magistrates had no cause of complaint against them.

At the end, however, the chairman of the magistrates delivered 'a most powerful address' and impressed on them the need to keep their houses 'orderly and respectable, so as to feel themselves superior to common beer-house keepers'. Eventually, after the publicans had apologised, and a memorial had been got up to support them, Cunnington said that he was satisfied and all the licences were renewed.[24]

The episode is worth describing, not simply because it involves William Cook and The Falcon, but because it gives them a certain place within Braintree society. The respectable citizens, especially the Dissenters, were worried about the disorderliness of the public houses and their perceived connection with a high level of crime. The publicans, who were men of substance, resented their 'prying' and 'espionage' and argued that, in the circumstances of a manufacturing town and, by implication, a large population of poorly paid weavers, there were no real grounds of complaint against them.

The newspapers and court records tell of several cases that the publicans themselves took to court, and these must represent only a very small fraction of the difficulties which they faced. In 1831 Guiver Sanders was woken out of his sleep by a man who called him 'bad names' and spat in his face, which so alarmed him that he called the night watchman.[25] And in 1834 a woman who had just been thrown out of one public house staggered into The Falcon and 'offered to sing for some halfpence'. When Mary Cook said that she would not have her there, the woman abused her and 'used very bad language'.[26]

This, then, was Charlie's home and background – a somewhat disorderly public house in what was then the dirty and poorly lit High Street of a bustling manufacturing town. His parents had sent him to school, for at least he could sign his name. But, in spite of their Independent connections in Stansted, they do not seem to have attended any church in Braintree, and when Charlie was baptized at St Michael's Church he was already eighteen months old.

In Stansted, as we have seen, most of the men in our direct line were the eldest surviving sons in the family, and they therefore took over the family business. Even the younger sons had been able to acquire a trade and several, like the elder Guiver, did very well for themselves. But Charlie was the youngest son of a publican and his wife who had died relatively young. He could not take over the public house, since only one child could benefit in this way, and he had not acquired any trade at all. It was this, more than anything else, that accounted for the collapse of the family's fortunes, or at least of our own particular branch.

Thomas, as the eldest son in the family, would normally have been expected to take over The Falcon, but he had stayed in Stansted when his parents moved to Braintree and in any event he had died young. So The Falcon was inherited by the next child, Mary, who was nineteen when Charlie was born and who married William Cook in the same year. The Cooks ran The Falcon until 1840 or 1841, and then moved to The Wheatsheaf, a much larger house, where they stayed until 1854. After this they went on to Black Notley, where William became a highly respected farmer and dealer. They were by far the most successful branch of the family, and one of their daughters married John West, the head of the brushmaking company. Mary died in 1865, but her children and grandchildren will appear again in this story, at the centre of the unresolved question of the identity of my grandfather's father.

Joseph, the next brother, was a carpenter, and was probably the same man as the Joseph Sanders who was an overseer of the poor in 1845. At first he lived with his family in the Coggeshall Road, but he is last mentioned in Braintree as a widower lodging at The Three Tuns in 1851.

Guiver, the next child, was a whitesmith, and he was joined in this trade by his younger brother, Henry, whose sons carried on the business. The older inhabitants of Braintree can still remember Sanders', 'a funny little shop', as one describes it, that stood in a corner of the Cattle Market until the 1930s.[27]

Between Guiver and Henry there was a sister, Esther, and another brother, William. In 1830 Esther gave birth to a 'chance child', but this is the last reference to her in Braintree. It is difficult to say anything with certainty about William, because there was at least one other William Sanders in the area at this time and it is usually impossible to know which of them is being referred to.

Charlie, we know, kept close to the Cooks, probably because they had helped to bring him up, and he was no doubt in frequent touch with most of his other brothers and sisters. Only one point of contact is recorded, however: when he married Jessamy Gray in 1851 his brother Henry was one of the witnesses.

10

The Dealer and the Gypsy: a Family of Poor Repute

I was told by my Aunt Mary when I began work on this book that 'We all come from the gypsies', and that she had been told this by her father and grandmother. I asked her if she could tell me more, and she said that when Lal, her sister, had begun telling fortunes from the teacups her father had said that it was the gypsy coming out in her. She knew that the gypsy in question was her great-grandmother, but she could not say more than this. With one exception, the rest of the family were unaware of their gypsy origins, and some suggested that Mary was 'romancing'.

In fact she was right, and the gypsy from who we all come was Charlie's wife, Jessamy Gray. She had been born at Isleham in Cambridgeshire in 1814, five years before Charlie. Her father Abraham was a tinker and a gypsy, but her mother, Mary Gammon, was descended from a long line of fenmen, watermen, labourers and their wives, people who had earned their living from the waterways and the wildlife of the Isleham fen. The Grays were a well-known gypsy family in East Anglia,[1] and there were at least two other families of gypsy Grays in the village. Many of their Christian names were ordinary and conventional, like Charles and Mary, John and Elizabeth, but others were exotic in the way of the gypsies, like Aquila, Cordelia, Meshach, Foundness and Mahala. Jessamy's four sisters who were baptized at Isleham were Silva, Lydia, Myrtilla and Mary, and her only known brother was named after his father, Abraham. Her own name, however, did not come from the gypsies, but from her maternal grandmother, Jessamy Gammon. Like Jessamine, it is a popular form of Jasmin, and it was often shortened to the more familiar Jessie.

The gypsies did not keep themselves entirely apart. The Grays were baptized, married and buried at the parish church, and several of them, like Abraham, took husbands or wives from outside their own community. But they led their own distinctive way of life, leaving Isleham each spring when the weather turned warm and wandering the roads until late autumn. They did not have caravans at that time, but tents made of poles and blankets which they strapped to the backs of their asses when they travelled and set up on the commons or in woods when they stopped. Since only the towns could support a tinsmith, or tinker, the work was ideal for a travelling craftsman and Abraham would go from village to village, mending pots and pans and kettles, while the women would offer to tell fortunes or sell goods like clothes pegs and wooden flowers. They would do seasonal work on the farms as well, like haymaking, harvesting and fruitpicking, and at certain well-known fairs and races they would gather with gypsies from all over the country. Later in the century, if not before, the Grays, with the Shaws, were the 'Gypsy entertainers of East Anglia', and T.W. Thompson has described the men, 'seated on raised platforms, and elaborately dressed in long, black coats, brightly coloured plush waistcoats, velvet knee-breeches, and smart top-boots', fiddling for the dancing from early morning until dark, while the women, 'in scarlet cloaks and queer little black bonnets, told the fortunes of the simple country people'.[2]

For those with romantic imaginations the gypsies embodied the spirit of freedom. But they were also a distrusted and even persecuted minority. They were often arrested as vagrants, and there were several cases in the Cambridge quarter sessions of families being convicted of 'strolling as gypsies', including, on one occasion, a family of Grays, and being publicly whipped for this offence.[3] Like many others, they were poachers on principle, refusing to regard wild birds and beasts as private property, and many cases are recorded of their poaching offences.[4] It was unlawful even to tell fortunes, or, to be more precise, to pretend to tell fortunes, for the lawgivers were careful in their wording not to support their pretensions.

By the early 1830s, it seems, all the Grays had left Isleham for good, for their names no longer appear in the parish registers. Why they left, and what happened to them all, we do not know. By 1839 Jessamy was in Braintree, where she added her mark as a witness to a marriage.[5] She had not given up the gypsy way of life, however, for a year later, in December 1840, she was arrested at the village of Pleshey, about eight miles south-west of Braintree, 'for pretending to tell the fortunes' of a woman there, for which she was sentenced to three months' hard labour.[6] Nor had she lost touch with her family, although the only evidence that we have for this is that many years later Alice, her youngest daughter, had a framed photograph on her wall of a man whom she called Uncle Gray and who, she said, had been very kind to her and given her a lot of china. Presumably this was Jessamy's brother, Abraham.

She settled in Braintree, however, and between 1844 and 1851 she had four illegitimate children there, one of whom died young. We know that Charlie Sanders was the father of the last two, and he was probably the father of the first two as well. On 23 March 1851 he and Jessamy were married in St Michael's Church, and seven days later they were recorded in the census as a respectably married couple, Charles and Jessamy Sanders, with three children, all of them with the surname of Sanders. Over the next eight years they had six more children, and one of these too died young. The last but one was my great-grandmother, Alice.

With a growing family, Charlie and Jessamy would have had little or no money to spare. They lived in a litle yard in Pound End, not far from the mills of Daniel Walters. It was a filthy and insalubrious area of tight-packed houses and tenements. Until the 1850s an open sewer ran through the streets. They shared a house with three other families and their rent was 1s. 3d. a week.[7] The people who lived with them were labourers, silk winders and rag gatherers, and their combined number was never less than ten and was usually nearer twenty.

At first Charlie was a labourer, but from 1849 onwards he described himself as a dealer in cattle, or simply as a dealer. So he earned his living by travelling around the country and acting as a middleman, buying and selling cattle at farms and markets, especially the Braintree market on Wednesdays, and hoping to make a profit on every deal.

As the children left school and went out to work they added to the family's income, at least for those years before they left home. At the time of the 1861 census Charlie and Jessamy were still living in Pound End, but in a house which they did not have to share with others; and by 1871 they had moved to the Notley Road, to a house which was close to the River Brain and to the engine house which supplied the town with water. Here their neighbours included not only silk weavers, but the engineer and two schoolteachers, a market gardener and a maltster. Two of the boys, Fred and Alf, were now helping Charlie with the business.

Charlie was now earning a good living, and in or around 1874 he and Jessamy bought a house and two cottages on Rifle Hill, in that part of the parish of Black Notley which formed the southern outskirts of Braintree.[8] Walters had set up a factory there, but had later moved it to their old site at Pound End. Evidently the Sanders took some of the property which had formerly belonged to the company. The house where they lived is now 7 Rifle Hill. It is a well-built, two-bedroomed house, and looks as if it has been cut in half, since apparently some other building was once attached to it. The other two cottages which they owned are now 3 and 5 Rifle Hill, and Fred, who eventually took over the business, probably lived with his family in one of these.

Charlie now described himself as a calf dealer, and for the first time his business was large enough to be listed in Kelly's Directory. If he was like Fred in later years, he would have travelled as far as the West Country for his calves, and he would have kept chickens and pigs and one or two milk cows, as well as a pony and trap.

Given the poverty of their early years, Charlie and Jessamy had done well in the world. But the Sanders were still a rough family, and Jessamy, as we shall see, did washing for other people at times. When she died in 1894 her death was reported in the *Advertiser* only because she had died suddenly of a heart attack and the case had to be referred to the local coroner. Charlie was still alive, but he was so little known that Jessamy was described as a widow.[9] Within a few months he was dead himself.

Jessamy was said to be seventy-six when she died. In fact she was almost eighty. Charlie's age was given, correctly, as seventy-four.

In 1893, a year before Charlie and Jessamy died, Alice, their youngest daughter, married Horace Galley in Bethnal Green. Horace was thirty-four and Alice thirty-five, though she said she was thirty-two. Probably they had only just gone to London. Horace, who gave his occupation as a herbalist, came from a respectable middle-class family in Braintree. His father was a foreman of mechanics and one of his brothers is said to have become a headmaster. The Galleys were deeply religious, and Alice's grandchildren later noted with respect that Horace was a sidesman in the Church of England and had several shelves of religious books. Whereas Alice spoke with a strong country accent, Horace's speech was more 'educated'. After the marriage Horace's family would have nothing to do with him. The Sanders were too much of a comedown for them and, worst of all, Alice had an illegitimate son who was then fourteen years old.

The best place to begin with Alice and her brothers and sisters is the census of 1861. All eight of Charlie and Jessamy's children were then living at home with their parents, and the census return is like the poor man's equivalent of a family portrait. Grouped around Charlie and Jessamy we have the three eldest daughters, Mary Ann (seventeen), Maria (fifteen), and Emily (ten), who were all silk weavers, and the three eldest sons, Charlie (nine), Fred (seven), and Alf (five), who were all at school. Alice was only three, and Tom, the youngest boy, was one.

None of these children, as far as the Galleys were concerned, could have lent the family any distinction. Mary Ann and Emily had illegitimate children and then left the area,[10] and Maria died of consumption when she was seventeen. Charlie, the eldest brother, became a silk weaver and then a labourer, and it seems from the 1881 census that he went to live with a woman in New Street and that they had at least two illegitimate children together. For some reason it was Fred, and not Charlie, who eventually took over the family business, and he was the only member of the family who married and whose children were all born within marriage. Alf and Tom remained bachelors all their lives. Alf, as we shall see, earned his living as a bird-catcher, and in 1881 Tom was described as having 'no occupation'.

All the children, it seems, were sent to school, but none, as far as we know, had any connection with the church. With their background this was not surprising. When Alice was baptized, for example, she was almost a year and a half old, and Alf and Tom were baptized at the same time.

All the sons were involved in petty crime, mainly 'trespassing in search of conies'. Poaching, of course, was a common offence, and in Black Notley in particular it seemed to the authorities that it was 'systematically carried on'.[11] The Sanders and their friends covered a wide area. With dogs at their heels or ferrets in their pockets they set snares in the local ditches and hedgerows and in several parishes around. Sometimes they were caught by police constables or gamekeepers, sometimes by the landowner's bailiffs or labourers. The prosecution usually took care to show that they were some distance from any public footpath, so as to deprive them of the defence that they were not trespassing, and to describe their dogs in great detail, so that they could not claim that they were unsuitable for poaching. Sometimes, when caught, they put forward some defence. When Tom and a friend were seen working a meadow with a fox terrier and a cream-coloured dog between five and six on a Sunday morning, they said that they were hunting rats, which they did every Sunday morning. Charlie once claimed that he was picking sloes, and once, when he was found at the bottom of a ditch watching a net in front of a rabbit hole, he said that he did not know whose net it was and that he had leave to be there, though he refused to say who had given it. Occasionally they resisted arrest. Fred threatened to break the jaw of a man who chased him in Great Waltham, and Tom, when accosted by a police constable in Black Notley, used 'very bad language' and threatened to hit him over the head. But generally they accepted what was coming to them, and did not even bother to appear in court. Charlie was the most persistent, or perhaps the most unlucky in getting caught. By 1883 he could be described as an 'old offender' and he was regularly given the maximum penalty of a £2 fine or two months in prison. He invariably paid and, like many others, he must have found poaching worthwhile.[12]

The Sanders were involved in other offences too. In 1870 Charlie was committed for trial on a charge of larceny from the person. He may well have been guilty, but his accuser was a man who had been going home drunk on a Saturday night and the evidence was too shaky to secure a conviction.[13] And in 1877 Fred was fined a shilling for assault, but for once the newspapers do not give any details.[14]

For the family, however, the most disturbing case must have been that which was scheduled for hearing in November 1882. Tom had been accused of assault, and the prosecutor was Jessie Sanders. This Jessie was probably not his mother, but his niece, his sister Emily's illegitimate daughter, who was then living with her grandparents. She was just sixteen, and Tom was twenty-two. We do not know the nature of the assault, because Jessie withdrew the charge and the case was never heard. No doubt the family had intervened.[15]

By the time of the 1881 census the only three children still living at home were Alf, Alice and Tom. Alice was then working in Walters' silk mills in Pound End, and her son Basil, who was then two years old, was being looked after during the day by his grandmother. On his birth certificate the space for his father's name had been left blank, and in later years there was a conspiracy of silence about the fact that he was illegitimate.[16] Alice's indiscretion was common at the time, but as working class morality became more 'respectable'[17] she decided to conceal it as a shameful secret, especially, perhaps, after her marriage to Horace Galley and her move to London, where she could begin a new life. With two exceptions, Basil's children were told nothing, not even that Alice was their grandmother. For the most part they were accepting and unquestioning – 'We just called her Aunt Galley. We never stopped to think who she was' – and even if they had wanted to know more they would have found it too awkward and embarrassing to ask questions.

At some point, however, the two eldest girls, Lal and Mary, were trusted to share the secret. Lal died in 1955, and who told her, and what was said, we do not know. But Mary was told by Aunt Galley herself that the father's name was Cook, that he came from a wealthy family with a big house and servants in Black Notley, that Aunt Galley had been in service with them, and that the family did not think that she was good enough for their son.

In 1881, as we know from the census, there was a family of Cooks in the Braintree Road in Black Notley, only about a mile from where the Sanders were living. It included George Cook, a widower of 44, and his son, also George Cook, aged 22. It is at this point that we re-establish the connection with William and Mary Cook, who had taken over The Falcon when Guiver died and who had later moved to Black Notley when William became a farmer and dealer. For George Cook, the 44-year-old widower, was their son, and so, in spite of the difference in age, he and Alice Sanders were cousins.

We know that the two families had kept in touch[18] and that they were still in touch at this very time. On Friday 5 November 1880, according to *The Braintree and Bocking Advertiser*, George's sister Emily came to stay with him. The Cooks were 'a well-known and respected family', but Emily had been living in London for a while and was now coming home with an illegitimate baby. She was distressed and agitated. The father, it seems, was living in Black Notley and she did not want to see him. She had been 'ruined', she said, and the affair was driving her 'crazy'. She also told her cousin, Mary Gentry, 'Don't let old Jessie come near me, for she's enticed me', and 'Old Jessie', said Mary, was 'a woman who washed her linen'. On the night of Saturday 6 November, Emily cut her throat with a razor.[19]

There was only one Jessie in Black Notley at that time, and that was Jessamy Sanders. She probably still claimed some gypsy powers, for when Emily spoke of enticement she seems to have meant something more like bewitchment.

So if Basil's father was really called Cook, the two George Cooks are the most likely possibilities. They lived in Black Notley and they came from 'a well-known and respected family'. There is no direct evidence that Alice worked for them, but she might well have taken a break from the silk industry to help them out and we now know that her mother did their washing. The older George Cook cannot be ruled out, but the more probable candidate is the son, who was only two years younger than Alice.

Basil is an unusual name, and we do not know why Alice chose it for her son. At first he attended the Anglican school, but when he was eight he went to the Junior Mixed School in Manor Street.[20] By this time the 1870 Education Act was in force, and he probably stayed there until he was twelve. He left school with a good command of figures, an ability to write a free-flowing letter, though with no punctuation and an arbitrary use of capitals, and not the slightest interest in any of the subjects he had been taught.

Alice was in London by February 1893, when she married Horace Galley in Bethnal Green. Walters had been laying off workers before finally closing down in 1894, and this could have been one of the reasons for her move.

Horace might also have wanted to leave Braintree in order to get away from his family's disapproval. Moreover, as we shall see, they had the opportunity of running a small shop in the Hackney Road.

Basil, it seems, did not go with them at once, for in May 1893 he was convicted with his Uncle Alf of gaming on the public highway – a common offence in Black Notley at the time.[21] We do not know exactly when he moved to London, but he was certainly there by 1898, since his daughter was born there in the following year. By that time he was an apprentice printer, a job which he thought would give him more scope than any he could get in Braintree.

11

Postscript to Braintree and Black Notley

Basil and his mother, like many others who migrated to London at this time, never lost touch with the relatives and friends whom they had left behind. Every year Basil went to stay with Alf for a week's holiday, and he usually took with him one or two of his children, who stayed with the Taylors, the next door neighbours. While there they always visited Fred and his wife Polly, who lived opposite in Charlie and Jessamy's old house.

Until this point we have had to rely almost entirely on documentary evidence. Now we can turn to living memory, and we can begin to see the family through the eyes of Basil's children, particularly Mary, who went to Black Notley more often than the others. We also have the testimony of two neighbours. Mercy Spearman, who is over eighty, has lived on Rifle Hill for nearly seventy years, and Bill Foster, who is in his seventies, has been there all his life.

For the first time we have a physical description – Fred Sanders, a thick-set, stern-looking man, of medium height, clean-shaven and dark-haired, and with a sharply pointed nose. Although he was well off, Fred normally dressed 'just like an ordinary farm labourer', according to Mary. On market days, however, he put on a tweed suit and stout leather gaiters, which Polly had to clean for him every week, and rode into Braintree on his pony and trap. Bill Foster remembers that in the winter he always wore a brownish overcoat, which was said to have cost him £50. 'He was out in all weathers in that.'

When Mary first visited Black Notley he was still in business as a calf dealer and was often away from home, sometimes going as far as the West Country in order to buy his calves. In a small paddock next to his house he kept one or two milk cows, as well as pigs and chickens. The children had been told that he was rich, and by their standards this was true. In addition to the house where he and Polly lived, he owned the two cottages next to The Rifleman public house. But according to the family he was 'a bit of a miser'. Although he was 'well off' he was 'tight with it'. 'He was always working, thinking about making money', and he 'always seemed to be grumbling – about getting too little money for his calves, about his food, about the weather.' The neighbours say the same. 'I don't think he'd part with much,' says Bill Foster, and Mercy Spearman describes him simply as 'mean'.

Aunt Polly was a plump, kindly woman, who made the children welcome and kept the house spotless. They had their main meal at midday. The first course, as was common in Essex at the time, was invariably suet pudding with gravy – 'to fill you up so as you didn't eat too much of the rest' – and there was always plenty of meat on the table. Polly, says Mary, was 'very nice, but she couldn't have had her own way very much. Fred was very domineering.' 'She was ever such a nice woman', Bill Foster says, but Fred was 'very strict with her'. The old man had 'a nasty temper'.

In 1933 or '34, when Polly was in her late seventies, Fred asked Mercy Spearman if she would clean the house for them. She did not want to, but he would not trust or employ anyone else, 'he was that sort of man', and so she agreed to do it for 2s. 6d. a week. She soon found that he did not trust her either. On the first day she found a coin on the floor, wrapped in fluff as if it had been there for some time. She picked it up and handed it over to him, but the same thing happened every time she went in. Her family were angry that having asked her to help he kept on testing her honesty in this way, and after a while they told her that she must take the money. So the next time she went she slipped it into her shoe and took it home. Fred did not say a word, and she never found any money again.

The story of Polly's death reflects even more badly on Fred. Mercy and one of the neighbours were sitting up with her and she died in the early hours of the morning. Fred was told and came upstairs, and 'The first thing he did, he slipped his hand under the pillow and took out her purse.' If he felt any grief, he did not show it. It was normal to pay people who sat up 5s., but Fred gave them nothing. 'I didn't mind', says Mercy. 'She was a nice old girl. I liked her.'

As for 'Old Alf', says Mercy, 'he was all right, different altogether to his brother', and Bill Foster says that he was 'very well liked'. He was a tall, thin man, with grey hair and a grey moustache. He wore a red choker, and was always smoking a clay pipe. His home was a four-roomed cottage, two up and two down, with a lavatory and a chicken run at the end of a long, narrow garden. There was a post in the front, and he used to spend hours leaning on it, watching the world go by. He had never married and, according to Mary, 'he never bothered much about food. Sometimes Mrs Taylor (his next-door neighbour) might cook him some potatoes in their jackets, and that would be a meal for him.' Basil and Alf used to go for a drink to The Rifleman at the bottom of the road, but normally 'Alf didn't like to mix. He was very quiet, was Alf, what you'd call a loner nowadays.'

In the census of 1881 he had been recorded as a man of 'no occupation', and in his will, drawn up in 1926, he described himself as being 'out of business'. In fact he made his living by catching birds, putting them in small black cages, and selling them in the local market or sending them to a pet shop in London. Bill Foster used to see him setting off with his nets and cages, and coming back with all sorts of birds, like redpolls, siskins, linnets and goldcrests. 'I'm a free man', he used to tell Mary: 'I can go out when I like and I don't have any master.' He was a poacher too, going mainly for pheasants, but he was 'much too artful to get caught'.

Occasionally, however, according to Bill Foster, he would put on a smart dark suit and a pork pie hat and go off to visit an uncle who was 'some big pot', 'a gentleman' in Chelmsford, who went by the name of Cook. Who he was we simply do not know, but clearly the two families, the Cooks and the Sanders, had remained in touch for over a century.

Neither Fred nor Alf was interested in politics, though, like Alice, they voted Liberal. But they were both very keen on sport, and followed the fortunes of Essex's cricket team. (Years later Neil Smith, one of Fred's great-grandsons, kept wicket for the county.)

Alf died in 1937, when he was eighty-one. For all his apparent poverty he left £557, half of which went to his nephew, Basil, and half to his brother, Fred. (Alice, his sister, was dead by then.) Fred died a year later at the age of eighty-four, leaving £1,638 to his daughter and two grand-daughters. After that none of the family had any occasion to visit Braintree again.

PART II
LONDON

Stratford:
1907–1931

12

The Galleys in Stratford

When Alice Sanders, or Aunt Galley as she came to be known, married Horace Galley in 1893 they were both living in the Hackney Road, close to Shoreditch Church. It is said that they ran a chemist's shop there but were unable to make a success of it. At the marriage Horace gave 'herbalist' as his occupation, but there is no mention of him in the trade directories of the time. By 1907 they had moved to Stratford, in what is now the London Borough of Newham, where they rented a house in Barnby Place.

They were comfortably off. Horace had a regular job with Howards, the manufacturing chemists, and Aunt Galley never had to go out to work. After some years at 3 Barnby Place they moved to number 7, where they occupied half of the house. The other half was taken by the Simkins, though usually only Mrs Simkins was there since her husband was away in the merchant navy.

By this time Basil had married Ellen Field and they were living with their children in Princes Court, a turning off Brick Lane in Bethnal Green. Aunt Galley went to visit them about once a month, and every Sunday Basil went to visit her in Stratford, taking one of the children with him.

Barnby Place was a small cul-de-sac off Bridge Street, close to the main shopping centre in Stratford High Street. There was a short terrace of brick two-storeyed houses on either side, and the Galleys' house was the end house on the left. Their front door opened onto the pavement. As you went in there was one room on the left, which was the Galleys' living room, and one on the right, which belonged to the Simkins. The stairs to the first floor rose straight ahead, and behind the stairs, at the back of the house, there was a small, stone-floored scullery which the Galleys and the Simkins shared. On the first floor there were three bedrooms, two of which belonged to the Galleys and one to the Simkins.[1] There was no bathroom, only an outside lavatory in the back yard. By the standards of the East End the Galleys lived spaciously. It is said that Aunt Galley's brother, Tom, lived with them for a few years, and we know that he died in Barnby Place in 1907. After that, however, they lived alone.

The showpiece of the house was the living room, which was crowded with furniture and ornaments. There was a heavy Victorian three-piece suite, a large china clock with matching vases, a gramophone on which records of music-hall songs were played, and a glass-fronted cabinet full of decorative china which 'Uncle Gray', Jessamy's brother, had given to Aunt Galley. This included several pint-sized drinking mugs, some thatched country cottages, the head of a man in a nightcap and a brightly coloured cockerel. Every space on the walls was covered with ornaments and pictures, among them photographs of Aunt Galley, Uncle Horace and Uncle Gray, and a large brown-framed reproduction of Millais' *Bubbles* which, thanks to the advertising of Pears soap, must have been the most popular picture in late Victorian England. Above *Bubbles* was a revolver in a wooden frame.

The pattern of the visits was generally the same. Basil and the child who was being taken that week would walk to Aldgate and catch the twopenny tram to Stratford. When they arrived they would be given tea and biscuits in the living room, and Aunt Galley would then prepare the Sunday dinner. If it was one of the girls who had been taken, she would be sent to a local Sunday school. If it was one of the boys, he would go with his father to watch the Sunday morning football at The Harrow public house. Horace meanwhile would go to church with his friend, Mr Brewster, a cheerful, red-faced man who always gave the children a penny. After the service they would go for a pint of beer before Horace came back for the meal.

Aunt Galley, like her sister-in-law, Polly, always served a suet pudding with gravy for the first course, and followed this with a main course of meat and vegetables with a sweet of a tart or a pudding with custard. There was usually more than could be eaten at the time, and later in the day Basil would take the leftovers back with him to Bethnal Green.

In the afternoon the grown-ups would have a sleep, while the child who had been taken would be sent to Sunday School. The pattern changed a little over the years, as some of the younger boys were able to get out of going to Sunday School. Bunny might play football with the local boys, George would watch the performing artists at The Adam and Eve public house, while Eddie remembers sitting in the living room making up stories or talking to *Bubbles*. At five o'clock they would all have tea, and the visitors would then take the tram back to Bethnal Green.

The Galleys were a striking pair. Aunt Galley stood about six feet tall, and when she went out she wore a hat piled high with feathers or imitation flowers or fruit. Her dark skirt swept the ground and she wore a white blouse, cotton on weekdays and satin on high days and holidays. She held herself upright and her walk was very 'stately', and she was often compared to Queen Mary. When she turned into Princes Court to visit her son's family the children would stop playing and become quiet.

She seemed even more imposing when Horace was with her, since he was only 'a little jockey sort of thing' who did not even come up to her shoulder. He wore a dark suit and a trilby hat and a white shirt with stiff high collars, and he always carried a stick. To the children he looked like 'a proper little chemist'. The force of the contrast is lost in the only surviving photograph of them, since Aunt Galley is sitting and Horace is standing, but even so her hat comes up to the level of his nose.

Several of the children were frightened of her. 'You wouldn't say a word out of place with Aunt Galley, or she'd give you one of her looks.' She was very 'forbidding' and stood no nonsense. In spite of her own background, or perhaps because of it, she had no hesitation in laying down the law for her grand-daughters. She was in Princes Court one lunchtime when Jess, who was then sixteen, asked her mother if she could go with the girls at work to see a show in the West End. Aunt Galley would not hear of it – 'Nellie, you can't let her go up there' – and so Jess was not allowed to join the party.

Horace was 'properly under her thumb'. He was 'a quiet old soul', 'very placid and inoffensive'. He was 'nervous' and 'timid', and he seemed 'cowed down'. She did not knock him about (a point, as we shall see, which it is necessary to make), but 'she was the guv'nor'. If he was late for his Sunday meal after his pint with Mr Brewster she would 'lead off at him' and 'give him a right ticking off'. But they seem to have been deeply devoted to each other, and when Aunt Galley went to rest in an armchair after dinner Horace would sing his 'Lally' to sleep.

The girls were all very fond of Horace – he was 'a dear old soul', says Jess – but Basil and the boys had little in common with him. 'We didn't find much to talk about to Horace,' my father says, and adds by way of explanation, 'He wasn't interested in football.' 'There was nothing wrong with old Horace,' says George, but after his opening cheery greeting he hardly had a word to say.

Aunt Galley, it is said, 'thought the world' of her son, and did all that she could to help him. And in spite of her strictness and her 'frightening' ways, she was always 'very good' to the children, which means that she was generous financially. Yet Basil and the children always called her Aunt Galley, and never mother or grandmother. Their true relationship was unacknowledged by the son and unknown by the children. Aunt Galley may have found this painful and distressing – we simply do not know – but she would probably have found honesty and candour even worse. It was only when she died in 1931 that her secret was openly made known.

Her property was valued at £370, and it was roughly divided between Horace and Basil. After her death Horace went to live with Lal and Albert, Basil's eldest daughter and her husband, since Basil said that there was not enough room for him at Princes Court, though Ellen would have been happy to look after him. Some of their furniture, however, was taken to Princes Court, and *Bubbles* was given pride of place on the wall above the fireplace in the parlour.

Horace lived on quietly for another two years. Shortly before he died he made a will saying 'I leave it all to Mary' (or 'I leave it all to Lal and Albert', for there are at least two versions of this story). But the will was invalid, since it was not witnessed and Horace did not say what 'it all' was. So the money went to his next of kin, to his brother, the headmaster, who had retired to Brighton, and his sister, who was the housekeeper of a magistrate in Braintree. Lal and Mary went to see her to try to persuade her to carry out Horace's last wishes. She would do nothing to help them. She was still bitter about Horace's marriage. Her mother, she said, had died soon afterwards, and it was the marriage that had 'broken her heart'.

12. The town of Braintree, as seen from the Notley Road in 1832.

13. Braintree High Street on market day, 1826. The Falcon is just out of sight as the street bends to the left, but the small black square is probably its sign. An aquatint from a painting by Robert Crane.

High Street, Braintree.

14.   The same scene, Braintree High Street, *c.* 1908. The Falcon is shown by an arrow.

15. Gypsies travelling. From Pyne's *Microcosm* (1802).

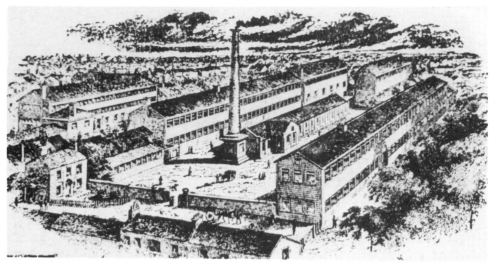

16.   The 'New Mills' of Daniel Walters at Pound End, Braintree, in 1875. Alice Sanders worked here as a millhand, and so probably did her sisters.

17.   Number 7 Rifle Hill, Black Notley, the house where Charlie and Jessamy lived, and later Fred and Polly. It clearly had some other building attached to it which has since disappeared, giving the impression that it has been sliced in half.

18. The workshop of Henry Sanders, which stood in the Market Square at Braintree, seen here *c.* 1900. The business seems to have been started by Charlie Sanders' elder brothers, Guiver and Henry, who both described themselves as whitesmiths, and to have been carried on by Henry's sons, George and Henry. Henry is said to be the man on the left with George to the right.

19. The Cattle Market being held in the Market Square, Braintree, *c.* 1900. The shop on the extreme right is Tribble and Son, harness makers. Next to that is The Bull public house, where Fred Sanders, and perhaps Charlie before him, used to keep his calves in the stables in preparation for the market, which was the high point of his working week. The little weather-boarded building in the centre of the picture is the workshop of Henry Sanders.

20. Horace Galley and 'Aunt Galley'. The only surviving photograph of them, taken on a day trip to Southend, probably in the late 1920s. 'They pose with a solemn sense of occasion, the ladies' toilet set squarely in the background, and the mirror image of the word ladies shows that the photograph has been printed back to front.'

Bethnal Green:
1899–1953

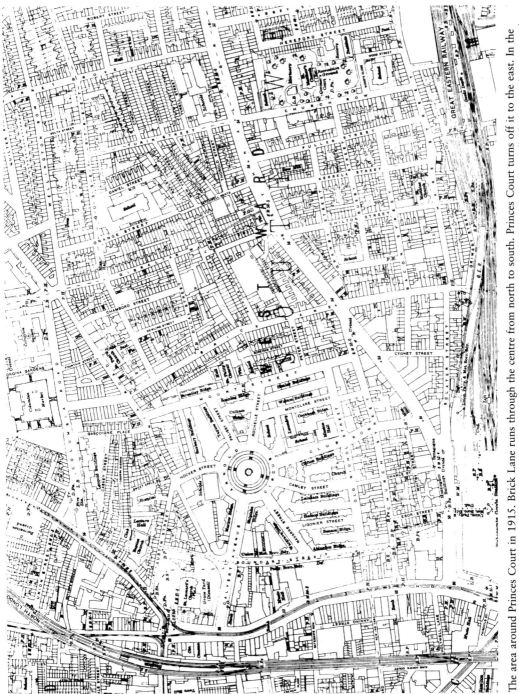

The area around Princes Court in 1915. Brick Lane runs through the centre from north to south. Princes Court turns off it to the east. In the west the Boundary Street Estate, centred on Arnold Circus, was built on the site of the old Nichol. The 'Mission Hall' shown on the corner of Club Row and Old Nichol Street is the Nichol Street Mission.

TABLE 3:
THE FAMILY IN BETHNAL GREEN

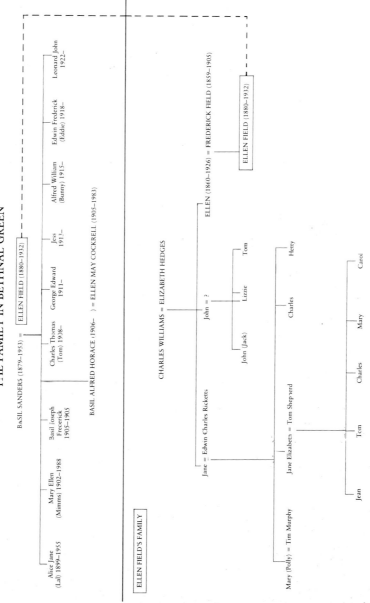

BaSIL SANDERS (1879–1953) = | ELLEN FIELD (1880–1932)

Alice Jane (Lal) 1899–1955

Mary Ellen (Mimms) 1902–1988

Basil Joseph Frederick 1905–1905

Charles Thomas (Tom) 1908–

George Edward 1911–

Jess 1913–

Alfred William (Bunny) 1915–

Edwin Frederick (Eddie) 1918–

Leonard John 1922–

BASIL ALFRED HORACE (1906–   ) = ELLEN MAY COCKRELL (1905–1983)

ELLEN (1860–1926) = FREDERICK FIELD (1859–1905)

| ELLEN FIELD (1880–1932)

ELLEN FIELD'S FAMILY

CHARLES WILLIAMS = ELIZABETH HEDGES

Jane = Edwin Charles Ricketts

John = ?

John (Jack)   Lizzie   Tom

Jane Elizabeth = Tom Shepherd

Charles   Hetty

Mary (Polly) = Tim Murphy

Jean   Tom   Charles   Mary   Carol

13

The Borough of Bethnal Green

The nineteenth century: the home of the Fields

At the time of their marriage in July 1899 Basil Sanders was living at number 7 Princes Court and Ellen Field at number 8. They had not yet settled permanently in the Court. A month earlier their eldest daughter, Alice, had been born in Haggerston and four years later their second daughter, Mary, was born in Shoreditch. By 1904, however, they were back in the Court, and they spent the rest of their lives there.

Western Bethnal Green, bordering on Shoreditch, was the home of Ellen's family. Her father, Frederick Field, was a carman, and her mother, also Ellen, was a boxmaker. She was their only child, and she had been born in Mount Square, a little court off Mount Street, only five minutes' walk from Princes Court. The Mount, as this area was known, bordered on, and was often taken to be part of, the Nichol, which Raphael Samuel has described as 'the most famous criminal slum in late-Victorian London'.[1] In Charles Booth's *Descriptive Map of London Poverty*, published in 1889, the whole of Mount Street, like most of the Nichol, was shown in black, the key colour for 'Lowest class. Vicious, semi-criminal'. Mount Square and Princes Court were coloured dark blue, which was only a little better – 'Very poor, casual. Chronic want'.

Ellen's grandparents, Charles and Elizabeth Williams, lived in the same house as her parents – in 1881 Charles gave his occupation as a seaman, but he was probably too old to go to sea any more – and her uncle and aunt, Edwin and Jane Ricketts, were only two doors away. By 1888 the Ricketts had moved to Princes Court, and the Fields probably followed soon after.

Bethnal Green

Princes Court, now known as Padbury Court, ran between Brick Lane[2] and Gibraltar Walk, and had been built in about 1790. On the left, as you entered from Brick Lane, there was a terrace of twenty houses. They had originally been built for the local silk weavers, since the industry set up by the Huguenots in Spitalfields had spread and become the mainstay of Bethnal Green. There were three floors in each house, and the top floor was given over to a large single room where the weavers could set up their looms. On the right there were six houses at first, and then an open space which was later filled by a cabinet-maker's workshops. Behind these was a privately owned burial ground, one of many in London, since the parish churchyards were much too small to contain the multitude of the city's dead.[3]

At the time when Princes Court was built it stood at the very edge of London's north-eastern development. On the other side of Gibraltar Walk gardens and orchards stretched eastwards towards the village of Bethnal Green and northwards to the village of Hackney. It was still an area where the merchants, manufacturers and professionals of the city could retire to enjoy the delights of the country. But as London expanded the gardens and orchards disappeared under a maze of crowded courts and narrow alleys, and the middle classes fled to the more salubrious suburbs, like Hackney, Highbury and Islington. A few pockets of relative 'respectability' remained around what is now Victoria Park, but for the rest Bethnal Green, like most of the East End, was abandoned entirely to the working class.

By the middle of the century it had already acquired a reputation for hopeless poverty and squalor, with the western part, according to one observer, exceeding all the rest 'in filth, disease, mortality, poverty, and wretchedness'.[4] Dickens placed the home of Bill Sykes in Bethnal Green, in one of 'the mean and dirty streets which abound in that close and densely populated quarter'. The pressure of population was unremitting, and was intensified by the influx of families made homeless by the development of central London, of unemployed labourers and craftsmen from the country, and, in the last quarter of the century, of Jewish refugees from Poland and Russia. On average there were always more than two persons to a room, and in the 1890s, even by the low standards of the time, about half of the population was living in conditions of overcrowding.[5]

From the 1850s the Metropolitan Board of Works had set about the task of providing underground sewerage throughout London, and the 1860s saw the first serious attempts at sanitary and housing regulation. But the laws were not strong enough to deal with neglectful vestries and obstructive landlords, and the poor, inevitably, did not help themselves, especially in an area like the

Nichol. John Reeves, a School Attendance Officer, reported in 1872 that the 'entire population' of the Nichol 'entertained an absolute dread of fresh air and cleanliness. . . . rooms and passages were reeking in filth for months and even years'.[6] In the 1890s one child in four in Bethnal Green died before reaching the age of twelve months. The death-rate generally was about a quarter as high again as in the rest of London.[7] In the Nichol it was more than twice as high.[8]

In his novel, *The Anarchists*, J.H. Mackay describes two friends walking around the area of Brick Lane one grey Saturday afternoon in the November of 1887. There were 'muddy pools of slimy filth' in the yards, with 'heaps of rubbish piled up in the corners'; the broken blinds on the windows swung loosely on their hinges; the cracked panes were pasted over with paper. They were importuned by a child prostitute and a drunken woman begging for money. The faces around them were old beyond their years. 'Whoever has once slowly sauntered through Brick Lane', Mackay wrote, 'can say that he has been grazed by the pestilential breath of want; whoever has gone astray into its side streets, has walked along the edge of the abyss of human suffering.'[9] More dispassionately, Charles Booth found that in the late 1880s 44.6 per cent of the population of Bethnal Green was living below the poverty line.[10]

The reasons for this are easy to discover. Silk weaving had long been in decline, and the free trade treaty of 1860, which had been so damaging to the industry in Braintree and Bocking, had hit the East End even harder. In 1824 the workforce in the industry had been 54,000. By 1880 it was down to 3,300. In Princes Court in 1881 there was only one weaver left. In the meantime, in the 1860s, after the change from wood to iron, the old ship-building industry on the Thames collapsed.

Apart from the distance from coal and iron, the main constraint on the growth of industry in London was the high cost of land, which made large factories prohibitively expensive. Labour, however, was plentiful and far in excess of demand. These conditions were ideal for the so-called sweated trades, furniture-making, footwear and clothing, where the process of production could be broken up and carried on in small workshops or people's homes, and where the entrepreneur could employ a small core of permanent workers and for the rest depend on casual labour, particularly homeworkers, who could be taken on or laid off according to demand.

In Bethnal Green, with the decline of the silk trade, there was a rapid growth in furniture making, which had developed there because imported wood was readily available from the docks. The borough was dotted with sawyers' yards and little workshops, like the one in Princes Court, and around the timber merchants, the sawyers and the furniture-makers there was a host of allied craftsmen and tradesmen like French polishers and varnishers, suppliers of cane and leather, and knob-makers and horsehair-twisters. Bootmaking was another common trade, though it was soon to be threatened by competition from the Midlands factories; and the East End 'rag trade' expanded very quickly, especially after the arrival of the Jewish refugees.

There were countless providers of goods and services – carmen, for example, like Ellen's father, who drove their horses and carts round the city, and whose occasional trips to the country provided days out for their children; stall-holders in Brick Lane and the Bethnal Green Road, who rose early to buy their goods in the London markets like Spitalfields and Covent Garden; rag and bone men and hawkers and artificial flower-makers. There were a few large employers, like Truman's Brewery in Brick Lane, Bryant and May's match factory in Bow, and several manufacturers of jams and sweets near the docks. But most employers in the East End had a workforce of less than twenty, and thousands were self-employed.

Many women took in washing or went out charring, but the most popular trade was box-making.[11] It was not enough to provide a living in itself, but it was useful for earning a few extra shillings and the work could be done at home and fitted in with the housework and shopping. It was also clean and, compared with jobs like scrubbing and washing, it was not physically strenuous. Even the children could lend a hand when they came home from school.

In the absence of large industry and with such a surplus of labour every tiny foothold in the economy was occupied and clung to tenaciously. The census for 1881 includes the following occupations for the residents of Princes Court – mattress maker, general dealer, dock labourer, seamstress, hawker, cigar maker, errand girl, bone turner, carman, sawyer, umbrella framemaker, laundress, locksmith, silk weaver, warehouseman, labourer, baby bootmaker, shoemaker, messenger, slipper maker, marble polisher, basketmaker, rope-maker, boot finisher, gilder, wood cutter, tobacco packer, chair polisher, milliner, traveller, chair maker, cane repairer, paper hanger, blind maker, razor grinder, wax doll maker, horsehair twister, fish dealer, rag sorter, packer, cabinet maker, charwoman, cigar box maker, french polisher, brushmaker and wine cooper. Some of these descriptions no doubt reflected regular full-time jobs, but others may have been based on no more than a day or two's work a week, or even a few hours. The errand girl might have been given only two or three errands to run, the boot finisher only a few pairs of boots to finish, and the seamstress only a few dresses to sew together.[12]

Below them there were many who could find no work at all, or who had no settled address since they could not afford to pay the rent. The cheap lodging houses were generally full, especially in the winter when it was too cold to sleep out. So too were the workhouses, though no one wanted to go there, for the governing principle was that they should be so comfortless and forbidding that no one would turn to them unless they were desperate. Most people in the workhouse spent only a few days there. They had been driven to seek shelter and support in a crisis, like desertion by a husband or father, and they came out as soon as they could get back on their feet, usually with the help of friends or relatives. But for the elderly and the infirm there was no escape. At the turn of the century one Londoner in five could expect a pauper's burial.[13] Charles Williams, Ellen's grandfather, was among them.

Many households were only kept going by weekly visits to the pawnbroker or the moneylender. Drunkenness and violence were common, especially on Saturday nights and between husbands and wives. Many women, inevitably, turned to prostitution, which exacted its own grim toll of disease and degradation. The lower end of Brick Lane and Liverpool Street Station were notorious haunts of 'brides'. Jack the Ripper claimed his victims in this area, and Ellen Field's mother had been born in George Yard, the scene of his first murder in 1888. Crime was endemic, and for many in the Nichol it was a way of life and children were brought up to it.[14] At the turn of the century the London County Council soberly reported that 'a large proportion of the inhabitants belonged to the criminal classes. Living in one street only [Old Nichol Street] there were at one time no less than sixty-four persons who had served varying terms of penal servitude.'[15]

Arthur Morrison's novel, *The Child of the Jago*, is set in the Nichol, and his Anglican pastor, Father Sturt, is closely based on Osborne Jay, the vicar of Holy Trinity Church. Jay believed that the criminal classes of the Nichol were so far beyond reform that they should be removed to penal settlements and not allowed to propagate their kind. Morrison agreed. For him the people of the Jago were 'rats . . . multiplying apace and infecting the world'. Anyone of any merit had escaped, leaving 'none but the entirely vicious'. The Jago, he wrote, was 'the blackest pit in London'.[16]

Morrison's metaphors were luridly distorted, and H.G. Wells felt compelled to remind him that the people of the Nichol were no different racially from those who sent their children to Oxford.[17] And Jay may have exaggerated his parishioners' criminality in order to attract more funds for his work. There were many ordinary, decent people in the area, like the Fields and the Ricketts, as we shall see. But even allowing for all this, the reality was bad enough.

Arthur Harding, who was born and brought up in the Nichol, acknowledged that 'The whole district bore an evil reputation and was regarded by the working-class people of Bethnal Green as so disreputable that they avoided contact with the people who lived there. . . . A stranger wouldn't chance his arm there.' And the Mount, the Fields' home, was 'as bad as the Nichol'.[18]

The Jago rats, Morrison said, were infecting the world, and the great fear of the law-abiding citizens of London was that, because of the pressures of overcrowding and unemployment, the 'residuum', the 'predatory' class of the East End, would infect the honest poor, the respectable working class, and that they would all rise up like new barbarians and overwhelm and destroy the civilisation of the capital. So the slums and rookeries had to be cleared and, just as missions were established in Africa, so missions were established in the East End to bring the light of civilisation and Christianity to people that dwelt in the darkness of ignorance.[19]

The most striking change was brought about by the newly formed London County Council. In the first of its major slum clearance schemes it razed the Nichol to the ground, flattening the area between Boundary Street and Mount Street and leaving only the buildings belonging to the churches and the London School Board. In place of the warrens of courts and alleys it created a system of roads radiating from a common centre, Arnold Circus. And in place of the insanitary and overcrowded tenements it built the Boundary Street Estate, a group of large barrack-like blocks of flats named after Thameside villages and towns, like Sonning, Marlow, Henley and Cookham, and opened by the Prince of Wales in 1900.

Several new parishes had been formed in the East End to meet the perceived needs of the growing population. Henry Walker, writing about Christian work in Shoreditch and Bethnal Green in 1896, was impressed by the Anglicans' 'conspicuous and commanding edifices' with their 'mediaeval massiveness of structure', but every Sunday they were largely empty.[20] The only exception was Holy Trinity Church in Old Nichol Street, for although he believed that many of his parishioners were unreformable Osborne Jay was a vigorous and popular minister. He was known as the Boxing Pastor because he had been a boxer himself when young and encouraged boxing among the men of his parish. Arthur Harding remembers him as a smiling six-footer.[21] My father remembers him simply as 'eccentric'.

The other churches had been quicker to adopt new methods, like mission halls where the services were less formal and restrained, open air services with portable harmoniums, and a wide range of supporting activities, anything to help the poor to see Christianity as their own and not as an unwelcome imposition by another class. The greatest innovators were the Salvation Army, with their uniforms, brass bands and citadels.

Among the churches in the area the most successful was the Shoreditch Tabernacle, the Baptists' stronghold in the Hackney Road. Every Sunday evening, according to Walker, it attracted a congregation of about a thousand of 'the better class of well-dressed working people'. Among the missions the most successful was the Nichol Street Mission, whose services were attended by two to three hundred. It had been started in 1836 by Jonathan Duthoit, a wealthy Huguenot silk manufacturer. It was non-denominational, but was supported and encouraged by the well-to-do Congregationalists of the Union Chapel in Highbury, where Duthoit had been a deacon.[22]

Nearly all the missions ran Sunday Schools, and even in the Nichol in the 1880s every child attended one school or another.[23] And many of them tried to relieve hunger and poverty, usually through soup kitchens for those who attended their services on a Sunday evening.

There were several other Christian foundations, like Annie MacPherson's Home of Industry on the corner of Club Row and the Bethnal Green Road, which gave industrial training to homeless boys and organised the emigration of several thousand of them to Canada,[24] and the Mildmay Mission Hospital in Austin Street, where the Anglican deaconesses were as concerned with spiritual salvation as with healing, and where the walls of the wards were decorated with Biblical texts and pictures.[25]

The Oxford House, in Mape Street, had been founded in 1884, at roughly the same time as Toynbee Hall in Whitechapel, and these two were the first university settlements in London. Under the guidance of its head, who was usually a clergyman of the Church of England, Oxford graduates and undergraduates came to live in the settlement for anything from a summer vacation to a few years, and became involved in community work and local government. The old model of the harmonious society, it was thought, with the gentry providing an enlightened lead and the working classes following deferentially behind, had broken down in the East End, where the gentry had abandoned their posts. The university settlements hoped to restore this model and to build bridges of Christian goodwill between the classes. 'The resident settlers', wrote one of the first heads of the Oxford House, 'are designed to take the place of the fugitive natural leaders.' Whereas Toynbee Hall had been inspired by the liberal ideals of Balliol and was mainly concerned with education, the Oxford House was inspired by the High Anglican ideals of Keble and concentrated on clubs for men and boys. Toynbee Hall became the training ground for politicians and social reformers, the Oxford House for Anglican bishops.[26]

Bethnal Green

The churches in Shoreditch and Bethnal Green, however, had little hold over the hearts and minds of the poor, and the same was true of the East End as a whole and in towns and cities throughout the country. It was a common observation that the working classes were not hostile to Christianity, but wholly indifferent to it. The children went to Sunday School, but when they grew up they only entered the church for baptisms, marriages and funerals. The London City Missionary in the Nichol had very little success. 'There may be a God, a Christ, a heaven, a hell;' he wrote, 'but these people are unmoved by the thought.'[27] In 1896 it was estimated in Bethnal Green that only about one in eighty attended either church or chapel.[28]

Among the middle classes going to church was the done thing: it helped to establish standing and respectability. Among the working classes it was not the done thing. The people of the East End, according to Bishop Walsham How in 1880, thought of religion 'as belonging to a wholly different class'. If a working man went to church he was marking himself off from his fellows in a very distinctive way: he was inviting attention and even ridicule for trying to get above his station. To go to a church, or even to a mission hall, you had to be well dressed. 'The Church worships respectability', wrote Keir Hardie, 'and puts its ban on poverty . . . I speak of no particular sect or denomination. I discern little to choose from in any of them.'[29]

There were more radical criticisms of the Church as well. George Lansbury argued that, instead of emphasising that the rich had a duty to help the poor, the Church should preach that the rich should 'cease exploiting and robbing the poor'.[30] And H.G. Wells condemned the university residents for indulging in no more than 'benevolent picknicking'.[31] Poverty would never be removed by mission halls and philanthropy. What was needed, it was argued, was a fundamental redistribution of power and wealth.

Yet socialism too failed to gain a hold, for the people of the East End were generally apathetic in politics as well as religion. London, it was said, was 'the despair of the Labour movement'.[32] 'It might be expected', wrote the London City Missionary in the Nichol, 'that the vast majority of people living in such abject poverty would be permeated with socialistic and revolutionary ideas: but this is not so. . . .'[33] It is not entirely clear why it was not so, but it was certainly difficult for trade unionism to develop in an economy which was based on small workshops, casual labour and homeworkers and where the advantages lay so heavily with the employers.[34]

A more powerful force for change was the primary education which was now compulsory under the 1870 Education Act. There was a strong emphasis on the three Rs, but the teaching was also shot through with the Christian and patriotic values which would produce dutiful and hard-working employees and loyal and enthusiastic citizens of the Empire. One of the simplest demonstrations of the advance in education came later with the silent films, when the literate children could be heard reading out the subtitles for their illiterate parents.

But in spite of the efforts of priests and ministers, university residents and teachers, for most East Enders the most important institutions outside the workplace were not the church and the school, but the public house and the music hall. Charles Booth found them much more drawn to 'pleasure, amusement, hospitality and sport' than to religion and education.[35] Some public houses were rough, especially on Saturdays, but most were simply places where the men in particular could get away from their noisy, over-crowded homes and have a quiet drink and a game of darts with their friends. Boxing was popular, and was encouraged as a manly sport by the Oxford House as well as by Osborne Jay, and the end of the century saw the rise of the professional football teams, like Tottenham Hotspur and Clapton Orient, which attracted many thousands of cloth-capped spectators every Saturday afternoon. Although street betting was illegal there were bookmakers in every area, and Princes Court, as we shall see, was one of their regular stands.

But it was the songs and turns of the music hall that gave the richest and most varied expression to what the East End found funny or sad or moving. They made fun of teetotallers and those who tried to rise in the world and who gave themselves airs and graces. They rejoiced in the pleasures of drink and gambling, and made light of the disasters that might follow. They were romantic about love but realistic about marriage. They were free from political and social rancour. And they had strong and insistent values of their own, like good neighbourliness and cheerfulness in the face of hardship. The audience took these songs back to their homes, and everyone had his or her own song, like a signature tune, which they would sing at family parties or in the public houses. They were not infallible cultural indicators, for they had to entertain, and what did not entertain they passed over in silence. Even so, through their humour and pathos, they can bring us very close to the heart of the East End's humanity.[36]

The twentieth century: the home of the Sanders

By the turn of the century several of the great battles of the Victorian reformers had been won or were being won. The streets of Bethnal Green were no longer covered with foetid mud, but were clean and well drained and at least adequately lit. Gas was being slowly introduced, water was piped to most houses, earth privies were being replaced by flush toilets, and public baths were provided on an increasing scale.[37]

The New Survey of London Life and Labour, published in the early thirties, referred to 'a vast improvement in the health of the London population during the last thirty years'. Between 1890 and 1930 the death rate was halved in Bethnal Green, and in the country as a whole the expectation of life rose by roughly ten years between 1910 and 1938 – from 52 to 61 for men and from 55 to 66 for women.[38]

Right up to the Second World War, however, much of the employment in Bethnal Green remained casual and seasonal. Furniture-making and its allied trades still occupied about a fifth of the working men, and was especially concentrated in the west of the borough. Of the other old London trades, tailoring was still widely carried on, especially by the Jewish population, but bootmaking had virtually disappeared. Many men were still dockers or porters, and an increasing number were employed in transport services of various kinds. About one in thirty were in the print, the trade to which Aunt Galley had Basil apprenticed. The general pattern remained that of small workshops on the ground floors or in the back yards of the small terraced houses or in disused cowsheds or stables. More women went out to work, mainly, according to *The New London Survey*, 'in the clothing trades, the paper trades and personal service'. The home industry of boxmaking came to an end.[39]

After the First World War there was a sharp reduction in working hours from an average of fifty-five a week to between forty-six and a half and forty-eight. Except for shopworkers, Saturday afternoons were free, and paid holidays slowly became the norm. In the late 1920s it was still reckoned that only one employer in twenty in Bethnal Green gave a week's holiday with pay. In 1938 such holidays were made legally compulsory for many classes of workers.[40]

After the hard times of the Edwardian period the First World War brought full employment,[41] and even during the Depression London did not suffer as badly as the rest of the country. For those who were in work there was a remarkable rise in the standard of living. By 1945 their average real earnings were more than a third higher than they had been in 1913. And even the unemployed in the Depression lived at roughly the same level as a family in work before the First World War.[42] It was just as important for the reduction of poverty that these rising incomes were spread over families that were getting steadily smaller. In England and Wales as a whole the size of the average household came down from 4.4 in 1911 to 3.7 in 1931 and to 3.2 in 1951.[43]

People were much better fed and, because of the rise in real wages, they had more money to spend on items such as fuel and light, clothing, household goods, tobacco, newspapers, transport, leisure and entertainment. The improvements were visible. The ragged, barefoot verminous children who had been a common sight in the Edwardian period were hardly to be seen at all by the end of the Second World War. Each succeeding generation grew up to be bigger and taller than the last.[44]

Housing aspirations changed. Children who had been brought up in rented rooms now wanted houses of their own. Between the wars rows and rows of semi-detached houses sprang up in suburban London, served now by the Underground as well as the buses, and among those who bought them were many young East Enders, like my parents, anxious to move into 'better' areas and improve their chances and their children's chances.

In Bethnal Green itself, however, most new housing was in the form of council flats, provided either by the borough or the London County Council.[45] Slum clearance continued slowly, but in the Second World War it was forcibly accelerated by the destruction of large areas in the blitz. Many new estates have been built since then, one of them in Princes Court, and the face of the borough has been changed beyond the recognition of those who used to live there.

Charles Booth and others had rightly argued that poverty in areas like Bethnal Green would never be eliminated if left to local resources and philanthropy alone. With the creation of the London County Council and, later, the rates equalisation scheme, the problems of the poorer districts were at last being tackled with the help of resources from the whole of London. More generally, with the gradual replacement of the Poor Law by the Welfare State, the resources of the whole nation were enlisted. At first provision was modest and limited, but it was steadily increased and extended. An old age pension of 5s. a week was introduced in 1908. In 1919 it was raised to 10s. and in 1946 to 16s. The National Insurance Act became fully operational in 1913. Sickness benefits and widows' pensions were provided, and for those out of work there was the dole, which was payable for a period of up to six months. After that the claimant had to rely on 'transitional payments', though from 1931 onwards, as an economy measure, these were subject to the means test, which aroused more bitterness than any other aspect of welfare provision.

But in an area like Bethnal Green overcrowding and poverty could not be eliminated quickly. In 1901 the population of the borough was 129,686. By 1931 it had gone down to 108,194, but even so nearly half were living at a density of more than two persons to a room. The proportion of persons living in poverty, though much lower than the 44.6 per cent recorded by Charles

Booth in the 1880s, was still very high at 17.6 per cent.[46] Children and old people suffered particularly; children because poverty bore most heavily on large families, and old people because, even with the pension, they inevitably fell below the poverty line if they lived alone and had no other resources. The aggregates and averages are bad enough, but they contained and concealed many individual cases of terrible hardship and distress.

In spite of these social conditions, and in spite of its growing power in the country as a whole, it was only after the First World War that the Labour Party began to make progress in Bethnal Green, and even then its success was patchy and uncertain. For the most part it held power in the local Borough Council, but on the London County Council it did not win the four seats for Bethnal Green until 1934, and it was 1945 before it gained the parliamentary seat for Bethnal Green South-West. The Liberal, Percy Harris, first won this seat in 1922, and for years it was the only Liberal seat in or within a hundred miles of London. Harris was a popular MP and had a well-deserved reputation of working hard for his constituents. In the opinion of Raphael Samuel, his 'mixture of vigorous but old-fashioned progressive politics with intense small-scale local politics was ideally suited to the conservative and precarious world of Bethnal Green.'[47]

Among many observers there were still fears of political turmoil, especially in the aftermath of the First World War and especially during the Depression. But there was less alarm in Bethnal Green itself, and in 1933 the Oxford House congratulated itself on the continuing 'absence of any political animosity in this area'.[48] Patriotism was still strong, inspired by what John Keegan has described as 'the inarticulate elitism of an imperial power's working class'.[49] Men flocked to volunteer in both world wars, and when the issue of fighting for King and Country was debated at a meeting for the unemployed at the Oxford House in 1933, 'the result was a unanimous vote in the affirmative' – 'a striking contrast', the House noted, to the outcome of the debate among 'their more favoured fellow citizens at Oxford.'[50]

The mid-1930s saw the emergence of Fascism. By that time there were about 150,000 Jews in the East End, of whom 20,000 lived in Bethnal Green. With their emphasis on Britain for the British the Mosleyites attracted strong support in the area, and Mosley himself, according to his biographer, Robert Skidelsky, 'established a strong emotional *rapport* with East London audiences'.[51] They set up several branches in the East End, including one in Shoreditch, but in spite of this they did not win a seat in either local or national elections.

The anti-Semitism to which they appealed, however, was virulent and widespread. James Robb, in his research in the late 1940s, found that more than four-fifths of the population of Bethnal Green was anti-Semitic to some extent, and he ranged them in degrees of prejudice from the extremist 9 per cent who believed that Jews were firebugs, swindlers, warmongers and traitors, through the slightly less hostile 31 per cent who believed that they were dirty, arrogant, cocky and pushing, to the more 'tolerant' 43 per cent, who merely believed that they were unscrupulous price-cutters who drove the English out of business, well-to-do and keen to make money by any means other than hard physical work.[52]

The churches in Bethnal Green, as in the country as a whole, continued to struggle and decline. Several of the Anglican churches were shut down, and so were some of the missions. In 1939 the Nichol Street Mission closed, not so much because of declining support, though its evening congregation had dwindled to about forty, as because its building had become structurally dangerous. The Salvation Army, however, became more active, and the Shoreditch Tabernacle, the Baptists' main centre, continued to be well supported.

The clubs attached to the Oxford House still tried to build bridges of goodwill between the classes, and in 1924 a new club was opened, the Cambridge and Bethnal Green Jewish Boys' Club. It was not attached to a university settlement, but was started by a group of Cambridge students in a converted public house behind the synagogue in Chance Street. Its aims were to raise Jewish youth from the impoverished conditions of the East End and, by encouraging the ideals of the English public school, to help them to integrate in English society. In 1938, in an attempt to foster better understanding in the face of Blackshirt propaganda, the club dropped 'Jewish' from its title and encouraged non-Jews to join.[53]

Apart from the Church, two other great institutions of the late Victorian and Edwardian period were in decline. The music hall slowly gave way to the variety theatre and the cinema, and all of them met increasing competition from the wireless. And the public house, though still important, was rapidly losing its custom. By the 1930s the consumption of beer was about half of what it had been before the First World War.[54] The change is perfectly illustrated by two photographs of outings from The Conqueror, the public house in Austin Street where Basil Sanders was one of the regulars. The first, taken before the war, shows thirty men of all ages on an open and ornate horse-drawn brake, gay with buttonholes, flags and a bugle. The second, taken after the war, shows fifteen middle-aged and elderly men in a plain motor-driven carriage. Only two of them sport buttonholes, and there are no flags and no bugle.

Bethnal Green

The coming of the wireless and the decline of the public house were both part of a change in which, outside the workplace, the home and the family were becoming the central focus of men's lives. There was more domestic comfort, even in Bethnal Green, and less reason for a man to seek refuge in a pub. With fewer children, more money and the support of the Welfare State, the nuclear family became less dependent on its relatives and increasingly turned in on itself. This change was slower in Bethnal Green than in many other areas, but it quickly reached its full development among the proud owners of semi-detached houses, many of them emigrants from the East End, in the expanding suburbs of London.

At first Basil and Ellen had fitted comfortably and contentedly into the popular culture of the Edwardian East End. They went to the music halls and the public houses together, came home and sang their songs. Then, around 1910, Ellen fell ill with 'heart trouble' and was cared for and converted in the Mildmay Hospital. She never went to the music hall or the public house again, and the Nichol Street Mission became her spiritual home. Basil was unmoved. His wife, he said, had 'gone barmy' at the Mildmay, and he continued to go regularly to The Conqueror.

For the eldest children their mother's conversion was crucial. The Mission was the most formative experience of their lives, and one of them went on to become an officer in the Salvation Army. But as Ellen's health grew worse and she had to retire more to her bed, the younger children were less influenced by her. They broke away from the Mission. One of the boys was drawn to the stage. Two of them became members of the Webbe, the boys' club that was attached to the Oxford House. And the youngest was elected as the captain of the Cambridge and Bethnal Green Boys' Club after it had dropped 'Jewish' from its name.

Over the years the Sanders in Bethnal Green moved slowly from penury and overcrowding to relative affluence and the luxury of occupying a whole house. Except a boy who died young and the eldest, Lal, who died in 1955, all of the children were still alive when I began work on this book, and the chapters that follow are based largely on what they have told us. Between them they form almost a microcosm of the borough of Bethnal Green.

14

The Family in Bethnal Green

When Basil married Ellen Field in 1899 she had just given birth to their first daughter, Alice. There was nothing particularly shameful in this. Charles Booth had noted that 'immoral relations before marriage among the lower classes' were 'not unusual' and were 'indulgently regarded', but that usually marriage was expected to follow, and did follow closely, on 'the indiscretions of the young'.[1] Even so, it was not something that Basil and Ellen wanted their children to know. Ellen told her daughter, Mary, that she was only seventeen when she was married and that Basil was only eighteen. In fact they were eighteen and twenty. She was obviously worried that if she told the truth, and if Mary did her sums, it would be seen that Alice had been born before the wedding.

They had ten children in all – Alice Jane (or Lal); Mary Ellen (or Mimms); Basil Joseph Frederick (who died of enteritis at the age of seven months); Basil Alfred Horace (my father); Charles Thomas (who was always called Tom); George Edward; Jess; Alfred William (or Bunny); Edwin Frederick (or Eddie); and Leonard John. Several of them were named after members of the family – Jess, for example, after Aunt Galley's mother, Jessamy Gray the gypsy – and George Edward was named after the two kings. 'My mother' he says, 'was very patriotic.' Between Lal, who was born in 1899, and Len, who was born in 1922, there was a gap as wide as a whole generation.

Basil was called Country George, or simply George, by his friends, but he was always known as Basil in the family. He was about five feet eleven tall, not quite as dominating as his mother, and he was powerfully built as well. At that time he must have stood out in Bethnal Green, where growth had been stunted through several generations by disease and malnutrition. Ellen, who had been born in Bethnal Green, was only about five feet tall. She was never strong, and in later years was continually pulled down by illness. 'She was a very small woman', Eddie says, 'you could have blown her over.' She was 'just two ha'porth of coppers'.

Basil was already a printer when he married, while Ellen gave no occupation, probably because she was looking after the baby. According to Mary, she had worked for a jam factory before she married, and she later worked for a few years in a laundry, specialising in the ironing of stiff white collars.

Her parents, Frederick and Ellen Field, were then living at 10 Princes Court. In all the surviving documents Frederick is described as a carman, but there is a tradition in the family that he was a muffin man, and that sometimes, when he went round the City with his tray of muffins on his head and ringing his bell, he would take his grand-daughter, Lal, with him. According to what his wife told Mary, he was 'always the worse for drink', and when he died of tuberculosis in 1905 he was only forty-five years old.

Granny Field, as she was known to the children, had a hard enough struggle to make a living for herself, but she also had to bring up the three children of her brother and his wife, both of whom had died young. In 1881 she had given her occupation as a matchbox-maker, but at the time when Basil's children knew her she was taking in washing for the neighbours and was the charwoman for Moore's, a tobacconist in the Kingsland Road. Her grand-children remember her as the soul of kindness. 'She was just lovely, very, very kind,' says Mary. 'She was marvellous, a good old stick, one of the best,' says George. She was always there to help her daughter with the cooking and the washing, and when Ellen was confined with another child it was Granny Field who took over the running of the house. In later years, when Ellen was ill, she used to come round early in the morning and get the boys out of bed for school. She was invariably kindly and cheerful, and very generous with what little she had. She would bring the children sweets from the tobacconist's where she worked, and 'she would give you her last ha'penny if she could'. She was not 'religious' at first, but later she became the caretaker of a little mission in Gosset Street. 'She wasn't much of a scholar,' says Mary: in fact she was unable to sign her name.

Granny Field had an elder sister, Jane Ricketts, who had lived in Princes Court since the 1880s and was now a widow with four children. She worked at home as a boxmaker, collecting the cardboard and glue from a firm in Peter Street, making up the boxes at home, and then taking them back to the firm. She was paid 2½d. a gross and she could make six or seven gross a day.

One of Jane's daughters, who was also called Jane, married Tom Shepherd, a cabinet-maker, and their five children became very close friends of the Sanders. Another, Hetty, was crippled and 'simple'. She could not work and had to be carried everywhere. She was always cheerful, and had a helpless fascination for pins and ribbons, begging them from anyone who came to see her and covering one side of her cardigan with them. A 'lady' from the Nichol Street Mission, Mrs Risk, 'took an interest in Hetty' and taught her some hymns, and she would sit and sing them by the window. 'You couldn't hold a proper conversation with Hetty', says Mary, but she was so loving and happy that 'it did you good to talk to her'.

For a time Granny Field lived on the top floor of number 8, while her sister and her children lived on the floor below. Towards the end of the First World War they all moved to Gibraltar Walk. They were only just round the corner from Princes Court, and the Sanders saw just as much of them as before. In spite of their closeness, some of the children did not fully understand the nature of the relationship between them. 'I never knew what they were to us,' Bunny says. And Eddie is equally confused: 'They're a right muddle on that side of the family.'

15

Princes Court

When the Sanders finally settled in Princes Court they took the top floor of number 11, the old weaver's workroom with two large windows overlooking the street. Ellen's parents lived next door, and no doubt her mother had recommended or 'spoken for' them to the rent collector for the Portals Trust, which owned the whole terrace of twenty houses on that side of the road. The six houses and the workshops on the other side were owned by another landlord, and they were usually occupied by Jewish families and businesses, the workshops by Cohens, the cabinet-makers, and then by Daniels, the upholsterers. Basil and Ellen spent the rest of their lives in Princes Court, moving after nine years to number 7, where they eventually took over the whole house.

The grey brick dwellings and workshops of the Court faced each other across a narrow cobblestoned street. Although they had three floors, the houses were very small, with only two rooms on the ground floor, two rooms on the first floor, and one large room on the top floor. The gardens at the back were no more than a few square yards of trampled earth backed by a high brick wall, and there were no gardens at the front, where the doors opened straight onto the pavement.

The Court was badly overcrowded. In most of the houses there were two or three families, and at any given time up to the Second World War there would have been about fifty children. The Sanders, with nine children, were matched by a few others, like the Juliers, the Barneys and the Streets, and most of the rest had at least two or three. Since newcomers were usually 'spoken for' by those who were already there many of the families, like the Fields, the Ricketts and the Sanders, were related to each other. And since the home was the responsibility of the women, who looked to each other for help and comfort, the original connection was almost invariably between mother and daughter and then, if there was more than one daughter, between sisters, with the men being merely the in-laws. The way in which it worked was simple. A mother whose daughter was about to get married would speak for her with the rent collector as soon as she heard that a neighbour had died or was about to move out. Or she might find space for her under her own roof, although it was recognised that this was not an ideal arrangement. Among others, Mrs Sullivan and Mrs Barney were sisters, and so were Mrs Mabley and Mrs Collins, Mrs Gray and Mrs Shepherd, and Mrs Cook, Mrs Main and Mrs Newman.

Many families had lived in the area for a long time, and the nature of the housing and the system of allocation made it possible, if opportunities arose, for a family's changing needs over the years to be accommodated in the same small terraced row. A young couple with a small family and little money, like the Sanders in the beginning at number 11, could take a top room for 2s. 6d. a week. As the family grew larger they would sooner or later get the chance to move to the first floor or the ground floor, either of the same house or another in the row, at a rent of 5s. a week. If their income increased as the children went out to work they could afford to take on more, perhaps a combination of the first floor and the top floor for a rent of 7s. 6d. And if they were very grand, they might take over the whole house for 12s. 6d. At the end, when the children had left home and perhaps the husband had died, the widow, like Granny Field, might want to move to the top floor again, perhaps with her daughter's family living below her. There were several widows at different times living on the top floors, like Granny White, Mrs Raines and old Mrs Fletcher. There was a lot wrong with the housing, but the way in which it could be divided and allocated made for stability and helped the community to keep together.

Basil's children can remember almost every one of their neighbours on their own side of the road, but very few of their Jewish neighbours on the other side. It was not merely that they kept themselves to themselves, but with a different landlord they were in a different network of speaking and being spoken for. It was only towards the end that the two communites 'mixed in'. There were always good relations with the Daniels, however, the upholsterers who took over the workshop from the Cohens. They possessed the only telephone in the road, and everyone could use it in an emergency.

At the top of the Court, on the corners with Brick Lane, there were two shops which were owned by Jews: Prices, who sold sweets, tobacco and newspapers, and Sugarbreads, who at first ran a general store but later sold secondhand clothing which they had bought and improved. On Sunday mornings Sugarbreads set up a stall on the pavement outside the shop. Apart from them, most of the shopping was done at the stalls in Brick Lane and the Bethnal Green Road, or the markets in Club Row and Columbia Road. The nearest pubs were The Gibraltar, or 'The Gib', in Gibraltar Walk, which faced the bottom end of the Court, and The Alma and The Duke of York in Brick Lane.

Next to the workshops, directly opposite the Sanders, was the small yard where Mr Sage, who lived below them, kept his cows, goats and pigs, and behind the houses at the bottom of the road, in an open space called the barracks, there were stables and sheds where Mr Sage and others kept their horses and carts. There was also a small smithy belonging to Mr Yearly, who, in addition to shoeing horses, made reels for firehoses which his wife then painted in their back garden. As well as the usual dogs and cats, several families kept rabbits, chickens and racing pigeons, and the cattle from the local dairies, one of them in Gibraltar Walk, used to be driven to London Fields to pasture every day. When Mr Sage died his animals were sold off, but it was many years before the stables in the barracks came down.

The Court was often noisy and crowded. Throughout the day there was the sound of hammering and sawing from the workshops, and there was a regular and constant traffic from the early hours of the morning when people began going to work. Those who were stallholders had to get to the markets early to buy the goods which they would sell later in the day, and the charwomen had to leave at five or six to clean the offices and shops before they opened. Mr Brandon worked at a wine warehouse near Tower Bridge: 'You could tell the time by him,' says George. 'Every morning, five o'clock, you would hear his old boots go bang, bang.' Later children set off for school and the women went out to the shops; horses and carts brought timber to the workshops and took finished furniture away; and straining men pushed barrowloads of timber, like old Joey Leman, a relative of my mother, who was out 'in all weathers, he used to be soaked; he walked miles and miles, he was a regular feature.' There were tradespeople like the watercress seller, the catsmeat seller and the rag and bone man, and the milkman trundling along his churn on a barrow and measuring out pints and half-pints into his customers' jugs. When the weather was fine some of the old people would put their chairs on the pavement or sit on their window ledges so that they could see what was going on and talk to passers-by. Neighbours often dropped in on each other to borrow something they were short of and to have a chat.

When the children were not at school they played in the street. The boys' favourites were football and cricket, especially at the top of the Court, where the road widened out and where my father still points to the dip in the cobblestones where he would try to pitch the ball when he was bowling. The girls played skipping and hopscotch, and they all joined together in games like 'he', 'tin can robber' (with each team having three shies at two tin cans against a wall, trying to knock them down and then catch the other side before they could put them up again) and 'black man's dark scenery' (with a child from one side hiding under a pile of old clothes and the other side trying to guess who was there). During the mussel season they made a grotto of dark shells, put lighted candles at the back, and begged passers-by to 'remember the grotto, please'.

Street betting was illegal, but at midday a bookmaker or his assistant regularly made his stand and took bets in the middle of the Court, and in the evening a small group of men waited to collect their winnings. Princes Court, in fact, was the local gambling centre. According to Arthur Harding, it was the territory of Jimmy Smith, who was given the job by all the local bookies of 'straightening out' the police. The bookies expected to be arrested now and then, but by paying their dues through Smith they would avoid being taken in too often. Sometimes they were given notice that the police would be coming and by agreement they would put up someone else to take their place, usually a man who was unemployed and who was happy to be paid a few pounds for standing in. Harding gives the impression that it was all a highly organised conspiracy between the bookies and the police, with even the magistrates turning a blind eye to what was happening.[1] The Sanders remember it differently, and it may be that the system changed over the years. According to them, the main bookmaker in the Court was Georgie Barker. He and Smith were partners, and Smith only stood out if Georgie Barker was away. Smith, they say, was a big, portly man with a gold watch-chain stretched conspicuously across his stomach. Georgie Barker, whom they came to know very well, was a red-faced man who 'lived off whiskey'. One day, when all the favourites at Sandown came in, Jimmy Smith 'put on his running shoes' and 'left Georgie Barker holding the bag'. They agree that the police were 'straightened out', but if there was a conspiracy it was not running very smoothly. Each bookie had to bribe the local constable himself, and even then he could not be sure that he was safe. Georgie Barker had a lookout at either end of the Court – Georgie Seabrook, at the top, was the bookie's lookout and had no other job until the Second World War – and if one of them gave the warning he would run through the nearest house, into the yard behind and over the brick wall at the back. His son, who helped him, was arrested once, since the police came without warning and in plain clothes, and he was so worried by the prospect of a heavy fine that he 'gave the policeman a wallop' and jumped onto a passing tram. But the system continued of putting up someone in Georgie's place. When Bunny was eighteen and out of work he made an arrangement to stand in, but his father intervened and stopped it.

During the Second World War it was no longer a paying proposition for Georgie Barker to stand out, since there were fewer race meetings and so many men were away. But he kept going on a smaller scale by collecting bets in pubs and from friends. Basil, who was then retired, used to collect a few bets for him from the neighbours and gave him the money when he called round in the afternoon.

On Saturdays a group of men used to play pitch and toss in the road. Like the bookie they had to run off if the police appeared and sometimes they did not have time to gather up their pence and halfpence and the children would dash out and pick them up. Every now and then fights would break out among them. 'There might be cheating and all that lark,' says George: 'fix the pennies and all that sort of thing.'

But most of the violence in Princes Court was between husbands and wives and it was worst on Saturday nights after the pubs had closed. 'It seemed as if it was a natural thing to do', says Mary, 'to have a go at each other. That's how they used to term it. That was their way of living, you see.' 'You can say nearly every Saturday night was a punch-up, you know, of different families,' says George. 'There'd be the Johnsons* down the bottom: or the Roberts* would be having a go with the woman next door, Mrs Jones* – they were nearly always at it – and there might be the Potts*, all like that, you know. And the Spencers* and the Browns*, they used to be at it.' Alice Goldsmith, one of the neighbours, describes how these fights used to start between her aunt and her uncle, Mr and Mrs Newton: 'My aunt used to drink. That was the trouble. And then she'd start nagging him and he couldn't stand it any more and he'd have a go at her.'

'Women used to get bashed about more than what they call wife-battering now,' says Eddie, and it was common to see a woman with a black eye. But in some cases the women gave more than they got. Like the Tates: 'She was a great big woman and he was a little man. She used to knock him about terrible,' says Mary. 'She used to sit on him,' says my father. Mrs Burnham, next door to the Sanders, used to knock her husband about, and as for the Stacks*, she had 'a fiery temper' and 'she'd knock him around more than what he would knock her.' In the end she threw him out of the house and locked the door on him.

* Indicates fictitious name

Mary and George still remember Mr Morris*, a big man who worked at Truman's Brewery, coming home late at night on Christmas Eve, 'drunk as a lord' with an unwrapped side of beef under his arm. He was singing 'Though your heart may ache and break, never mind' – 'singing it as loud as anything', says Mary, 'pitch dark', and he was 'as happy as anyone'. But when he got home his wife was waiting for him. 'Crash, bang, wallop!' All the neighbours came out to see what was going on. 'I'll give you "never mind",' and she got hold of the beef and slung it up the turning, and she pushed him out of the house and slammed the door. So he had to spend the night sitting on the kerb. The Morrises had another spectacular row during the peace celebrations at the end of the Second World War. 'Jimmy Morris,' says George, 'that's the eldest son, he was trying to stop his father hitting his mother, and they was chasing all up and down the street. Talk about peace celebrations!'[2]

Several of the children were badly beaten by their fathers. Mr Morris 'would take his belt' to his children, 'many a time', says Mary, and 'the Johnsons would as well.' 'Some of the poor sods down there', says George, 'it used to be a bit tough, really.'

Bethnal Green was notoriously a 'rough' area, and it was an age when boxing was encouraged as 'manly'. My father remembers going to watch the champion from his school fight the champion from another school: 'we all went to cheer him along.' There were fights in the streets between boys from different areas, and some of the boys, says George, were 'right tearaways'. But there was very little involvement in organised crime of the type described by Arthur Harding in *East End Underworld*. Bobby Harris* was called in sometimes by one of the local gangs when they wanted to sort someone out, but he was not really a member of the gang.

There was only one man in the Court who had served long periods in gaol and who was regarded as a regular criminal, and that was Mr Spencer.* He was 'a right tea-leaf', says George, and the story that is best remembered of him is that 'he was the one who cut the tail off the cat because the cat give him away.' 'He was doing a job, a burglary, and the cat give the alarm.' For the ordinary man or woman about his or her business, however, the East End was not a dangerous area. Doors were never locked during the day, and all the women agree that they never had to worry about being attacked as they walked the streets – 'it wasn't like it is now.' When Mary read Arthur Harding's *East End Underworld* she commented that she had never known 'it was as bad as what it was. Not until I read that book.'

The overall pattern of work in Princes Court was typical of western Bethnal Green and, although there were changes over time, with a gradual shift towards regular employment, there was still a wide variety of jobs and many people were employed on a casual basis. During the inter-war period there was only one major employer for the men in Princes Court, and that was Truman's Brewery in Brick Lane. At least four of the Sanders' neighbours worked there from time to time: Mr Clark, Mr Morris, Mr Perryman and Mr Holt. During the Second World War several of the men went to work at Woolwich Arsenal, like Charlie Main and Georgie Seabrook, the bookie's lookout. The old Bethnal Green trade of furniture making was still well represented in the Court. Mr Collins, for example, was a cabinet-maker, Mr Evans and Mr Dennis were upholsterers, and Alfie and Charlie Cook were French polishers. Some of the Jewish families on the other side of the road were tailors, and there were at least two tailors on the Sanders' side: Mr Tate, the man who was sat on by his wife, and Mr Arnold, who made men's trousers in his own home. There was only one bootmaker left, Mr Clark, but the Smiths ran a small leather shop in their own home: 'they used to get cuttings of leather and sell them for handbags and all that.' There were several carmen, like old Mr Seabrook, who worked for Pickfords, Mr Newman, who worked for a firm in Spitalfields Market, and Mr Gray and his son, who worked for the railways. A few of the men were porters, like Billy Hall in Brick Lane and Jackie Kemp in Spitalfields Market.

Several people in the Court ran their own stalls, usually in Brick Lane or the Bethnal Green Road. The most successful among them were the Putneys, 'the catsmeat people', who bought their meat from the horse market in Middlesex Street, cut it up in a shed at the back of their garden, put it on skewers, and then sold it from a stall on the Kingsland Waste or hawked it around the houses. They were 'well off', 'they had a good trade', and they occupied their whole house. Mr Kelly went round with a horse and cart buying up secondhand clothes which he then sold from a stall in Brick Lane. Mr Burrows followed the same line of business, but he did not have a horse and cart and carried a large basket over his arm instead. Mr Sage travelled around on his horse and cart buying secondhand furniture.

Several of the Sanders' neighbours sold fruit and vegetables which they had bought at Spitalfields Market, like the Mableys, who ran a greengrocer's stall, and the Bonners, who ran a fruit stall, both in the Bethnal Green Road. Young Towser Barney specialised in bananas and Mrs Horton sold watercress. Mrs Powell used to sell flowers at Liverpool Street Station, where she regularly took her position with a big basket in front of her. Old Mrs Fletcher used to stand at the corner of Brick Lane selling odd bits and pieces like pins, laces and matches which she had bought from a wholesale store in Houndsditch, and her daughter-in-law sometimes stood next to her selling beetroot and lettuce from a small table.

Mr Julier used to deliver cardboard boxes, wheeling them around on a huge iron contraption which he kept in Mr Sage's yard. Mr Horton was a rag and bone dealer and Mr Greenleaf a rag sorter. Mr Yearly, as we have seen, made iron reels for firehoses. Bill Sullivan was a window cleaner, Mr Hall was in the navy, and Mr Stannard caught birds, like Alf Sanders in Braintree, and sold them in Club Row Market. Later, one of the Juliers' sons became a taxi driver, while one of the Shepherds' sons 'rose hisself' to become the manager of a string of garages. But many of the men had no regular jobs, especially during the Depression. At different times Mr Smithson,* Bobby Harris* and Mr Street, for example, were all odd job men and labourers. Harry Smithson,* one of the sons, 'used to be at the Duke of York, picking up glasses', says George. There was 'nothing essential about him. Last time I see him he was picking up glasses in the Well and Bucket in the Bethnal Green Road.' He was 'a potman', says Bunny, 'casual like.'

In the early years several of the women made matchboxes, like Jane Shepherd and her daughters. Others, like Granny Field and Mrs Newman, were charwomen. Mrs Walker, whose husband had been killed in the First World War, took in mangling at 1½d. a dozen. Mrs Julier, 'she was a very clever businesswoman', says George. She used to buy secondhand clothing at the church jumble sales and sell it to the Sugarbreads at the top of the road. One woman was said to be a prostitute.

Many of the children did odd jobs, like cleaning shops, taking barrow-loads of wood from one workshop to another, and lighting fires for the Jews on their Sabbath. 'I think', says Eddie, 'that everybody that was in the East End at that time, they tried to earn a bit of money somehow or the other.' 'You had to, didn't you', says my mother, 'because the men didn't earn much.'

A few of the older people had been able to retire on their pensions, like old Bill Gill. 'All he used to do', says George, 'get up in the morning, sit out on the window ledge, and as soon as it was twelve o'clock, straight over to The Duke of York, stop in there, closing time, come back home again, have his dinner, up again out there, that's all he done practically every day.'

Several families could only get by with a weekly loan from the pawnbroker. They washed their clothes and pawned them on Monday, and redeemed them on Friday so that they could wear them over the weekend. The Morrises left their best suits with the pawnbroker for the whole year, and took them out only for the sports day at Truman's Brewery. Others depended on the moneylender, who charged a penny on a shilling each week. As for hopping, according to Eddie, 'It was only the really poor that went. Down our road there was only one family, the Potts. They used to pile up an old van, and all the boys would have their hair shaved. And when they come back they used to give us all apples that the farmer had given them. So that week we always had apple tarts and dumplings.'

There were many in the road who did not live to see old age. Basil, who reached his seventies, was one of the lucky ones, but Ellen, who suffered from a heart condition, died when she was fifty-two. For most families the diet was poorly balanced, and many lives were shortened by excessive drinking. Some people, like Ellen's father, Frederick Field, Mrs Perryman and one of the Sages' children, died of tuberculosis, an illness that was associated with overcrowding – 'They always thought once you got TB you was finished', my father says – and diseases like scarlet fever, measles and diphtheria were still dangerous, especially for children. 'The ambulance used to come round', says Jess's husband, Fred, 'and they used to bring the kids out with hoods over their heads. We kids used to stand around: "Who's it going to be this time?"' Lennie caught scarlet fever when he was two and had to spend nineteen weeks in hospital. My father had it, less seriously, when he was ten, and was in hospital for two or three weeks.

Several people in the Court suffered from physical disabilities of one sort or another. Mrs Powell and Towser Barney had only one eye; old Mr Evans had a wooden leg; Harry Evans was a cripple; and Dummy Clark, who had 'a lovely personality', was deaf and dumb. Safety standards at work were very low and, as my mother says, 'you didn't have the same treatment as you have today.' Because of the danger of septicaemia the hospitals were quick to amputate, and the London Hospital was known locally as 'the butcher's shop'. When Lennie was four or five he was playing with some bigger boys who put him on top of one of the high boxes for electricity that used to stand on the pavements. He fell off and broke his left arm at the shoulder. He was rushed off to the Mildmay, but they could do nothing for him and so he was taken on to the London Hospital. The doctors wanted to take his arm off, but Basil refused to sign his consent. 'And a good job he didn't,' says Jess, since Lennie became one of the best sportsmen in the family and still has almost the full use of his arm.

There was a lot of mental illness too, and several who would have been sent to mental hospitals today were kept and cared for in their own homes. Some were backward from birth, like Hetty Ricketts, Ellen's cousin, and Billy Johnson,* who was cross-eyed, knock-kneed and generally retarded. Several other children, as George puts it, 'were a bit on the mental side'.

Old Bill Sullivan, who was a window cleaner, was suffering from the effects of the First World War. He was 'a right character, he was', says George. He used to come into the street wearing all his medals and brandishing a sword and charge up and down as if he were attacking the enemy. Or sometimes he used to think he was still bombing the Germans: 'he'd go up to the window and drop bottles out.' If he had cleaned your windows one week and you did not let him clean them the following week, he would throw mud at them; and once Daniels, the upholsterers, upset him by employing another window-cleaner, and he raised such a disturbance that the police had to be called in. Sometimes he was 'all right' and he was always 'quite harmless', but in the end he became unmanageable and had to be sent to an asylum.

Alf Burnham, who lived next door to the Sanders, was 'a funny-looking man' who always wore a bowler hat. While his wife was alive he had been dominated by her: he had been 'like clay in her hands,' says my father, 'like putty.' But when she died, says George, 'he went berserk. He didn't go mad', it was more 'freedom like'. But there was a very uncertain line between madness and Alf Burnham's particular form of freedom. Sometimes, in the evening, he would put his hats on chairs in a ring and talk to them as if they were guests. 'Come on. Have another drink. Drink up! Drink up! Do you want some sausages or what? What do you want? Do you want some eels?' It was a form of entertainment for the neighbours. Charlie Main at number 5 would come into his yard and throw a few pebbles at the window, and Alf would rush out: 'Who done it? Who done it? Interrupting our party! Leave us alone. We're not interfering with you.' And Charlie Main would dash back into his own house. He often went down to the prostitutes at Liverpool Street Station, and two once came to visit him in the Court, much to the annoyance of Mrs Julier, who bawled them out and sent them packing. He never spent a penny if he could help it. His normal meal was an Oxo cube with stale bread, but sometimes Mary would cook him a dinner and the neighbours might give him meat if it was beginning to go off. His wife had been a model of cleanliness, but after she died he slept under coalsacks. At one time he had collected bets for Georgie Barker and had been paid half a crown a week. When he died a sack full of half crowns was found in his bedroom.

There were several neighbours whose senility was more incapacitating than Alf Burnham's. The old woman who was known as Aunt Sarah went 'nutty' after her sister's death and allowed her rotting food and filthy rooms to be taken over by fleas, bugs and rats. Like Bill Sullivan, she had to be taken to an asylum. Mrs Raines, on the top floor at number 10, did not lose her mind, but became depressed and committed suicide.

It was difficult to maintain high standards of cleanliness in the Court. None of the houses had hot running water, and most people had a bath once a week in the scullery. Some used the public baths, like those off the Kingsland Road, where my father used to go, or, later, those at York Hall. A bath there cost sixpence, and a clean towel and a bar of soap were provided. There were long queues on Friday evenings, with people getting themselves clean for the weekend. One of the reasons for the popularity of the boys' clubs was that they provided showers free of charge.

Ellen worked hard to keep the house clean, but bugs appeared from time to time in all the houses of the Court, and many children had to go to school with their legs covered in bites. Several of the wives, like Ellen, used to paint the walls with naphthalene, and they would brush it on the springs of the beds every year. Not everyone bothered, however, and every now and then one of the houses became so badly infested that the Council had to be called in to fumigate it. The Smithsons* were the worst offenders. They were 'a right scruffy lot', says George, and according to Eddie one of the boys was nicknamed Soapy 'because he always wanted a blinkin' wash.'

At the schools the children's heads were regularly inspected by a nurse whom they called 'Nitty Nora'. If any of them had nits they were taken to the Cleansing Centre in Brick Lane and had all their hair shaved off and were given a bath.

The front doorstep and the pavement in front of the house were always scrubbed clean. To have failed in this would have been a public disgrace. When George moved next door to number 8 his wife Cath was so conscientious about this that she used to scrub up and down the road way beyond the limits of her own house. But in one case the concern with cleanliness, or at least with the appearance of being clean, was expressed in a way that struck everyone as odd: Mr Main, at number 5, always used to carry onions in his pockets 'to take off the smell of his feet'. 'His feet used to smell terrible,' says his daughter, who still keeps up with Mary: 'He used to go to the doctor's. He used to wash 'em every day, but we couldn't do anything for him.' He would say to his children 'You'll always remember me when I die, won't you?' According to Mary, he had an onion in each pocket, and 'he used to come in our kitchen and he used to say to me "Do you want these? I've had 'em all day. I'll have two fresh ones tomorrow." Dad'd say, "I'll have them if they're all right." '

Another mainstay of respectability was religion. Every child in the Court was sent to Sunday School, though among the adults there were very few who went to church. Old Granny White went to the Salvation Army, and Mrs Chapman, Ellen's friend, attended St Matthew's Church in Church Row. The Cooks, who were Irish, went to the Roman Catholic Church in Old Nichol

Street. Ellen, until the children grew up, was the only adult who went to the Nichol Street Mission.

A lot has been said and written about the warmth, the friendliness and the neighbourliness of the East End. No doubt it has gained from the glow of nostalgia, and from comparisons with the coolness and primness of London suburbia. But we cannot deny the evidence of the people themselves. The Sanders all speak well of their neighbours, and recall many acts of kindness and friendliness. There was certainly a powerful sense of community. When Mary went shopping for her mother almost every face was familiar to her. She met neighbours from the Court or nearby streets, people she had known at school or the Mission, people she had come to know through them, and others she had come to know through her brothers and sisters. Even today Bunny still insists on living in Bethnal Green because 'he wants to bang into one of his mates whenever he turns a corner'. People knew a lot about each other. When Basil wrote letters to his sons in the war he told them all the news about the neighbours as well as the family. If any of the children meet someone today who lived with them in Princes Court they start talking at once about the people they knew. All this is the same as village gossip, but there was one great difference between Bethnal Green and the village, and this was that everyone in Bethnal Green had the common bond of being poor and working class. The middle classes, in spite of the settlements, were never a significant presence. All the talk was held within the same framework of shared circumstances, values and interests.

Arthur Harding, looking back on his East End childhood, claims that it was 'a much happier world than it is today',[3] and Eddie says the same: 'People were much happier in those days. I don't think I ever saw anyone miserable.' But it is impossible to assess the happiness of a whole community. There could have been very little happiness for wives who went in fear of their husbands or for children who were regularly beaten by their fathers. Old Mrs Raines, who was lonely on her top floor, was so miserable that she lost the will to live. And there were those who found Bethnal Green intolerably constricting. If you wanted to 'better yourself', or even to have peace and quiet, you had to move out. The Sanders were probably luckier, and happier, than most. They never suffered extreme deprivation; there was little or no violence in their home; and, for the most part, they were not socially ambitious, and did not feel badly hemmed in by the limitations of Bethnal Green.

16

The Home

To reach the top floor of number 11, the Sanders' first home in Princes Court, you had to push open a trapdoor in the ceiling at the top of the stairs. As you entered, the windows were on your left and there was a fireplace with a small oven opposite. The old weaver's workshop had been divided into three compartments by curtains, which could be drawn open or closed as the family wanted. The compartments at the sides were bedrooms, and the compartment in the centre, with the fireplace, was the living room.

The floorboards were bare and, apart from the beds, the main pieces of furniture were a scrubbed wooden table and a few hard, straight-backed chairs. There were no armchairs or wardrobes. Clothes were hung up on hooks or packed away in chests of drawers. Without gas or electricity, all the cooking was done in the oven or over the fire, and the room was lit by paraffin lamps and candles. In order to get water the family had to go down two flights of stairs to a standpipe in the back yard. The toilet too was in the yard, and both the standpipe and the toilet were shared with the Sages and their two children, who lived on the first floor, and the Brandons and their four children, who lived on the ground floor. For this accommodation they paid 2s. 6d. a week. The four eldest boys were born at number 11. Basil Joseph, the first of them, died there.

By 1913 there were five children in the family and their single room was badly overcrowded. In that year the first floor of number 7 fell vacant, and the Sanders took the opportunity to move there. They now had two rooms at a rent of 5s. a week. On the floor below lived the Juliers with six children, and on the floor above old Mrs White, who belonged to the Salvation Army and was fond of singing hymns. When she died a few years later they took over her room in addition to their own, and the rent went up to 7s. 6d. With the arrival of four more children, however, they were just as overcrowded as before. The top room was divided into two bedrooms, one for the girls and one for the boys (at one time my father, Tom, George and Bunny all slept in the same bed, two at one end and two at the other); Ellen and Basil slept in the kitchen on the first floor; and the two youngest, Eddie and Len, were put in a corner of the living room. Lal married and moved away in 1920 and Mary in 1924, but Mary's marriage soon broke down and she moved back with her son Ronnie, who was then aged two.

By that time water had been piped to the first floor and gas had been installed, so that they could now use lights with gas-lit mantles and a gas cooker as well as the coal fire and stove. Under a covering roof in the yard outside there was an old copper in which Ellen did the washing on Monday mornings. The boys, when they were at home, had to light the fire underneath it and keep it going with wood shavings, chippings and offcuts from the workshop across the road. After the washing had been done Ellen cooked her puddings in the copper.

At some time during the war Ellen had become the landlord's caretaker for Princes Court. This meant that she received all the rents from her neighbours on that side of the road and paid them to the landlord's agent when he called on the Monday morning. She also passed on any complaints, and generally acted as an intermediary between the agent and the tenants. She allowed the agent to use her living room as an office, and while he counted the money and signed the rent books she gave him a cup of tea and biscuits. In return for these services her rent was halved.

In most families the rent was the woman's responsibility, and several wives handed it over on the Friday evening so that their husbands could not spend it on drink on the Saturday. Others were not so careful, and had to visit the pawnbroker on the Monday morning before they could get enough money together. If they fell behind by more than a month they were evicted. The Juliers were 'put out' during the First World War and their place on the ground floor was taken by the Halls. Basil did not like the idea of having so much money in the house over the weekend, but it was never lost or stolen. Nor did he like the involvement in his neighbours' personal and financial affairs that the job necessarily brought with it, but there was very little unpleasantness.

The landlords were the Portals Trust, but Ellen's dealings were entirely with their agents, F. and R. Rutley, who managed many other properties in London. When Lal was married she eventually moved to one of their houses in Tottenham, and much later Jess and Eddie did the same. George, when he married, moved next door to number 8. His wife, Cath, came from Wales, and since there was no one of her own family locally it was Ellen who spoke for her with the agent.

In 1925 there was a fire at the house. Late on the afternoon of Sunday 4 January, George tripped over as he was carrying a candle upstairs. Some curtains caught light, then the Christmas decorations, and within seconds the fire was blazing fiercely. George ran off to call the fire engine, but the rest of the family was trapped in the room overlooking the back yard. Basil called out for help, but when no one came he decided to jump. There are several versions of what happened: that he caught himself on the clothes line or on the wireless aerial, or that he jumped onto the shed and the roof gave way. In any event, he broke his leg. By this time the neighbours were coming round, and one by one the rest of the family jumped to safety. Then the firemen came and put out the blaze. There was not much damage, and the fire only rated a few lines in the miscellaneous columns of *The East London Advertiser*. Under the heading 'A Big Jump' it was reported that Basil Sanders had jumped from a first-floor window, 'receiving severe injuries to his legs'. In fact he had broken only one, but he had to spend three months in the Bethnal Green Hospital, where a metal plate was inserted to join the bone.

This was a turning point in Basil's life, since the doctors diagnosed high blood pressure and warned him that he must not drink. He gave up going to The Conqueror and he also, it seems, gave up sleeping with his wife. After this she slept upstairs with the girls in one room, the older boys slept upstairs in the other room, and Basil slept with the younger boys on the first floor.

In 1929 the Halls moved out and the Sanders took over the whole house. This was the height of their domestic arrangements. 'We thought we was real posh,' Eddie says. 'That was real luxury,' says Mary. For the first time they had a proper 'parlour', the front room on the ground floor, which was one of the great hallmarks of working class respectability. It was not used much, especially in the winter when a fire had to be lit, but it was generally reserved for special occasions, like entertaining visitors. It was the repository of the family's most valued possessions. When Aunt Galley died in 1931 her three-piece suite was installed there, and her clock and the matching vases were set up on the mantelpiece with *Bubbles* on the wall above them. There were several framed photographs in the room, like Ellen 'in her prime' and Bunny getting a prize for football, together with a picture of a country scene. The china ornaments were souvenirs from the seaside, mainly Southend and Clacton, and odd bits and pieces picked up from the stalls in Brick Lane. There was a piano, which only Lal could play, and a gramophone with records of music-hall songs and hymns.

In the rest of the house the furniture was still sparse. In the main living room at the back there was a high-backed wooden chair for Basil, but the rest of the family still had to sit on ordinary dining chairs. Carpets and rugs now covered the floors, but there were still no wardrobes, only chests of drawers. In the women's room at the top there was a photograph of one of Ellen's old friends with the inscription 'Gone but not forgotten'.

They now had the exclusive use of the back yard, where Basil kept rabbits and chickens and where the boys turned the ground to dust by playing football and cricket. An old ivy covered the wall at the back, but that was the only vegetation.

Yet for all their 'poshness' they were still overcrowded, with eight people, and for a time ten, in five rooms. They were conscious of their neighbours as well, since the walls were so thin that they could hear them very clearly, especially when voices were raised. Rents had gone up but, because of Ellen's services to the landlord, they only paid 6s. 6d. a week.

Ellen did not live long to enjoy the luxury of possessing the whole house, for she died of heart failure in 1932. Mary then took over the running of the house, and shortly afterwards Basil had to retire because of ill health. Except Bunny, the remaining children all married and moved away over the years, the last being Mary, for the second time, in 1947.

With Bunny out at work all day, and generally out with his mates in the evening, Basil spent much of his time on his own. But there were always people in and out of the house. Several of the children, especially Mary and Len, came round regularly to give him a hand, and every day several of the neighbours came in to place their bets with Georgie Barker. There were always visitors over the weekends. He had his wireless, and when the weather was warm he sat out on his window ledge and chatted with the people who went by.

At various times the family had kept pets, including one of the chickens that outlived all the rest. Basil did not have the heart to kill it, and for several years it used to strut around the house after him. During the war he was given Nobby, a small black mongrel to which he became very attached. Every afternoon, after Georgie Barker had come to collect the bets, Basil would take a rest on his bed with Nobby on a cushion by his side. And that was where he died, of a heart attack in his sleep, one January afternoon in 1953.

Bunny stayed on in Princes Court for a while, but after a few years the whole terrace on that side of the road was pulled down to make way for a new estate.

21. The Nichol: Boundary Street, Bethnal Green, *c.* 1890, shortly before it was demolished.

22. A court in the Nichol, *c.* 1890.

23. George Yard (now Gunthorpe Street), seen in 1979. 'Granny Field' was born here in 1860. Jack the Ripper murdered his first victim here in 1888.

24. 'Feeding the Hungry'. Sketches of the Nichol Street Mission from *The Illustrated London News*, 17 April 1886.

25 (above) and 26 (below). Two outings from The Conqueror in Austin Street, the first before the First World War, the second after. In the first Basil Sanders is seated on the brake, second from the left. In the second he is second from the left at the front. These two photographs are a perfect illustration of the decline of the public house over this period: see page 102.

27. The men's ward of the Mildmay Mission Hospital, c. 1910, with Biblical texts on the walls and beams. It was at the Mildmay, about this time, that Ellen was converted. According to Mary, one of the deaconesses entered the date on the flyleaf of a new Bible and added the verse 'I will lift mine eyes unto the hills from whence cometh my aid'. Years later Ler's wife, Anne, had a minor operation at the Mildmay and remembers seeing the text 'I will never leave thee, nor forsake thee' as she lost consciousness under the anaesthetic.

28 (above). Ellen Field and Basil Sanders on their wedding day, 1899.

29 (left). 'Granny Field', *c.* 1915. She normally wore an apron of sacking, but put on white for the photograph.

30. The family in 1928. From left to right, back row: Jess, Bunny, Tom, my father, George. Front row: Lal, Ellen, Lennie, Basil, Eddie, Mary.

31.   Princes Court (now Padbury Court), a photograph taken in 1951 a few years before these houses were demolished. They were built *c.* 1790. Number 7, where the Sanders lived, is on the extreme left. The window of their front parlour is to the right of the door. At the bottom of the Court is The Gibraltar public house.

32.   Brick Lane market, 1932.

33 (above). Some of the children of Princes Court, *c*. 1924. 'We just happened to be playing out there', says Jess, 'and they come and collected us.' In the back row, from left to right: Larly Main, Jimmy Cook, George Sanders, Neddy Dennis, Johnny Hall, Ernie Collins, Dolly Kemp, Rosy Shepherd. In the middle row: Charlie Main, Harry Newman, Willie Nobbs, Bunny Sanders, Wally Shepherd, Teddy Collins, Nellie Clark, Alice Gray. In the front row: Eddie Sanders, Lennie Sanders, held by Jess Sanders, Billy Austin, held by Suey Austin, Albert Austin, Jimmy Austin, held by Alfie Austin, Tommy Tresadern, George Shepherd, Tom Shepherd, Sam Shepherd, Bobby Perryman.

34. In the back yard of 7 Princes Court. At the back: Jess and Bunny. In the front: George, Lennie and Eddie.

17

Earning a Living

Basil did not talk about his work, and his children never knew exactly what he did. On his death certificate they described him as a retired compositor. In fact, as their own birth certificates make clear, he was a skilled machine printer, and the machine that he operated was a Cropper machine. This was used mainly for printing items like letterheads, handbills and notices. It worked on the principle of two vertical plates coming together, with a block of type on one plate and the paper to be printed on the other. The printer supplied the power by operating a treadle with his foot, and he inserted and removed each paper separately by hand. A man who was quick could print about a thousand pieces of paper in an hour. After each run he had to remove the block of type and put in the block for the next job, but he did not have to arrange the type himself. So for most of the day Basil would be standing in front of his machine, pushing the treadle up and down with his foot, putting sheets of paper between the plates as they came together and removing them as they came apart, taking care not to get his fingers caught between the plates, but no doubt under pressure to go as fast as he could. Under an agreement reached in 1919 the working week was 48 hours, and there was a week's paid holiday each year.[1]

No one in the family knew how much he earned, but it must have been nearly £2 a week by 1914 and about £4 a week by 1930. According to Mary, he gave his wife £1 a week for the housekeeping, and kept the rest for his drinks, his cigarettes, his snuff and the Spurs.[2] He could certainly have given more, but as the breadwinner he was held to be entitled to his pleasures. It is said that he always worked for G.E. Jackson and Company, but the firm was only founded in 1905. They were then based in Finsbury Market, but around 1910 they moved to Dysart Street, at the back of Finsbury Square.

Basil walked the mile between his home and his work, and he had just enough time to come back for his dinner at midday. One of the children had to keep watch for him, and as soon as he appeared round the corner from Brick Lane they called out to Ellen so that she could have his meal ready for him when he came in. In 1929 Jackson's moved to Southgate Road, Islington, and Basil's walk, if anything, was slightly longer.

The firm was not unionised,[3] which did not worry him, since he was generally content with his terms and conditions, but he did have one cause of complaint. It seems that a job fell vacant which he should have had, but instead it was given to 'one of the Governor's relations'. He was unhappy about this and Ellen, without telling him, wrote to Mr Jackson to complain. 'She thought she was appealing to the good nature of the man,' my father says, 'and the man had no good nature apparently. He was one of the old Victorian bosses.' Mr Jackson called Basil to his office and told him that if he received any more letters like that he would 'kick him downstairs'. And Basil was so angry about his wife's interference that when he came home that lunchtime he picked up the ends of the tablecloth and hurled his meal in the air.

Apart from that there was no trouble, and at least Basil had a steady job and a regular income. He worked for the firm for about thirty years and when he had to retire in 1933 – he was suffering blackouts because of high blood pressure and it was dangerous for him to go on – he was given a pension of ten shillings a week which he continued to get until he died.

With a growing family Ellen could no longer go out to work, but the children were all expected to bring in some money even while they were still at school. Mary earned half a crown a week for cleaning a Jewish salt-beef shop, and my father was paid threepence a time for cleaning all the shoes in a secondhand shoe shop in Brick Lane. On Saturdays several of the children earned a few pence as 'Shabas goys', lighting the lamps or the fires of those Jewish neighbours whose religion forbade them to do it for themselves. Bunny and Eddie were given the occasional sixpence for pushing barrowloads of wood or furniture for Mr Daniels in the workshop across the way – one of the workmen would pull on the shafts and the boy would push from behind – and there was always the odd penny or halfpenny to be earned by running errands for the neighbours.

As soon as the children left school at the age of fourteen they went out to full-time employment, and any money which they earned between then and getting married was handed over to their mother. At first she might give them a shilling a week for themselves. As they grew older they would be given more.

The three girls all went into 'women's work'; they were all poorly paid, and they all left work when they married or soon after (though Mary had to return to work when her marriage broke down).

Lal, the eldest, was one of the many women who were caught up in the war effort. Along with 25,000 others, she was employed in the munitions factory at Woolwich Arsenal. This was not traditionally women's work, but with the demands of war and so many men away in the army this is what it became. She worked in 'the yellow room', where the TNT which the women poured into the shells made their skin go so yellow that they were popularly known as the Canary Girls. It could also result in severe poisoning, and Lal suffered badly. The family are convinced that it was because of this that her health was so poor later: 'they reckoned it had damaged her inside'.[4] After the war she worked as a clerk for a firm in Ironmongers Row, but she married in 1920 and did not work long after that.

Mary began work in the men's tailoring department at Dickens and Jones. Her cousin, Jean Shepherd, was a court dressmaker there and had looked out for a vacancy for her. She trained there for three months, earning 2s. 6d. a week, but then she went on to Debenham's, where she worked as a blousemaker on piecework. She had to give it up when her mother became ill and she was needed at home to look after the family, but when her mother recovered she became a clerk in an office close by, in the Bethnal Green Road. She stopped working after she married in 1924, but when her marriage broke down and she returned to Princes Court she began work as a charlady for the Associate Bank of New York in Old Broad Street. It was a job she could fit in with helping her mother, leaving the house at five every morning and coming back by midday. At first she cleaned the stairs for 14s. a week. Later she became the canteen supervisor.

Jess began work as a dressmaker for Black and Chilterns in the City Road, where Mary knew the manageress. She earned only ten shillings a week, since the women, as she says, were paid less than the men. Then she made handbags for Kings in Finsbury Square, and again she earned only ten shillings a week. In 1937 she married and moved to Tottenham.

Although Basil worked in the print, where recruitment traditionally ran in families, he did nothing to get his sons into the trade. It is suggested that he did not want his wife and children to find out how much he was earning. It seems more likely that he was content to leave these matters to his wife. 'Mum done all the worrying over us,' my father says, and it was Ellen who found a job for him with Mr Pugh, an ironmonger in the Holloway Road who was a supporter of the Nichol Street Mission. 'Mum thought the boys would do better if they could get with a Christian man, under Christian leadership,' Mary explains. Tom was also employed by Mr Pugh, and so were two other boys from the Mission. Mr Pugh probably thought that in taking these boys he was getting a more reliable type of assistant, and he had the advantage of knowing them personally in advance. 'When I first met Tom', he wrote later, 'he was dressed in very short petticoats and from that day to this I have never heard him say an unkind word or do a shady deed.'

Pugh Brothers were at 95–101 Holloway Road, and Mr Pugh was the sole proprietor. They advertised themselves as Motor and Cycle Agents, Furnishing, Ironmongers, Wholesale Dealers and Factors, and Sole Manufacturers of 'Pugh' Gas Fires. At first my father was a messenger and odd-job boy, earning 15s. a week. He went on to be a shop assistant, selling cycles, tools and radios. His hours were from 8 a.m. to 7 p.m., six days a week, except Thursdays, when he had the afternoon off, and Saturdays, when he worked until 9 p.m. After the first year he had a week's paid holiday each year.

When he had left school the headmaster had confidently recommended him as 'a thoroughly honest, respectable and hard working lad', and he was always conscientious and dependable. He joined the Ironmongers' Assistants' Association, where he heard lectures from manufacturers of electric lights, lawn mowers, vacuum cleaners and addressing machines.

He was aware, only too well, of his boss's absolute control. At two minutes to nine on a Saturday evening Mr Pugh might come round and order his assistants to straighten up some boxes on the top shelf at the back or to clean out some inaccessible corner. 'You couldn't do a thing in those days,' he says. When Mr Prince, the manager, deliberately left half a crown on the floor he picked it up and handed it to the cashier. 'Otherwise', he says, 'I'd have been out on my ear.' There was, of course, no union.

Shop assistants were not well paid, but they might well have 'prospects' of becoming managers later. By the time he was nineteen my father's wages had gone up to 35s. a week. Mr Pugh thought well of him but, since all the managers were comparatively young, his prospects were not very encouraging. So they both decided that it was time he moved on, and in 1926, on Mr Pugh's recommendation, he took a job as an assistant with Thos. Gunn Ltd., 'Wholesale Ironmongers and Electrical Engineers', at their branch in Queen Street, EC4. Within a year, however, Gunn's ran into difficulties and he was made redundant, and after that he had jobs with several ironmongers. His pay varied. Gunn's, for example, paid him 35s. a week: Richard Melhuish's of Fetter Lane paid him 50s. And the hours were sometimes different from Pugh's. At Gunn's, for example, he had to work on weekdays from 8.30 a.m. to 7 p.m. with one hour off for dinner, and on Saturdays from 8.30 a.m. to 1 p.m. Gunn's warned him that no salary would be paid 'if absent through illness or any other cause'. Melhuish's told him that he would have to wear brown overalls with stiff white collars 'and we shall be glad if you will provide yourself with same.'

He would probably have continued as a shop assistant if he had not met my mother. She 'nearly had a fit', she says, when she found how little he was earning, and told him that they could never get married on that. So they went together to see Dickie Pearson, the Superintendent of the Nichol Street Mission, who worked for the Royal London Mutual Insurance Society and was in charge of its Islington office. Through him my father bought an insurance book and became an insurance agent, which meant that he now had the right to collect premiums from the hundred or so policy-holders listed in the book and to receive a commission on each premium collected. His book cost him £325. He had £65 available, mainly from my mother's savings, and he borrowed £260 at 7½ per cent interest. Since he had to pay this back at £1 a week, and since his income on the book was only about £3, at first he was earning less than before. But there were possibilities, which he realised, of gaining new business, and by the war he had paid off the loan and was earning £5 a week.

Most of his clients had life or endowment policies on which they paid a shilling or two a week, and his round was concentrated in Highbury, Stoke Newington, Stamford Hill and Hoxton. He went out collecting on Mondays and Tuesdays and on Friday evenings and Saturdays, when people had just been paid, and he travelled by tram on an all-day ticket which cost a shilling a day. On Thursdays he paid in his money to the branch office in Islington. He took Wednesdays and Sundays off, and for the rest of the time he tried to get new business. He enjoyed the work and became very friendly with many of his clients. For some of them he was the only white collar worker they knew, and they would ask him to write letters for them to the local council or to fill in a form or draw up a will. He also joined his trade union, the Royal London Staff Association, which would later provide the basis for a new career.

Unlike my father, Tom never settled at Pugh's. Religion was the all-absorbing centre of his life. He had attended the Mission regularly, but he had also been drawn to the open-air services that were held by the Salvation Army's cadets from their training college in Clapton. He had joined their Bible class, and soon he felt that he was being called to become a Salvation Army officer. The strongest opposition came from his mother, who would have preferred him to be connected with the Mission. He argued that the Army would give him more scope, but she was not persuaded, and for a long time he had to hide his Salvation Army uniform. Basil, of course, thought the whole idea was ridiculous. 'He thought I'd taken leave of my senses,' says Tom. But he did not bother to argue against it.

Ellen in the end was won over, and so Tom went to the college in Clapton and became a Salvation Army cadet. He completed his training, and on the evening before he left for his first posting in Glasgow there was a special farewell service at the Mission. Mr Pugh could not attend, but sent a letter to wish Tom 'great success in his new sphere which I consider the highest of all callings, "Direct Service".'

By the standards of the time Mr Pugh was not a bad boss. His wages were no lower than the average, and very few employers gave a week's paid holiday. It was a common practice for employers to dismiss their young employees as soon as they became entitled to a man's wage and to replace them with school-leavers,[5] but neither my father nor Tom was treated in this way. Mr Pugh may have kept them under strict control, but in this he was no different from most other employers, and at least he felt some kind of Christian responsibility for them. No doubt the two boys were ideal employees, but it is possible that Ellen was right and that they did do better with him than they might have done elsewhere. They certainly did better than their younger brothers in these early stages of their careers.

For George, Bunny, Eddie and Len there was no question of working for Mr Pugh – they were not the best-behaved lads at the Mission – and they all found jobs for themselves, relying on advertisements or tips from friends. Unlike my father and Tom, none of them settled down to any steady employment, and they moved rapidly from job to job, sometimes of their own accord and sometimes because they were 'given the push'.

George, in my father's disapproving comment, 'was always flashing in and out of jobs'. He began in the City, in the Lombard Restaurant. 'Nice job that was, in the kitchen', he says, 'peeling spuds and all things like that. And then there was a bit of a two and eight with one of the blokes there. We had a right fight and we both got the sack. And then I sort of drifted around, you know.' At one point he got a job in a warehouse of Jeremiah Rotherham's in Shoreditch High Street. He got on well at first, but then, he says, 'I fell foul of the geezer there. He was one of them blokes, you know. There was a real Dickens atmosphere there, you know, Dickens's. If you was in you was in, if you wasn't you wasn't. Anyway, I couldn't stand it. I was always having rows with him and I just got the sack.' After that he 'drifted from job to job', and there were many times when he was 'in between sort of thing'. He earned a few shillings on the side, as we shall see, by doing turns in the clubs and the pubs and the variety halls.

Bunny, who had passed the scholarship and had gone to the central school in Mansford Street, might have been expected to do better, but he left when he was fourteen and 'If you left there when you was fourteen you haven't got no school character. All I got was the half-term report. Well, the chap when I was fourteen was the football teacher, and his remarks were: "Bunny Sanders is an honest, trustworthy, reliable boy, and is to be congratulated on his excellent captaincy of the football team." And when I went out to get a job, first thing they used to ask you was "What's your school character?" I said "I haven't got one." They'd say "Haven't you got nothing?" And I'd say "Well, I've got this half term report." And the chap looked at it and he said "We don't want no footballers here. 'Op it".'

His first job was with an engineering shop in Ironmongers Row, 'putting holes in for screws, terrible job, all day long the same thing. I lasted there about two and a half days.' Then he heard about another job as a messenger boy with William Lea's, the printers in Worship Street, and he started there, 'nice and clean', at a wage of 12s. a week. But he was sacked when he reached 'the great age of sixteen' and became entitled to a man's wage, 'which was too much'. 'I don't know if I got the sack for messing about. I don't think I did. But everybody got the sack. They'd make any excuse up, you know. A bit of bad time-keeping, anything.' After that he 'just drifted from job to job', with occasional spells on the dole.

Eddie had so many jobs between leaving school and the age of twenty that he cannot remember them all. He worked as a sweeper-up for a cabinet-maker's in the Hackney Road, as a vanboy for the East London Rubber Company, as a warehouse boy for a pipe firm, and as 'a kind of storeman' for an engineering firm making cigarette machines. 'I did all right there', he says, 'but I got the push. I can't remember why. They gave you the push for anything then.' His best job was working for Sloans Electric in Golden Lane. 'I was sort of in charge of their electric lamp department. They gave me the push when I became sixteen because they didn't want to pay me a man's wage. After that I was on the dole for a bit.'

Lennie began work as a messenger boy in 1936 for 14s. 10d. a week. Then he became a glazier, but this was interrupted by the war, when he worked on firewatching and demolition – 'nothing steady, day to day sort of thing.' He earned a bit more as a footballer with Clapton Orient, occasionally playing for their first team during the war when, as he says, all the clubs were short of players. He never became a professional. 'There was no sense in being a pro because you got thirty bob a game whether you was a pro or amateur.'

Except Lennie, they all spent time out of work. After his marriage to Cath in 1931 George was unemployed for about two years. He was 'on the labour', or on the dole, for six months, and after that 'you got slung off, and you just relied on relief.' To qualify for this he and Cath had to go through a means test, which was carried out by an official from the Public Assistance Committee. Before the official came: 'Anything worth pawning, you got rid of it', 'any grub in the house, get rid of it.' In answer to his questions they told him that they had no money, that their parents were not giving them anything, and that they had nothing, like a piano, worth pawning. But he was a 'crafty bloke', up to 'all sorts of tricks', and after he had inspected the house he asked if he could have a cup of tea. George was quick to spot what he saw as a trap and told him 'We ain't got no tea.' In this way they passed the means test, and they were given tickets for what they needed – tickets for groceries, for bread, for meat, and for coal in winter. The rent was paid as well. But if they wanted anything special, like a pair of boots for one of their boys, they had to make a special application, and even when this was granted they had to go where they were told to go and 'you got what they give you, no messing.' It was 'hard going', an embittering experience. He tried to get a job through the Oxford House, but they 'didn't seem to want to know.'

One by one, however, they all settled down. Shortly before the war George got a job testing petrol tanks at Heston airport, close to Heathrow – 'Good little job it was' – and he stayed in and around the airports for the rest of his working life. As for Bunny, he 'found the electrical line'. He had got a job as an electrician's mate at 25s. a week, and bought the books on electricity which were being published in serial form by Paxton's. He finished the course and with one short break he remained an electrician, serving with the RAF during the war, and finishing up with the Admiralty in London. In 1938 Eddie, when he was twenty, decided to 'make a career' for himself. So he followed my father's example and, with the help of Dickie Pearson at the Mission, he became an agent with the Royal London. He was called up in the army in the following year, and Lal, his eldest sister, did his book for him in the war. When he came out he took it up again, but he 'wasn't making much of a go of it' and so he gave it up and became a postman. Lennie after the war became a taxi-driver, and he is still a taxi-driver today.

After their early years, therefore, as messenger boys, warehouse boys or shop assistants, drifting from job to job or drawing the dole, by the time they were thirty all the men in the family had settled in the work which they were to follow for the rest of their lives – my father in the Royal London, Tom in the Salvation Army, George at the airport, Bunny as an electrician, Eddie in the Post Office and Lennie as a taxi-driver.

Although London had not suffered as badly as some other areas during the

Depression, unemployment was always a threat, and the employer had almost unfettered control. Young boys could be sacked for 'nothing at all', or simply for reaching the age of sixteen and becoming entitled to a man's wage. Even a good employee with more than twenty years' service, like Basil, could be threatened with being kicked downstairs when his wife wrote a letter of complaint. Those bosses who abused their power were condemned as Victorian or, in George's words, 'real Dickens', but to most workers, and certainly the Sanders, it seemed that very little could be done about them.

It was different after the war, with full employment and stronger unions, and none of the men was out of work for any length of time. Meanwhile Basil went on collecting his ten shillings a week from G.E. Jackson and Company, and when he died it was noted with approval that a company representative attended the funeral.

In Stansted, as we have seen, there was a marked economic advantage in being the eldest son in the family – and in Braintree in being the eldest daughter – and even in Bethnal Green, where there was no family business to be taken over, my father, the eldest son, probably did better financially than any of his brothers and sisters. He was the only white-collar worker among them (apart from Tom in the Salvation Army), and he was the only one who went on, as we shall see, to move to the outer suburbs and to buy his own house, though Tom and his wife bought their own house when they retired. Moreover he and Tom, together with the three girls, were the children who were most influenced by the Nichol Street Mission, and he has remained a committed and active Christian all his life.

He himself ascribes his upward mobility to the driving ambition of my mother, and this was obviously a powerful factor. But it was he, and not anyone else, whom my mother chose to marry and drive on, and he responded to her influence and pressure. Once again the connection between seniority in the family and worldly success and respectability seems too strong to be coincidental.

18

The Standard of Living

Basil and Ellen's standard of living improved dramatically during their married life, and the most obvious sign of this was their move over time from the top floor at number 11 to occupy the whole house at number 7. To a certain extent they were carried along by rising standards in the country as a whole, at least from the beginning of the First World War. Their experience was also part of the normal cycle of a working family's life: they were hard up while the children were still at school and became more comfortable when they went out to work. They benefited from two other changes as well: Ellen's becoming the caretaker for the landlord, which saved several shillings a week in rent, and Basil's abstention from drink after the doctors had diagnosed high blood pressure. My father and Tom, who are both religious, see Basil's enforced teetotalism as the great turning point in the family's fortunes. After he had given up going to The Conqueror, they say, 'it was a much better home life', 'everything was lovely', and for the first time he and Ellen could afford such things as a piano and holidays by the sea. There is obviously some exaggeration in this, but it is not entirely fanciful.

The Sanders were very poor at first, but they were better off than many others. Basil had a regular job and Ellen was a careful housekeeper. She watched every penny, and never had to resort to the pawnbroker or the moneylender. She guarded against emergencies as well. She drew out penny insurance policies for each of the children to cover any possible funeral expenses, and she kept these policies carefully up to date.

The children did not go hungry, though in the early years Lal and Mary, the two eldest, used to queue up for their breakfasts at Father Jay's, and on Sunday evenings they attended the service at 'Mac's', Annie MacPherson's Home of Industry, where Mary would go forward at the end and be given a ticket for three jugs of pea soup during the week. Things were not much better during the war, when Tom was sent to Bishopsgate each week because bread was a few pence cheaper there. For their tea they had only plain bread and butter, with jam as a special treat once a week.

The youngest children, however, think that they were wonderfully fed. 'We were lucky,' says George. 'I'll say that about our Mum and Dad, God bless their souls. We always had three square meals on the table.' When they got up in the morning there would be porridge or bread and dripping, 'something like that, and a nice cup of tea'; they could take a sandwich to school if they liked; when they came home at midday there was 'a lovely hot dinner, especially in the winter, all stew and all that lark' – sheep's tongue and brains on Tuesdays, Jess remembers, and steak and kidney pie on Saturdays – and for afters they might have spotted dick; and for tea 'bread and butter, jam, and a bit of cake', and sometimes kippers or bloaters. On Friday evenings, if they were lucky, they would be sent to the pie shop in Brick Lane and get a bowl of pie and mash, or a saveloy, a faggot, pease pudding or jellied eels. Basil's special treat was a half a sheep's head. Eddie, it is true, went to a soup kitchen once, but it was 'for a lark more than anything', and certainly not need. And he did not dare tell his mother he had gone, for if she had known 'she'd have proper cleaned me out.'

The children were decently clothed, even if they had to wear each other's cast-offs. Tom remembers that they 'used to be glad of jumble sales', and sometimes Ellen bought shoes from the pawnshop when people were unable to redeem their pledges. Mary ascribes her bad feet to this. In the week they wore woollen jerseys, and we can see what they wore on Sundays from the only photograph of the family as a whole, which was taken in 1929. Basil disliked being put out of his normal routine – 'it was a right palaver getting ready,' Jess says – but at least he could wear his everyday suit with the trousers shiny at the knees.

Aunt Galley helped out. When Mary passed the scholarship, for example, it was Aunt Galley who made it possible for her to go to the grammar school by buying her new school clothes, and she bought Bunny a new suit or coat every year. She even paid 4d. a week for violin lessons for George.

The eldest children had no birthday parties when they were young, and if they received a present, which was very unusual, it would be an article of clothing. The first birthday that my father celebrated was his twenty-first. 'We never got excited about our birthdays,' Tom says. But Lennie, the youngest, always had a party, with cakes, presents, 'the lot'. 'They made a real fuss of me,' he says.

It was the same with Christmas. The eldest children hung up their stockings, but all they found on Christmas morning was an orange, a bag of sweets and a bright new penny. They could not afford poultry for their Christmas dinner, though sometimes they would have a rabbit which they had fattened in the back yard. In later years it was very different, with toys in the children's stockings and a chicken or turkey for dinner. For the younger children Christmas was 'marvellous'.

Holidays improved as well. At first Ellen did not have holidays at all, while Basil would take Mary for a week to Braintree. My father, Tom and George all went on holidays subsidised by the Children's Country Holiday Fund, a scheme started by Canon Barnett of Toynbee Hall. An official from the fund would come round to the school each week and collect 6d. from each child up to a total of about 10s. The child would then be entitled to a fortnight's holiday in the country, staying with local people. Later, through the landlord's agent, Basil rented a cottage for an entire month at Pitsea, Ashingdon or Rochford, and Ellen went down with the children and Basil joined them for a week and at weekends. Otherwise they had the occasional day trip to Southend.

At the end of her life, by the standards of Princes Court, Ellen was well off. She had more than £100 in Post Office savings, an account with the Midland Bank in Great Eastern Street, and a substantial 'divi' with Williams, the grocers. Her last act, before she died, was to buy a wedding present for my parents, a three-piece suite from Mr Daniels across the way, which she was able to pay for in ready cash.

It was only a few months after Ellen's death that Basil had to give up work, but with the support of those children who were still at home he was fairly comfortable and he never felt the need to give up part of the house in order to bring down the rent. He inherited not only Ellen's savings, but considerable sums, probably about £400 in all, from his mother and his Uncle Alf. In addition to his firm's pension of 10s. a week and the old age pension of 16s. a week, he earned a few shillings by collecting bets for Georgie Barker, the bookmaker.

In his last years, however, he had no savings, but was living from week to week. He gave his grandchildren a shilling each for their birthdays, and we knew that he was not well off because our aunts and uncles gave us half a crown. When he died he left no property, except the contents of the house, and his children had to whip round among themselves to pay for the funeral. Bunny, who stayed on in Princes Court, did not want all the old man's bits and pieces, and as we sat in the parlour after the funeral George was given Aunt

Galley's clock and the matching vases and Eddie laid claim to *Bubbles*. These are our family heirlooms. I was given an old pen-knife, which I liked very much at the time, but I have lost it since.

19

Education

When my father and my aunts and uncles talk about their education it is as if they are relating their experiences in some remote foreign country which they had visited in their youth and which they had never seen again. It was a strange and unfamiliar land, full of signposts to places whose importance they had to take on trust, like the plays of Shakespeare and the Napoleonic wars. The teachers, its settled inhabitants and rulers, had exercised complete power over them. Some had been kind and helpful, others fierce and intimidating. They had tried to instruct them in the country's topography, but apart from the three Rs, which the children had needed in order to get jobs in the world outside, there was very little that they had laid hold of and made their own.

The first four children, including my father, went to St Philip's, a church school in Mount Street. The last five went to Daniel Street. They do not know why the change was made. Both schools were mixed. Mary and Bunny passed the scholarship at the age of eleven, and Mary went on to the Central Foundation School in Spitalfields and Bunny to Mansford Street Central. The other children stayed at the elementary school. All of them left at the age of fourteen.

They were taught reading, writing and arithmetic, geography, history, scripture, nature study, painting and drawing. There was no organised sport at St Philip's, but during the breaks the boys would play football among themselves on the small concrete playground. They had very few outings. My father's class was taken to see a ship at the West India Docks, and to a performance of *A Midsummer Night's Dream*, 'only local', at Mile End. They were not taught the facts of life, but had to pick them up for themselves. (One of the boys came home worried one day because he had kissed a girl and thought that this might make her pregnant. And another did not find out 'what was what' until he was 18 years old.) They were taught hygiene, though, and during the food rationing of the First World War special visitors advised them what food they should eat and told them that they should chew it slowly and thoroughly.

According to my father, history was a 'good subject'. It was mainly a procession of kings and queens and wars and battles and it did not extend further than the rise of the British Empire. The only novelist they mention is Dickens, and they generally read Oliver Twist. Apart from seeing *A Midsummer Night's Dream*, they read Shakespeare in class and learned certain passages by heart. My father remembers 'the seven ages of man, isn't it? The baby, the schoolboy wiping his nose on the way to school, the callow youth. We used to recite that. And we used to recite the Battle of Agincourt one.' He also learned 'the Crimean War one, the Charge of the Light Brigade.' At Daniel Street they did acting too, which George in particular enjoyed: 'when I was at school, I was very good at Shakespeare, you know, Julius Caesar, and I done the quarrel scene with another fellow.' As a result 'I won the whatsname, I won a big Shakespeare book.' 'We learned a lot of songs too', my father says, like "Cherry Ripe" and "Hearts of Oak".'

Discipline was strict, but not brutal. My father was caned twice on the hand for being cheeky. My mother's sister, Ivy, who also went to St Philip's, was caned once for talking. 'You didn't have to do much to get caned in those days. Mr Millie was fond of using the cane. He used to be in the army.' 'They used to tell you to put French chalk on your hand,' my father says, 'then it wouldn't hurt so much. But down it used to come, wallop!'

Their model was in part the public school, and Daniel Street even had its own school song, drawing its inspiration from Daniel in the Old Testament:

> In Babylon there lived a youth whose praises men did sing,
> Because he had interpreted the visions of a King.
> Daniel his name, prayer his help, God his willing aid,
> He saw the truth, he saw the faith, his glory cannot fade.

The chorus was:

> Daniel Street must live up to its name,
> Daniel Street must always play the game.

The patriotism which motivated the teaching of history and the choice of songs and poetry was let loose completely on Empire Day, 14 July, when the entire school went in the morning to the church hall in Mount Street. The scouts were there in their uniforms, and the children wore rosettes of red, white and blue and carried Union Jacks. Pageants were mounted: in one year Mary took the part of Britannia, in another year she was Ireland. The headmaster made a speech, and there was Scottish dancing and the singing of patriotic songs – 'Rule Britannia', 'Land of Hope and Glory', and the song that had been specially composed for Empire Day:

> What is the meaning of Empire Day?
> Why do the cannons roar?
> Why does the cry 'God Save the King!'
> Echo from shore to shore?

At the end the national anthem was sung and the school was given an afternoon's holiday.

This patriotism, unlike most of the teaching, reinforced what the children felt and believed and what they had been taught already. George Edward, as we have seen, had been named after the two kings, and explains this by his mother's patriotism. And after the First World War one of the poems which Mary recited at family parties was 'The Old Iron Kettle', which her sister Lal had given her as a present. It is the story told by the mother of a young soldier who had braved enemy fire to get water in an old kettle for a comrade who was dying of thirst. The old kettle, dinted by bullets, now hangs from her mantlepiece, and a friend suggests that she should get rid of it:

> 'What, part with that dear old kettle?' she said, and her eyes grew dim:
> 'If I come to my very last farthing I wouldn't part with him.
> You say that it's battered and rusty, and of use to me no more,
> Worth well perhaps three halfpence at a secondhand dealer's store.
> But to me that dear old kettle has a worth that can never be told,
> A value that could not be greater if it were made with gold.'

And she then gives the account of her son's bravery as he went to get the water:

> 'The bullets whizzed around him fired by the sleepless foe.
> They made the dints in the kettle, but God preserved my Joe.
> And when the King, God bless him, heard what my boy had done,
> He sent a cross with some ribbon, and said it was nobly won.
> So the sign of his Sovereign's honour is shining on his breast,
> And I've got the poor old kettle, and I think I like it best.'

Bethnal Green

Mary says that this poem always went down well, and she can still recite it with an intensity and fervour that can bring her audience close to tears.

Basil, typically, was less committed. He did not volunteer for the First World War, and he was relieved when his employer managed to get him exempted on the ground that he was involved in printing for the War Office. Later, at the time of George VI's coronation, he asked his children to put out the flags, like everyone else in the road, but he was not caught up with the excitement of the occasion. 'If we don't put them out', he told Eddie, 'we might get some stones thrown through the window.' But he was not opposed to the monarchy: 'he would never say anything against it.'

Neither he nor Ellen encouraged the children in their studies. The only books in the house were the Bible, *Christie's Old Organ* (a popular religious book), and the few volumes which the children were given as prizes or presents. Basil read nothing except the newspapers, and later perhaps some football annuals that had been given to the boys at Christmas. Ellen read the Bible regularly and she took a religious magazine, *The Life of Faith*. Neither of them read novels. According to Eddie, they were 'too busy' to read books. It was 'such a different kind of life', says Tom: there was 'no real privacy'.

Mary, as we have seen, only went to the grammar school because Aunt Galley paid for her new school clothes. She wanted to stay beyond the age of fourteen but her father refused: 'You can get all those ideas out of your head. You're going to work when you're fourteen and that's that.' Because she went to a different school her neighbours regarded her as 'stuck up' and her brothers and sisters called her 'Clever Clogs'. If they wanted an answer to a question, 'Oh ask her, she'll know, she'll know.' Going to Spitalfields, she says, 'made a difference to me. I could have gone further, it made me want to do different things', like being a teacher or a missionary. When she left school she and a friend used to go to evening classes in Daniel Street where they learned elocution and gymnastics. 'I wanted to speak better,' she says. 'I wanted to be different in myself.' She bought books on grammar and syntax, but her mother thought it was all wrong: 'It's no use trying to be what you can't be. Don't bring those books into the house. You're not going any further.' She knew that her mother was speaking from the kindest of intentions, but she was frustrated and upset and used to cry for hours. 'I often used to wish we were rich.' She left her evening classes when she was eighteen or nineteen, and that was the end of her formal education.

Bunny, who also passed the scholarship, received, as he says, not 'the slightest bit of encouragement'. He was not ambitious, like Mary, and he had no wish to be different. On the contrary: 'I didn't really want to go' to the

Central School, he says, 'because all me mates were round Daniel Street.' But looking back, he thinks he should have been given more advice. 'When you got to the third year it was up to you to decide whether you wanted to go Industrial or Commercial. I did show a talent for Commercial, because I've always been good at figures, very good at mental arithmetic and everything else. Always. But no one advised me to go into it. I asked my father and he said he didn't care what I done.' So 'I went into Industrial because all the boys was going into Industrial, all the boys who played football, all the lads. . . . No, I never got no encouragement as regards school.'

Eddie was given some help, but only fortuitously through some cigarette cards on English history that his father passed on to him. 'The teacher was surprised that I knew so much, but I'd picked it up from the cards.' And Lennie says much the same as Bunny: 'If you done it you done it off your own bat, sort of thing.'

In religion, however, Ellen gave every encouragement to the children, and the eldest at least responded fully, while Basil gave the boys his love of sport, especially football and cricket. It was not an impoverished legacy.

20

The Nichol Street Mission

We do not know exactly when Ellen was converted at the Mildmay, but it must have been around 1910. After short periods at the Gibraltar Walk Mission,[1] which closed down, and Annie MacPherson's Home of Industry, which moved, she settled at the Nichol Street Mission, which became her second and spiritual home. 'We used to practically live round the little Mission,' says Jess. It was Ellen's 'happiness', says Mary: 'it took her away from everyday life.'

By the time the Sanders became connected with the Mission it no longer provided free breakfasts but concentrated instead on its evangelical work. The Sunday evening service was the highpoint of its life, and there were morning, afternoon and evening Sunday Schools. The midweek activities included a Weeknight Service of Praise and Prayer, the Young Ladies' Club and the Women's Meeting, the Cubs, Scouts and Rovers, the Girls' Life Brigade, the Cripple Parlour, the Band of Hope, Christian Endeavour, the Hospital Savings Association, the Penny Bank and the Monthly Fellowship Meeting. There were annual treats and outings for the Sunday Schools and, shortly before Christmas, a Sunshine Party for the cripples, when toys and clothing would be handed out. The list of activities is impressively long, but while several hundred children attended the Sunday Schools the Sunday evening service drew only a hundred adults, a number which had gone down to forty by the end. Most of those who went were women.

The Mission's President was the minister of the Union Chapel in Islington, but it was the Superintendent who really ran the place. From 1924 it was Mr McPherson, a member of the Union Chapel who eventually became a partner in a firm of City stockbrokers; and from 1928 it was Dickie Pearson, who was a deacon of the Shoreditch Tabernacle and worked for the Royal London Mutual

Insurance Society. As well as McPherson there were several Congregationalists, most, if not all, from the Union Chapel, who helped the Mission in one way or another, like Miss Dorothy Erlebach, a voluntary worker for the Country Holiday Fund, who took the Sunday School registers and ran needlework classes at the Mission during the week; Mr Summers, a bank official, who ran the evening Sunday School, and his wife, who organised the Women's Meeting and the Hospital Savings Association; Miss Coulson, 'a lady of independent means', who helped to train the young Sunday School teachers; Mr Pugh, the ironmonger who employed my father and Tom, and who played the cornet for the children on Sunday evenings; and Ted Houghton, a cabinet maker from Hackney, who ran the morning Sunday School.

Ted Houghton, it is said, had 'a hard life', but for the most part these Congregationalist helpers were well-to-do members of the middle classes, living in the more affluent parts of Highbury and Islington. 'They were definitely a different class from us,' says Mary. Dorothy Erlebach and Miss Coulson were 'ladylike, highly educated'; Mrs Summers was 'a lovely lady, really nice'. And, like the gentry in Stansted in the eighteenth century, they were generally referred to as Mr or Mrs or Miss, and not by their Christian names. But there was no feeling of being patronised. The Union people all 'mixed in'. They were all 'very, very good'.

The local people, especially the Sanders, became increasingly involved in the leadership of the Mission. My father became the assistant secretary, ran the cubs and the scouts at different times, and eventually he and my mother took over the evening Sunday School from Mr Summers. His diary for these years records activities at the Mission four or five times a week. My mother set up and captained the Girls' Life Brigade at the Mission; Mary ran the primary Sunday School in the afternoon; Tom was a Sunday School teacher; Lal ran a stall to raise funds for the Mission and took over the Hospital Savings Association from Mrs Summers.

Although connected with the Congregationalists, they did not regard themselves as belonging to any particular group. 'We didn't take up any denomination,' Mary says: 'we just went by the Bible.' They did not practise infant baptism – children were 'dedicated' to God – but they did not practise adult baptism either.

Ellen believed that the Bible was the literal and inspired word of God, and so at first did most of the children. Mary, in fact, still accepts the Genesis story of creation, but my father says that he has now changed his mind: 'as you go on in life you see things differently.' Ellen, as we have seen, was converted at the Mildmay, and Mary and Tom can also point to a particular moment of conversion, Mary when she was ten, at a Scripture Union meeting at the Mildmay, and Tom when he was thirteen, at a special evangelical service at the Shoreditch Tabernacle. For my father 'it seemed to be a gradual process. We got immersed in the Sunday School, and then we worked through, you see.' For Jess it was gradual too. She looked up to her mother, she says, and followed her example.

They were not fierce or doctrinaire in their religion. They knew that they were saved and that they were going to heaven because Christ had died for them on the Cross, and that, they believed, was all they needed to know. For them, and for the rest of the Mission, Christianity was a simple, practical affair. They tried to obey the great scriptural injunctions to love God and to love their neighbour, but they also followed the petty Sabbatarianism and narrow prescriptions of the evangelical Christianity of their time. They were not allowed to go to the shops or to do any unnecessary work on Sundays. The girls could not sew or knit, and Ellen would not pay the milkman on that day, though they thought that Mrs Cox, the mother of Mary's second husband and the strictest of all the people at the Mission, was carrying things too far when, even as an old woman, she walked two miles to and from the Sunday service because she thought it wrong to use public transport.

They did not drink alcohol. The eldest children took the pledge at the age of ten or thereabouts – 'I promise to abstain from all intoxicating liquors or beverages' – and they attended the Band of Hope every week, where they watched magic lantern shows on the evils of drink, 'what it did to the families', says Mary. They did not gamble: Ellen would not allow cards in the house, and McPherson, the Superintendent, was so worried that his stockbroking investments might be regarded as gambling that he wrote a booklet to argue that they were not. (The President of the National Savings Committee wrote the introduction.)[2] They did not go to the cinema or the theatre, which made it particularly distressing to Ellen that George wanted to go on the stage. They did not dance, though folk dancing was allowed, in the teeth of Mrs Cox's opposition, for the Rovers and the Girls' Life Brigade. They did not smoke, though smoking was permissible. They were thrifty too: Ellen saw it as part of her Christian duty to be careful with the family's money, and it was in the same spirit of Christian stewardship that the Mission had a Penny Bank for Christmas savings and a branch of the Hospital Savings Association.

All this sounds grim and forbidding and yet, so far from being sternly authoritarian, Ellen was a gentle, affectionate woman. She told the children what she expected of them, but 'she didn't lay down the law'. She always made visitors welcome, and she took genuine pleasure in the success of others. She cared deeply for her family and friends, and every night, before going to sleep, she would kneel on the mat beside her bed and pray aloud for up to half an hour, remembering them all by name. (Jess used to lie in bed wondering when she was ever going to stop.) Many years after her death Mr Pugh surprised my father by describing her as 'an angel on earth', since 'he wasn't a man to talk like that'. But my father fully agreed with him, and the older children all acknowledge that she was the most influential person in their lives.

They also speak warmly of the 'wonderful times' they used to have at the Mission. Their Superintendent usually preached about once a month, but for the most part they had preachers sent out by the various evangelical societies. Some of them were 'real cards', says my father, who would get very 'worked up' and 'flow away' in their excitement. Once a quarter the Rovers took the service, and they often took the midweek service as well. Lal's husband, Albert Moore, might be the speaker, or my father, who recorded in his diary the texts or themes on which he spoke, like 'The Long Journey in Life', or 'The Faith of the Centurion', or 'He sat where they sat and he was astounded'.[3] 'I used to say how he didn't realise until he sat in a person's place what they were suffering or what they were thinking. How, when you put yourself in somebody else's place it alters your attitude to life. And I used to develop from there.' Or 'I might talk about Jesus said "Follow me" and go off on that.'

They chose their hymns and choruses from *Sacred Songs and Solos*, compiled by Ira Sankey. They were 'mainly of a cheerful character', my father says, and those that were not tended to be sentimental. Many of them looked forward to the rewards of heaven, like

When the roll is called up yonder I'll be there

or

We're marching to Zion, to glorious, glorious Zion,
We're marching through Emmanuel's land to fairer worlds on high.

Others spoke of the strength and support that came from God in this life, like Ellen's favourite, which she often sang as she worked in the house:

Strength for each trial and each task,
What more, my Saviour, could I ask?
Just as I need it, day by day,
Strength for today, just for today.

A prayer meeting followed the service. At one stage, in a manoeuvre to make the whole congregation attend, it was held before the final blessing 'so that people couldn't get out', but 'the people didn't like this' and it had to be held afterwards. Ellen and Mrs Cox were the two who prayed most. 'To be quite honest, it was too much really,' my mother says: 'they used to go on and on.' 'They'd stand up and pray,' says Jess, 'and you'd never know when they'd sit down.'

Sometimes the Mission conducted open air services in Gibraltar Walk, and once a year it held an evangelical campaign with a specially invited preacher. It would also send groups to the meetings organised by the combined evangelical societies at places like the Assembly Hall in the Mile End Road, where hundreds of people crowded together to hear the most celebrated Gospel preachers, like the Wood brothers and Gypsy Smith. 'He was a gypsy boy,' says my father, 'and he'd got converted. He was very emotional, the tears would roll down his cheeks. And he could sing, he had a lovely voice.'

Ellen was very active in the Women's Meeting, and persuaded several of her neighbours to go who would never have gone to the Sunday service. In a typical evangelical simile, Mrs Summers told Tom that the Women's Meeting had been 'like a sinking ship' and that his mother had 'rescued' it.

My father found his fulfilment in the scouting movement. As the cubmaster and then the scoutmaster of the troop attached to the Mission, the King Arthur Troop, he went on special training courses and his week's annual holiday was always a camp. But what he enjoyed most was being a Rover Scout. There were about twelve Rovers in all, including Albert Moore, Lal's husband, Frank Blanchard, who had come from a middle class family in North London, and Frank Daborn, a probation officer attached to Toynbee Hall. Apart from their normal scouting activities, they specialised in giving concerts. They performed for the Sunday School children and the Cripple Parlour at their annual treats, for the old people in the local workhouse and the down and outs in the Whitechapel lodging house in Flower and Dean Street. Albert was their star performer. He 'had one of those faces that could make people laugh', and he sang music-hall songs like 'My Old Dutch', 'If you can't pay the rent they'll bung you in the bunhouse by and by' (which went down particularly well in the workhouse) and 'Oh it's a windy night tonight' (the song of a drunk coming home late and thinking that, because 'everything's a-going around' and 'the lamp-post now is touching the ground', it must be a windy night). My father used to sing his family piece, 'Keep right on to the end of the road', Frank Blanchard and Frank Daborn played the piano, and they all took part in choruses and various sketches, like 'The Madhouse', when they would play out the part of madmen, 'The Savages', when they would paint themselves up and dance in a ring and yell, or 'The Hospital', when they would perform mock operations, pulling out long strings of sausages from a screaming patient hidden behind a sheet.

In all the activities of the Mission the devotional commitment and social concern were enlivened by a simple enjoyment of the comedy of life, and my father and my aunts and uncles still laugh aloud and slap their hands on their knees when they remind each other of various incidents – like my father as a boy falling asleep behind the organ when he was supposed to be pumping it up, and at the end of the sermon the organist pedalling, bomp, bomp, bomp, and not a note coming out; old Tom Williams and Lil Woodcock vying with each other as to who could sing the loudest and getting redder and redder in the face (and 'old May Poole used to squeak away too'); the young boys who threw in firecrackers during the evening service and the excitable lady preacher screaming and clutching her heart as if she had been shot; the woman from Shacklewell Street at the prayer meeting who started gabbling in strange tongues, which put Albert, who was leading the meeting, in such a panic that he rushed out of the room; Tom Corrigan, my father's friend, rising at a prayer meeting and calling out 'Dear Lord' – and then, clutching his back, 'I've got the cramp'; Albert falling through some rotten boards on the stage at one of the Whitechapel lodging houses ('one minute he was there, the next minute he was gone'); and another of the Rovers, Syd Aarons, when the curtains opened at a concert for 300 children and he saw all those faces looking up at him, 'getting the wind up' and running from the stage and refusing to go back on. 'Oh, we had lots of fun at the Mission.'

Apart from this spontaneous enjoyment, 'cheerfulness' was almost a moral duty, and one of the worst things that you could say of anyone was that he or she was 'miserable'. At one of the Rovers' variety concerts their first item was 'We introduce ourselves', their second 'And then convince you that we're "Happy".' Even the cripples were encouraged to be cheerful, and the programmes for their 'Sunshine Parties' are full of little verses and exhortations like:

> May we be happy when alone
> And cheerful when in company

And

> Gloomy shadows oft will flit
> If you have the wit and grit
> Just to smile a little bit.

Bethnal Green

My father is still fond of quoting the verse:

> Two men looked out through the prison bars,
> One saw mud, the other saw stars.

In many ways the Mission and the scouting movement were a continuation of my father's education, and organising services, meetings, concerts and camps, giving talks and sermons, singing solos and acting in sketches, gave him the confidence and self-assurance that helped him later when he became a trade union official. The Mission was also, through his contacts with Mr Pugh and then Dickie Pearson, the means of his getting work and starting a career.

Although one of the most powerful motivations for mission work was the fear of political unrest, there is no evidence that the Congregationalists of Highbury and Islington were impelled by anything other than a sense of Christian duty. No political views were ever expressed from the pulpit, and my father cannot remember any political discussion in any Mission context. Mr Pugh, it seems, had no interest in politics, and the same was true of Dorothy Erlebach. The Sanders, as we shall see, were Liberals, and Dickie Pearson, who was a Liberal, became Mayor of Bethnal Green and a member of the LCC. When one of the Sunday School teachers left to join the Socialist Sunday School, 'we thought that was terrible', says my father. But Ted Houghton was 'a red-hot Socialist', McPherson was a Socialist at this stage of his career (though he became a Conservative after his rise on the Stock Exchange), and there were others at the Mission who supported the Labour Party. With the emphasis on respectability and Christian love, however, there was always an underlying suspicion of anyone who advocated class conflict and confrontation, and of 'extremism' in any form. Even the pervading ethos of 'cheerfulness' militated against those who were discontented with their lot.

The Mission, says Mary, 'encouraged us to be different', and Ellen and her eldest children were regarded as 'different' by their neighbours in Princes Court. Ellen, it was said, was 'a real lady', as if some of the Union Chapel gentility had rubbed off onto her, and the eldest children were different from their younger brothers, who were less receptive to the Mission's influence. All of them, but particularly Mary and my father, softened the rough edges of their Cockney accents. It is possible too that Mission influence, as well as Mission patronage, made my father and Tom more acceptable as employees, since, unlike George, Bunny and Eddie, neither of them spent more than a week or two out of work.

But respectability imposed its burdens, and not everyone was strong enough to bear them. My father's first girl-friend was Rosy Taylor.* She was 'very jolly', 'she liked a laugh and a joke', and she played the piano for the Girls' Life Brigade. In 1928, after they had been going together for more than three years, she told him that she had to leave him since she had fallen in love with someone else. She did not say who it was, but about a year later Mary discovered that the man involved was her husband, Bert Wooding.

Bert had not been brought up in the Mission, but he had been welcomed and accepted as Mary's young man and then her husband. He became the scout master and the assistant secretary and was one of the Mission's leading workers. He was good-looking, a man of great charm. 'You couldn't help liking him,' Mary says; or, as Lennie remarks, 'he was the Gary Cooper of the Nichol Street Mission.' He and Mary had gone to live in Stoke Newington and they had a son, Ronnie. Rosy Taylor, it emerged, was not Bert's only liaison, and when Mary found out what was happening she broke down. With my father's help she took legal advice, and one evening, when Bert was away, she moved with Ron from Stoke Newington to Aunt Galley's home in Stratford. Bert said he wanted Mary to come back to him, and Ellen was distraught and begged her to go. But Mary felt that she could no longer trust him and so in 1929 they were formally separated and Mary returned to live in Princes Court. It was not quite the scandal that had overwhelmed Josiah Redford in Stansted, but the Sanders, and the Mission, were badly shaken. Mary is convinced that it hastened her mother's death and Bert, of course, left the Mission completely.

Ellen, in fact, died in July 1932, with all the family gathered around her. A memorial service was held for her at the Mission, and they sang her favourite hymn, 'Strength for today, just for today', though she would no longer need strength for any day. Her march to Zion was over. The Mission which had been her second home was packed with family, friends and neighbours. It was the first service there that Basil had attended.

* Fictitious name

21

Live and Let Live

Ellen prayed for her husband every night, that he might be converted, and it was a source of great unhappiness to her that he did not share her faith. Did he believe in God at all? 'He never talked about it,' says Mary, but in her view, 'he didn't believe in anything: he didn't believe there was a God.' 'I think he was rather under the impression', says Eddie, 'that Mum done enough for both of them.'

But he was not hostile to Christianity. 'I never heard him say anything against religion, or for it,' says Tom: 'He seemed neutral.' He respected his wife's beliefs, and he supported her insistence that the children should go to Sunday School, though after her death he was prepared to compromise. He allowed Len, for example, to play football on Sunday afternoon as long as he went to Sunday School in the morning.

All this fitted in with his own philosophy of tolerance and forbearance. 'If you can't do no good, don't do any harm': he was always telling the children this, and he spelt it out in full on a birthday card to Mary:

> If you cant do no Good Dont do any Harm.
> To Live and Let Live we all know is a charm
> Return Good for evil is a saying Old and True
> Take my Tip its the finest thing to do.
> You know I know just as well as you
> Its know use Bearing annamosoaty
> If you got an enemy Treat him as a brother
> For we are all as good as good as one another.

But while he did not interfere with the religious side of his family's life, he expected not to be interfered with himself. He would not allow any religious argument in his presence, and when Tom made a point of inviting him to the Mission's Sunday evening service he brushed him off dismissively. For a time Lal and Mary, with their mother's approval, used to invite all the children from Princes Court to a service and 'a little sing-song' on the top floor of the house. This was too much for Basil who, in George's words, 'got a bit niggly' and 'put a block on it'. Normally he was quiet and easy-going, but there was a strong underlying resentment of people who might think that, because of their Christianity, they were better than him and a contempt for what he regarded as fraudulence and hypocrisy. He had no time for Mrs Cox, and if she came back to the house after the evening service he would usually go off to another room. He did not like her son, Bert, either, and he showed it in his humour, which was not entirely good-natured. The old lady had always said that she wanted a funeral with horses and plumes, but when she died, after the war, Bert found it impossible to arrange this. 'You'll get in trouble when you die,' Basil told him. 'She'll give you a right ticking off: "Why didn't you give me a funeral with horses?"' And in reacting to Mary's troubles he combined condemnation of Bert Wooding's insincerity, as he saw it, with a certain vindication of himself: 'I wouldn't do a thing like that. And I wouldn't think a man who was supposed to be this and that at the Mission would have done a thing like it. That's your Christianity.' 'Yes', says Mary, 'he flung that up in my face.'

Apart from his indifference to religion and, as we have seen, to education as well, Basil taught the boys nothing by way of practical skills, probably because he had none himself. But what he did pass on to them was his love of sport. Mary is particularly sharp about this: 'I think football came first, and cricket. Regarding teaching the boys anything, nil. Soon as they were old enough, go with him to football or cricket, and my mother had to get on, or we had to. My brothers didn't do much, I can tell you that for nothing.' The boys themselves would not argue with this. 'The only thing he used to talk to me was pure sport,' says Len: 'he drummed in football and cricket to us.' Basil had played football himself, probably for one of the Sunday morning teams, and he went to see the Spurs regularly right up to the time of his accident. He was just as keen on cricket, though he had probably never played it seriously. He often took the boys to see Essex play, either at Leyton or, during their holidays, at Southchurch Park in Southend. He enjoyed racing, though only Bunny followed him in this, and he played darts for the team at The Conqueror.

Of all his sons, Basil was particularly attached to Bunny and Len, probably because they excelled in sport. According to Len, Bunny had the more natural talent, but he lacked dedication and did not train. He had trials once for the

Orient and was invited to join their amateur team, but he preferred to play for Barking. He had also captained his school's cricket team, and still remembers his embarrassment when he and his team received medals from Douglas Jardine, the England captain, and he had to wear a pale pyjama top because his father had been unable to provide a white shirt. Len 'achieved higher', as Bunny says, because he played a few games for the Orient during the war. But for the most part he played for Leyton, officially as an amateur, but in fact for 3s. 6d. a game. He was also good at cricket and had trials for Essex, but they were only willing to take him on as an amateur to see how he made out, and he could not afford it.

At mealtimes sport was the main subject of conversation, which the women accepted with a good grace on the whole, since they thought it was only natural for men to talk about sport. Basil even remembered his children's birthdays by the matches that were being played at the time. 'I'll always remember the day you were born', he told Eddie, 'Spurs were playing Liverpool, away.' The most remarkable story, however, is of Eddie's homecoming after the war. He had been away for five years, going with the Eighth Army round South Africa to Egypt, and then back through Italy and Greece. His troop-carrier had almost been sunk near Gibraltar; he had nearly been killed by shells in the desert; he had fought in the battle of Alamein. As he walked proudly down Princes Court in his uniform he was greeted by a huge banner stretched across the street: 'Welcome home, Eddie and Bunny Sanders'. One of the neighbours, Mrs Cook, who was sitting on her front doorstep, rocked back in surprise as she recognised him. He knocked on the front door of number 7, and his father opened it.

'Hallo, Dad'.

'Hallo, son, come in.'

He followed his father down the passage to the back room, and as they sat down his father turned to him and asked 'Going down the Spurs on Saturday?' Even Eddie, who was as fanatical about football as his father, was taken aback by this. 'Not "How are you?" or anything like that, but "Going down the Spurs on Saturday?"'

But it was not merely that sport was important to Basil. On other subjects he had very little to say, and it was sport that made communication possible for him. He rarely expressed his feelings openly, nor for the most part did his sons, but in their talk about football and cricket the impulses of affection ran through the exchanges of their shared enjoyment and interest. Moreover, unlike religion and politics, sport was a safe subject for conversation in the house, since it did not give rise to disturbing arguments or uncontrollable rows.

22

On and Off the Streets

George was the first of the children to reject the Mission. 'Well, I'll be fair,' he says: 'What done me for Missions, you see, Mum was very strict. . . . Three times a day, whether you liked it or not, you had to go. When I got older, about fifteen, I used to say "No. If I want to go I'll go. If I don't want to go I don't go."' 'To be honest', says Eddie, 'George, Bunny, Lennie and me were fed up with religion to the teeth. We were all brought up on the Mission. I don't think any of us was dead against it. But we were against being too religious. Mum . . . never preached it, but we had to go.'

It is no coincidence that none of the four youngest boys stayed with the Mission, for as her health became worse and she became more of an invalid Ellen's influence over the children weakened. Bunny says that he 'can't remember much of Mum', Eddie points out that he was virtually brought up by Lal, and Len says that he can remember nothing at all of his mother, although he was ten when she died.

Apart from this, George was a restless and independent spirit. 'I was a bit of a tearaway, I was,' he admits: 'and I was always up to tricks, different tricks, here and there.' He stayed out late, got involved in fights, hung around cafes on Sundays, and was given more good hidings by his father than any of the others. 'George was a bit of a wild 'un,' says Eddie. 'George broke loose,' says Tom. He 'fell into bad company', he was 'on the streets'. He had gone into the Scouts at the Mission but, he says, he 'hadn't taken to it'. And he went to the Webbe Institute, one of the boys' clubs run by the Oxford House, but he 'didn't stick to it long, because it was too overcrowded, to my opinion.'

There were strong artistic hankerings in George. As a boy he had been taught the violin and the piano, though again he had not stuck to them, and at Daniel Street School he had won a prize for acting Shakespeare. For a time he went to the Oxford House Book Club and took part in readings from Shakespeare there, but again he did not stay long. As he says himself, he was always 'in and out' – in and out of clubs and societies, in and out of debt, in and out of work, in and out of trouble. 'George always had mad brainwaves', says Mary, 'doing silly things. I suppose he was young, and full of trying different things and that.'

For some reason which now seems obviously mistaken he thought that George Sanders was not a suitable name for a man who wanted to make a career in show business, and so he called himself Al Maynard, after Ken Maynard, a cowboy film star. He did comic dances and sang the latest hits, like 'Virginia' and 'She's got eyes of blue'. His mother, of course, disapproved, and he told her as little as possible of what he was doing. She did not even know his stage name, and when letters for Maynard were delivered at the house she sent them back: 'Not known at this address'. He went in for talent competitions at the London Music Hall, the Star, the Brixton Empire, the Foresters, 'all over'. He was successful once, at the London, and he 'could have gone with an act called the Piccadilly Trio, a sort of continental act, a semi-ballet, semi-comedy', but he was under age and Ellen would not sign the papers. Eddie saw him once on the stage at the Olympia, when a talent competition was held in the interval. He specialised in 'double-jointed dancing', says Eddie, and did a good turn, but he did not win, even although he had a lot of mates in the audience who clapped him and made a lot of noise.

He never really made the grade on the stage, and when he appeared he was always 'bottom of the bill'. For the most part he did his turn at clubs and pubs at 7s. 6d. a time, with 2s. 6d. extra if he got an encore. For a time he palled up with a friend called Dicky Leach and they performed as the Eccentricity Boys, with singing and 'eccentric dancing'. Later he went busking with a group called the Luna Boys, who worked the cinemas and theatres on Saturday nights. They would do The Stall in the Charing Cross Road, then 'nip down' to The Gaiety and the Drury Lane Theatre, then 'shoot up' to the first house at the Palladium, and then back again, after a drink, to the second house at the Holborn Empire. There would be two queues at the Holborn, and 'you'd work one queue, then work the other queue'. It was 'all run properly' by 'a bloke called Sticks', and the buskers would each be called on in turn – the Luna Boys, 'the old barrel organ, bloke on the drums, and a bloke on the old sax'. And you had to arrange with Sticks to leave a bottle of brown ale in the gentleman's toilet for 'the old copper'. Otherwise you might get run in for obstruction.

Bunny was the next to rebel against the Mission. Apart from the compulsory Sunday School, what he detested most was being sent on Saturday to a shop in

Austin Street to collect the flowers for the Mission on Sunday. He was always 'given the bird' by his mates as he walked back, laden with flowers, to Princes Court. 'I always seemed to fall for that job,' he says. At the Scouts at the Mission he could not stand the uniform, but when he was fourteen he joined the Webbe, which he took to at once. As if Bunny was not distinctive enough, he was given a new nickname, Slosh, after an Edmonton boxer, Slosh Saunders. Eddie also had no enthusiasm for the Mission, and like Bunny he joined the Webbe, where he was given the nickname of Little Slosh.

The Webbe, on the corner of Hereford Street and Hare Street, just a few hundred yards from Princes Court, was one of two boys' clubs run by the Oxford House. Bunny and Eddie went the full course: after the junior club (for ten to fourteen-year olds) and the senior club (for fourteen to eighteen-year olds) they went on to the Oxford House Club for men in Mape Street. The Webbe was open every evening and its managers, the residents from Oxford and some 'old boys', organised a wide range of games, from boxing and football to table tennis and chess, and ran a small library and a drama group as well. At the end of the evening there would be a hymn and a prayer, but attendance was not compulsory and not many went. A committee of the boys' representatives helped to run the club and maintain discipline. At summer weekends there were camps in the country, and once or twice a year parties of boys visited Berkhamsted and Chigwell, the two public schools which were associated with the club. From 1929, because of the increasing membership, the boys were divided into four houses – Queen's, Oriel, New and Merton – run, it was reported, 'on the same lines as the Public School system, but with no geographical divisions, of course'.[1] The Webbe belonged to the Federation of Working Boys' Clubs and took part in all its sporting and dramatic competitions.

The Oxford House Club for men was very much a continuation and development of the Webbe, with sporting activities and a cafe, library, lecture room and entertainment and dancing hall. What it did not have was a bar, since alcohol and gambling were forbidden.

Earlier heads of the Oxford House had included Winnington-Ingram, who went on to become Bishop of London, and Canon Dick Shepherd of St Martin-in-the-Fields. Michael Seymour, who was in charge from 1922 to 1936, was the first lay head, and for most of this period, from 1926, Sir Wyndham Deedes was the vice-head. Many students came and went as managers, but the one whom Bunny and Eddie remember best is Ken Carey, who was later ordained in the Church of England and returned as the House's chaplain.

Bethnal Green

The House had illustrious support. Seymour was a member of the MCC and could invite celebrities like Patsy Hendren to hand out the prizes for sport. In Oxford there was a powerful governing committee, chaired for some time by Lord Hugh Cecil. In 1928 Queen Mary visited the premises, and in 1932 the Prince of Wales and the Duke of York. In 1935, at the House's Jubilee service, the sermon was preached by the Archbishop of Canterbury.

The House held close to its original ideals. The High Church tradition remained strong, and Ken Carey was only one of several past residents who went on to be ordained as an Anglican bishop. And there was the same determination as in the Victorian period to bring about a better feeling between the classes. The contacts between the Webbe and Berkhamsted and Chigwell, for example, were encouraged in the hope that they would help to break down the barriers between the 'toughs' and the 'toffs'. But the aim was not equality, but a balanced harmony, and many of the residents still saw themselves as the benevolent squires of Bethnal Green. They became involved in local welfare and educational organisations, they ran a free legal service, 'The Poor Man's Lawyer', and during the Depression they provided an employment agency. In 1927 Michael Seymour, as a councillor of the People's Party, or in other words as an Independent, became mayor of Bethnal Green.

The managers of the Oxford House claimed to be politically neutral. Political discussion, like alcohol and gambling, was 'prohibited' in the Oxford House Club for men, and in 1931 they described it as a place that was 'unspoilt by Alcohol and Party Politics'.[2] They seemed to imagine that in being Independents they were not taking a political role at all, and that they could be 'completely free from political shackles, . . . put the public welfare before party considerations, and . . . humbly try to set an example of fair play and moral courage.'[3] But they had a high regard for the Liberal Percy Harris, whom they described as a 'clean fighter', and they sometimes formed electoral pacts with the Liberals in order to keep the Labour Party out. In 1928 they ascribed the Socialists' lack of success in Bethnal Green to the influence of the Church and the Oxford House,[4] and five years later they claimed some of the credit for the continuing 'absence of political animosity in this area'.[5] Their response to the Mosleyites was not entirely straightforward. They published a sympathetic account of East End anti-Semitism, though they explained that they did not necessarily agree with it all. More typically, they said they were 'heartily sick' of all the political battles.[6]

Michael Seymour stressed the cultural mission of the House, cultural, that is, 'in the best and most generous sense . . . the opportunities . . . for living a fuller spiritual and intellectual life . . . the enjoyment of literature, art, music;

the desire of beauty.'[7] Concerts were organised, and plays, lectures and films. At the Webbe the drama group on Sunday afternoons was attended by twenty to thirty boys, including Bunny and Eddie. But their motives were not all that they seemed. 'To be quite honest', says Bunny, 'I used to go up there to dramatics in the first place because you also got the run of the billiard room as well.' 'It was all craftiness,' says Eddie: 'You did your bit, and then you could slip upstairs for table tennis and have a free cup of tea.' In 1931 the Webbe reached the finals of the Federation's dramatic competition with the 'Banquet Scene from Macbeth' and the 'Murder of Banquo'. In the first Bunny took the part of Macbeth, and in the second he was one of the murderers. They did not win, and Bunny was told by one of the judges, Lady Carrington, that he was 'too mechanical' in his speech. 'I didn't give enough emotion. I found the words very hard to say at times.'[8] *The Oxford House Magazine*, however, reported that 'the dramatic moments really interested the actors, and if Banquo was stabbed with perhaps more than his fair share of "trenched gashes" he was at any rate uncomplaining, and Lady Macbeth tried hard ... to adapt a naturally cheerful disposition to the circumstances of the play.'[9] The trenched gashes, Bunny remembers, were inflicted with home-made wooden swords, one of which fell apart in the performance. And, though memories are uncertain on this point, it seems that the Lady Macbeth with a naturally cheerful disposition was Abraham Basilinski, now better known as the actor Alfie Bass. It was Bunny who had introduced Alfie Bass to the club, and he 'got very popular there. But funny enough he didn't have as much success acting-wise as what I did. And he was a lot better as you know, now.'

But the reason for the boys' clubs' popularity was sport, and the residents reluctantly admitted this: 'Games of every description are the attraction . . . . Indeed, for the great majority of boys they are the only purpose for which a Club exists.'[10] It was certainly the sport that drew Bunny and Eddie. 'These boys' clubs was a complete new outlook on life,' says Eddie. 'You went there. They gave you a pair of plimsolls and a vest and a pair of shorts, and you'd play cricket, football, and you'd have table tennis, you had billiards, snooker, and you had a bath every night of the week if you wanted it, showerbath. And you had all these sporting personalities coming to the club.' Bunny excelled in almost every sport, and in the best public school tradition was awarded his first team colours for football and cricket. When the Prince of Wales visited the Webbe he asked to be introduced to the best billiards player. Bunny, however, was not there, and so they introduced him to Eddie instead. The Prince shook his hand and asked him if he could play billiards, but he was so 'dumbfounded' that he could not reply.

But there was more to sport than this. 'There is much to be learnt in playing the game,' said *The Oxford House Magazine*. 'Team spirit and all that it implies is the greatest lesson, and from team spirit springs Club spirit.'[11] Team spirit, loyalty, self-sacrifice and discipline, all this provided training to be a good citizen. Eddie was conscious of being taught the ideals of 'fair play, good sportsmanship and all that palaver', and one of the presents which he gave me as a boy was an illuminated and framed copy of Kipling's 'If'.

He and Bunny were untouched by the religious influence of the Webbe, nor did they break through the barriers of class. The House magazine claimed that real friendships developed between the toughs of the Webbe and the toffs of Berkhamsted and Chigwell, but when I asked Eddie if he could remember any such friendships he replied, 'Of course not. They were a different class altogether.' Bunny is not quite so dismissive. There were a few friendships, he says, but 'I never had any that lasted, and I don't know anybody who did.'

Although the Oxford students all 'mixed in', Bunny and Eddie tended to look up to them with respect rather than to regard them as equals. Many of them were 'famous people later on . . . and they was all well educated people.' 'They were friends as far as the club was concerned, but not friends like you normally had friends.' A few years ago an old club member died, and Bishop Carey came to conduct the service. 'He remembered Bunny and me,' Eddie says. He even remembered their nicknames, Slosh and Little Slosh. 'I think it's marvellous for a man in his position to remember people like us.'

Although the older boys helped to keep order, discipline was always a problem. There was a lot of what Bunny calls 'skylarking about – breaking up equipment and all that.' At one of the club dances there was so much fighting that a newly arrived young resident in charge thought a riot was going on and wanted to call in the fire brigade.[12] The usual punishments for disciplinary offences were warnings, suspensions and, in the worst cases, expulsion.

On the whole, though, the Webbe was seen as an institution that helped to keep the boys out of trouble. In almost any talk on the club, 'keeping us off the streets' is a phrase that comes up time and time again. Eddie says that the clubs were particularly important when the boys were unemployed: 'What saved us at that time was the boys' clubs. Otherwise we'd have been out on the streets' – which, of course, was precisely where George was at the time, and where he was generally regarded as having fallen into bad ways.

Len, the youngest, instead of joining the Webbe, went to the Cambridge and Bethnal Green Jewish Boys' Club. Unlike the Webbe, the Cambridge had a club for infants, and Lennie went there with a Jewish friend when he was only eight years old. 'I loved it so much,' he says. 'I thought it was fantastic.' After going all the way through he became a manager of the club, and he is still a manager today.

When Lennie joined in the 1930s the two leading men at the club were George and Rowland Lotinga, who came from a wealthy and long established Jewish family. George, who was the club secretary, had an art gallery in New Bond Street, and Rowland, who was one of the managers, became a company director. They were helped by several others, including Harry Moss of Moss Bros. and John Diamond, later Chief Secretary to the Treasury in the first two Wilson governments, and they were supported financially and in other ways by many of the leading Jewish families in the country, like the Samuels, the Rothschilds and the Josephs. In the same way as the Oxford House, they were able to arrange visits by leading sportsmen, like the cricketer Herbert Sutcliffe and the footballer Arthur Rowe, and politicians like George Lansbury and Percy Harris.

There were many Jewish clubs which did not allow non-Jewish members. The argument was that social intimacies would lead to intermarriage, which in turn would lead to assimilation, and that was anathema to the Jewish establishment. From the start the Cambridge had been more liberal than this, but it had not set out to break down the barriers between Jew and non-Jew. Lennie was one of only a dozen or so non-Jewish members. And it maintained its distinctive Jewish identity. It had a service conducted by a rabbi on Friday evening, played its football on Sunday, ran a class on Jewish history during the week, and was affiliated to the Association of Jewish Youth. But the rise of Fascism convinced the Lotingas that they had to adopt a more positive policy. Segregation, they argued, led to ignorance and misunderstanding and was one of the main causes of hostility and unrest. So in January 1938, in spite of the misgivings of Basil Henriques and others, the club dropped the word Jewish from its name. It remained affiliated to the Association of Jewish Youth, but Christian services on Sunday evenings were now held as well as Jewish services on Friday evenings, and the football matches were moved from Sundays to Saturdays. By the end of the year 80 of the club's 320 members were non-Jews, and its annual report claimed that 'From every point of view the Club has been the GREATEST POSSIBLE SUCCESS – so-called problems of religious or racial character between boys of different religions just do not exist.' Even the *Jewish Chronicle* reported that the experiment was 'working out very well'.[13]

The club's activities, says Len, included 'everything, you name it: photography, first aid, woodwork, all games, indoor games like table tennis, snooker, billiards . . . badminton, football, handball, cricket, running, chess, dramatics, everything.' The boys who were elected as the club's officers met every week with the managers to organise the club and exercise discipline, and a club magazine and a news-sheet were published.

In spite of the different religious emphasis, the club's ideals were very similar to those of the Oxford House – sportsmanship, public service and loyalty to the Crown. Its aims, as defined by Rowland Lotinga, were for its members 'to be good English Citizens, to carry out all that that implies, to remember always that they are members of the Best Country in the World, and of the best Club in the World, to "play the Game" in all walks of Life, and to serve God, King and Country.'[14] The four houses of the junior club were Sandringham, Balmoral, Windsor and Buckingham, and those of the senior club Gloucester, Kent, Cornwall and York. George Lotinga encouraged the boys to join the Territorial Army, which caused some upset since, as Lennie says, 'you don't often find Jewish boys in the army'. One of the first boys from Bethnal Green to be killed in the war was a Jewish boy from the club, and he was given a memorial service with full military honours at the Bethnal Green synagogue.

Good sportsmanship was continually drummed into the boys. A good sportsman, wrote Rowland Lotinga in an article on football, 'should always be generous in defeat and MODEST in victory: to come straight to the point – I mean when you have just scored a goal, *don't* rush round the scorer and cheer him or clap him. It is absolutely downright bad sportsmanship to applaud in any way when *your* side has scored. . . . I know other clubs do it. I know professional teams do it, but I also know that no DECENT side does it.'[15] There was a particularly strong emphasis on not arguing with the umpire, and Alec Waugh was quoted: if you are given out wrongly, 'you will turn straight round and walk towards the pavilion'.[16]

Any other sort of behaviour would be unsportsmanlike and un-English, and for Jewish boys in Bethnal Green at that time there were serious dangers in appearing to be un-English. The club's activities were sometimes disturbed by Mosley's Blackshirts, and one writer in the club's magazine was worried that some of the boys seemed to be unaware of the causes of anti-Semitism. He urged them to eliminate what he regarded as one of the worst provocations: 'I refer', he wrote, 'to "flashy conspicuousness". Don't dress flashily! Don't act flashily! Don't talk flashily! Keep discipline! Don't do anything that will make someone an anti-Semite!'[17] After a lecture at the club one of the boys wrote a review in which he said how pleased he was to find a Jewish speaker who did not wave his arms in the air.

The jargon in the magazine and the news-sheet was the jargon of the public school: 'At long last we have been able to don our footer togs again. . . . Now then, you chaps, let us have a strong finish to the season. . . . Here's good luck to you fellows.' But there was a wide gap between the language of the magazine and the behaviour in the games rooms, and instilling public school ideals was as tough at the Cambridge as at the Oxford House. The disciplinary offences recorded in the officers' minute books include fighting, disobedience, swearing, writing filthy words in the attendance book, laughing and turning the lights on and off during prayers, throwing electric light bulbs out of the door and breaking the piano. Len was given several warnings, and on three occasions he was suspended for a week, once for 'general misbehaviour', once for 'general rowdiness', and once for 'disobedience' to Rowland Lotinga. This was not an unusual record.

Like Alfie Bass at the Webbe, however, Lennie became very 'popular' at the club. He became captain of the football and cricket teams, and in 1939 and 1940 he was elected and re-elected as club captain. 'It didn't matter that you wasn't a Jew,' he says: 'If you was a member of the club, that was it.' The businessmen associated with the club encouraged the development of the most able boys and sometimes employed them and helped them to get on. 'If I'd been good in education', Len says, 'they'd have made sure they found me a position. . . . But there was no point trying to make something out of someone if it wasn't there.'

To a certain extent the fears of the Jewish establishment were realised: social intimacies did lead to intermarriage. During the war it was the duty of the older boys to take some of the younger ones home at night. Len was made responsible for young Tony Hiller, and Mrs Hiller always invited him to come inside for a meal. He became friendly with her daughter, Anne, and in 1942 they were married. But in this case intermarriage did not lead to assimilation, except in part for Len. 'I know I'm not Jewish officially', he says, 'but my wife is Jewish, my son is Jewish, and my home is a Jewish home.' Given his background it is a surprising development.

23

Politics and Prejudice

Granny Field voted Liberal, and so did Basil and Ellen. 'We were all Liberals down the Court,' says my father, though obviously with some exaggeration. 'The Liberal Party was the only one we really knew in Bethnal Green,' says Eddie.

If the Liberals were the only party they knew, Percy Harris was the only politician, and everything they say about local politics supports the view that the Liberals' success was heavily dependent on Harris's popularity and hard work. 'Percy Harris was very well liked,' says my father: 'The Liberals did so much for the people down there. They made themselves available.' George, who was no Liberal himself, describes Harris as 'top of the bill', and remembers how he arranged for several years' outstanding widow's pension to be paid to one neighbour, and how he managed to get one of his mates out of the army because he had volunteered when he was under age. Every Friday Harris would be at his local office in Kerbela Street to listen to his constituents' problems. 'They idolised Percy Harris in Bethnal Green.'

Ellen belonged to the Liberals' Saving Club, and several of the children went to the Liberals' Christmas parties. At election times they displayed Percy Harris's posters in their windows, and when he came round canvassing he was given a cup of tea and biscuits in Ellen's parlour. In the streets the children joined in the popular election chant (for Jonah read Harris's opponent at the time):

> Vote, vote, vote for Percy Harris
> Kick old Jonah down the stairs.
> If it wasn't for the law
> We would punch him on the jaw,
> Oh we won't vote for Jonah any more.

Another version seems to have had a Tory opponent in mind:

> Vote, vote, vote for Percy Harris,
> Kick old Jonah down the stairs.
> With his high topper hat
> And his belly full of fat,
> Oh we won't vote for Jonah any more.

Apart from their high opinion of Percy Harris, Mary believes that her parents reacted against the Labour Party because in those days 'it was too communistic'. They took *The Daily Sketch* and *The News Chronicle*, which was strongly Liberal, and on Sundays they took *The News of the World* and *Lloyd's News*. According to my father, they regarded *The Daily Herald* as 'a terrible paper', but this may reflect his own views as much as theirs. Beyond this it is impossible to find out what opinions they held, because Basil would not allow politics to be discussed in the house. Like religion, it was best left alone, since it led to too much unpleasantness. Eddie thinks that his father was right, because 'People who follow these parties, they're at one another's throats all the time.'

But there was no great pressure for any talk about politics, since most of the children were not interested and were content to fall in with their parents' views. 'I don't think, to be quite honest,' says Bunny, 'that politics was very much to the front with any of the members of our family,' though he makes an exception of George. Mary confesses that she does not understand them and my father, apart from a dislike of 'hotheads' and 'trouble-makers', rarely takes a strong political line. He was once asked to become a Socialist candidate for the local council, but he would have nothing to do with it: 'At first the Labour Party in Bethnal Green was a bad circle, a group of malingerers lining their own pockets.' Tom says that he was not interested in politics and adds, with some pride, that the Salvation Army is non-political. Jess is the same, and Bunny claims that any interest that he had in politics was killed when he worked as an electrician in Government service after the war. 'You see what goes on there. You lose all faith in 'em.' And he tells the story of Ernic Bevin and his wife who, when they moved into Carlton House Gardens, had the position of a bell push in the bathroom altered six times – 'You know, up a bit higher, down a bit, all that business' – and of Mrs Churchill, who had the old gas kitchen in 10 Downing Street ripped out and replaced by an electric kitchen. 'The money that goes and the way they spend it!' Eddie is equally uninterested: 'I'm no expert in politics and never shall be. Once they're in power they're all the same.' Len voted Labour, but this was because Anne was 'strong Labour' and he voted the way she told him. As for himself, he 'didn't care twopence for politics.'

George was the only exception to all this indifference and apathy. At first he threw in his lot with the Labour Party, but they did a few 'strokes' that he did not like and then, 'to be fair with you, I was a bit of a Communist.' He ascribes this to the bitter experience of being unemployed for so long and to the fact that he had several good Jewish friends at a time when the Communists were leading the fight against the Fascists.

Except George, then, the Sanders were in the main unconcerned about political issues, and they generally supported the Liberals because they saw it as the natural thing for people in their position to do. In spite of the glaring inequalites of society they did not think that they had any cause for complaint. Basil had always had a regular job and, as they moved from one room to occupy a whole house, they felt that they had done very well for themselves. They accepted society as it was, and did not seriously envisage that it could be ordered in any different way. They were respectful of authority and suspicious of those who set themselves up against it. Whereas the Liberal Party was made up, as they saw it, of decent, conscientious, respectable people like Percy Harris and Dickie Pearson, the Labour Party, in spite of its idealism, had too many hotheads and firebrands. The Socialists were critical of the capitalist order and articulate about their discontent. The Sanders were neither discontented nor articulate. The fact that George, the most volatile of them, was the only one to take up with the Labour Party merely confirmed them in their view of the political world.

Basil's reaction to the Mosleyites was characteristic of him. He detested the excitement and violence which they brought, but he never argued against them. 'He kept out of it,' says my father, 'he was neutral.' 'He'd avoid trouble, would Dad,' says Jess. 'The only thing he'd agree with them,' says Bunny, '– I think most of us did, well, not most of us, but most East End people did, I think there was a little bit of anti-Semitism in all of us. A little bit, I don't say a lot, a little bit, because no doubt they was jealous the way they got on.'

Living in an area where anti-Semitism was so strong, it would have been surprising if the Sanders had not been affected by it. By that time, as we have seen, there were about 20,000 Jews in Bethnal Green, and there was a strong concentration in the west of the borough. In Princes Court there were Jewish families on the other side of the road, and there were clusters of Jewish settlement all round, especially in Boreham Street, which was known as Jews' Alley, and the Boundary Street Estate. Many of the local shops were owned by Jews, like Prices and Sugarbreads at the top of Princes Court, and most tailoring and furniture-making concerns were in Jewish hands, like the workshops opposite the Sanders.

So the first charge against the Jews was that they were 'taking over'. And they not only 'took over', they 'got on'. 'I think actually they took most of the business really,' says Mary. 'That was the beginning of it. You seemed to see a Jew used to prosper while a Christian used to fail. People got the idea with Jewish people, they used to get on.'

And the way they got on aroused comment too. They were seen as clannish, dishonest and given to sharp practice. 'They helped one another, you see, of their own faith,' says Tom, and my father agrees: 'You will always find a Jew will help a poor Jew. That's how they get on.' There was no real friction with the Jews, says Jess, 'but if one of them sold you something that was no good it always seemed as if they were trying to do you.' And the main argument that George found being used by his mates was that the Jews were undercutting. Their shops sold goods more cheaply than their competitors and as employees they were prepared to work for less. There was also the criticism, which George confronted, that you would never find a Jew on the roads, navvying. They were happy to make money, it was said, but not to do any hard physical work.

There was the inevitable hostility against newcomers, strangers, regardless of their attributes. They were commonly called 'the dirty Jews', and there were fights between Jewish and Gentile boys for no better reason than that they belonged to different groups. 'We used to fight against the Jews 'cos we was Christians,' says George: 'Go round Boreham Street and sort the Jews out, sort the Yids out.' The children used to shout out 'Old Bobela' at the old woman, wrapped in a shawl, who sold fruit in the shop next to Prices. And Jess as a girl used to go down Jews' Alley in particular in order to play Knock Down Ginger with her friends. Speaking of his mates who were sympathetic to Fascism, George says that 'it was sort of born into them' to be against the Jews. 'It was the kind of thing you grew up with, you know,' says my father. 'They was a kind of another race of people and I think subconsciously people didn't take to the Jews. Unless they were particular friends of yours you never mixed with the Jews.'

There were many good personal relations. The children who worked as Shabas goys say that the Jewish families were 'very good' to them. Jess used to be given 'a great big lump of motza' at holiday times, and George was given smoked salmon and salt beef sandwiches. The Prices, the shopkeepers, were 'very nice people'; Alfie Bass was very popular at the Webbe; the much-admired Percy Harris was a Jew. George had several close Jewish friends; 'and if you've got a Jewish friend you've got a Jewish friend: they're good. Mind you, there are some that are a bit dodgy. There's always good and bad.'

Lennie was actually pro-Semitic – 'I think Jewish people are warmer than Gentiles. Definitely' – and he thought that Anne's mother, together with his own father, was the most wonderful person he had known. Anne's family, the Hillers, lived in Cookham Buildings, part of the Boundary Street Estate. They were not orthodox, and in fact Mrs Hiller sent all the children to an evangelical mission for the Jews in Brick Lane, which was run by some Jews who had been converted. They were not sent for any religious reason: 'Lots of Jews went,' Anne says: 'We were very poor and they were very good to us. They used to give us clothes and food. Of course, they were trying to convert us.' In earlier years the leaders of the Jewish mission had a hard time with the rest of their community. My father remembers them attending one of the Nichol Street Mission's open air services and being spat on by the orthodox Jews as they passed by.

Anne's family had no objection to her engagement to a Gentile, especially as they knew Lennie and liked him. But there are two different accounts of Basil's reaction. The first comes from Len himself:

'The first thing I done, when I wanted to get engaged, I went home to my father and "Dad", I said, "I'd like to get engaged." So he said, "What's the problem?" So I said, "Well, you know she's Jewish." So he sat there for a minute, sat on his chair, a big high chair, and he says "Do you love her?" I said "Certainly", and he said "Don't worry about anybody else in the family. You bring her round here and if she's good enough for you she's good enough for me." That was it. That was my father.'

The second comes from Mary, who was looking after her father at the time:

'He didn't like Jewish people. Not really. Because when Len and Anne got married, Anne's mother came to see Dad. And when she went my father said, "Well, they'll get married, whatever I say. They want to get married, they'll get married. I don't like mixed marriages. I wouldn't want any of my grandchildren to be Jewish."'

Basil would obviously have been happier if his son had got engaged to a 'Christian' girl. Even in Lennie's account there is the acknowledgement of a problem, and Basil had to sit in silence for a minute before he accepted the position. But Annie and her mother made it easier for him. They came round to see him almost every day, and after Mary had left to get married they often brought him food and helped him in the house. He quickly became very fond of Anne, and she was very fond of him.*

Relations between Jews and Gentiles in Bethnal Green were full of complexities and contradictions, of theories and philosophies that were only half thought through and feelings and attitudes that were only dimly understood. The young boy who went out 'to sort out the Yids' in Jews' Alley could later support the Communists because of his sympathy for his Jewish friends. The old man who did not really like Jews became deeply attached to his Jewish daughter-in-law. They all held their belief that the Jews were a different race and ascribed to them particular racial characteristics, and they all had Jewish friends and acquaintances whose characteristics were completely different. In all this they were representative of many others.

---

* This part of the book has aroused more comment in the family than any other. Lennie remains convinced that there was no trace of anti-Semitism in his father and is upset by any suggestion that there was. George comments that you might get the impression that the old man was anti-Semitic because when neighbours criticised the Jews he would nod his head and say nothing, but in fact he was simply avoiding argument. Most of the others, however, agree with the account.

35 (left).   A Cropper hand at work. An illustration from 1877.

36 (below).   The premises of G.E. Jackson and Company in Dysart Street, at the back of Finsbury Square.

37.   My father as a young man, *c*. 1930.

38 and 39. The interior and exterior of Pugh Brothers, the ironmongers in the Holloway Road who were my father's first employers, seen here probably *c.* 1910. When my father first joined as a messenger boy it was his job to arrange the display outside the shop before it opened.

40. My mother (fifth from the left in the middle row) with the Girls' Life Brigade at the Nichol Street Mission. *c.* 1930.

41. A cub camp at Laindon, Essex, *c.* 1930. In the back row, from left to right: Charlie Shepherd, Jean Shepherd, my father, Lily Corrigan, Tom Corrigan.

42.   Bunny (second from the right at the back) in the Oxford House football team, 1936–7. Morley, one of the university managers, is at the back on the left.

43.   Eddie (second from the right in front) in the 'Occasionals' football team for the Oxford House, 1936–7.

44. Boys queuing outside the Cambridge and Bethnal Green Jewish Boys' Club in Chance Street. A photograph taken in the late 1930s.

45. Herbert Sutcliffe, the English cricketer, autographs a bat at the Cambridge and Bethnal Green Jewish Boys' Club in 1938.

46. Lennie, in the white shirt, camping with the Cambridge and Bethnal Green Jewish Boys' Club near New Romney in Kent, *c*. 1936. At the back is George Lotinga.

47. Lennie (87) as a member of the Cambridge and Bethnal Green Jewish Boys' Club under-16 cross country team in a race organised by the Association of Jewish Youth.

48. Sir Percy Harris with a group of children from the Stewart Headlam School in a 'Bethnal Green Pageant' at the York Hall, February 1935.

49. Dickie Pearson (Superintendent of the Nichol Street Mission) as Mayor of Bethnal Green.

24

Husband and Father, Wife and Mother

According to Eddie, Basil was 'the Guv'nor', and my father, when talking of a disagreement between his parents, says that 'the woman was very much a back number in those days'. It was Ellen who ran the home or, as Eddie revealingly puts it, his father 'let Mum look after the family'. When it mattered, however, Basil's word was final. As the breadwinner, his needs and requirements came first, and he demanded a reasonable standard of service. 'Dad was a man like this,' Mary says, 'you had to have his meals on the table when he came home.'

Looking back, Tom says that he lies awake at night thinking what a hard life his mother had. 'It's not very nice to say it, but my father didn't have much consideration for her.' Mary is more forthright. She points out that he never let Ellen know how much he was earning; he only gave her £1 a week for housekeeping; he was regularly out at the pub; and he gave very little help in bringing up the children. He was 'not unkind', she says, but he was 'inconsiderate' and 'selfish', especially in view of Ellen's poor health. 'My mother was a wonderful women.' She was 'very calm' and 'very placid', but in Mary's view, 'You can be too calm. Then you're put on.'

Yet Tom says that his parents were always 'very friendly', and Mary admits that 'in *their* way they were happy', though she adds that it would not have been her way, or 'a good many more people's way today'. By the contemporary standards of Bethnal Green, in fact, Basil was a very good husband, and George, making these standards explicit, and referring to the violence between many husbands and wives, says that his parents were 'sort of ideal'. There were other 'united couples', like the Collins, but his parents were 'about the best of the lot'. Basil had the occasional temper, but, apart from the time when he threw his lunch in the air after Ellen had written a letter of complaint to his boss, the children cannot remember any 'rows' between them.

There was an underlying tension about religion, as we have seen, since Basil did not accept that people who went to the Mission were necessarily better than himself or anyone else. And in particular he felt that Ellen spent too much time at the Mission, especially if she was not at home when he came back from work. Mary represents him as complaining 'You think more of the Mission than what you do of me.'

On the whole, though, they lived contentedly enough together. There was a mutual respect between them, and neither tried to dominate the other. Basil provided a regular wage: Ellen ran the home economically and efficiently. She did not come between him and his sport: he did not interfere with her religion. But again, to the modern perception, they were not very close, and the phrase that the children repeatedly use is that 'he went his way and she went hers'. Their relationship was more a sensible, pragmatic accommodation between two people who were really very different from each other than the close loving partnership that is looked for in marriage today.[1]

For most children at that time the father was a more distant figure than the mother, but this was particularly true for the eldest Sanders. Tom feels it most strongly: 'Now I look back, he was very remote, really. He just went out to work, and when he came back he went round to the pub. We didn't really know him, or at least I didn't.' It was only after his accident in the fire that Basil began to stay at home in the evenings, and for the younger children he was a much stronger presence. Lennie, in fact, 'idolised' him. 'To me', he says, 'he was on a pedestal, top of the tree, 100 per cent.' He was honest and straightforward, there was no 'side' to him. He was slow to make friends, and he could not stand people who were 'hooky, you know, not straight', but 'If he liked you, you had a friend for life.'

Ellen's relations with the children were the reverse of Basil's. For the eldest, as we have seen, she was the most powerful influence in their lives. Mary describes her as 'a wonderful woman', and my father and Jess agree with Mr Pugh that she was 'an angel on earth'. 'She really lived her religion,' says my father. 'She'd help anybody. She was never envious. If people got on she was always pleased for them. She always had a smile for you.' Tom describes her as 'a very kind, gracious woman, very jolly and happy'. But towards the end of her life she was virtually an invalid. She still looked after Jess very lovingly, but for the boys she was more remote and ineffectual.

She still made sure that they all went to Sunday School, but according to Eddie she was 'never strict – she wasn't big enough.' It was Basil who was the disciplinarian. He was not violent: unlike many of the fathers in the Court, he only handed out the occasional good hiding and he never used a belt. 'It wasn't brutality,' says Eddie, 'but he had a tongue. I think every member of the family can say they were scared of him.' My father says much the same: 'You might get a clout, but we were so scared of him we never went so far.' 'He was a big fellow,' says Tom, 'he put the fear of God into us.' With the younger boys he was more lenient. Bunny was given 'a couple of wallopings' for being 'saucy' to his mother when she asked him to get the flowers for the Mission, but he thinks that his father should have been stricter with him. 'If he'd given me a few more wallopings when I was a kid he'd have done me more good. Or kept me in line better, you know.' And Len, the baby of the family and his father's favourite, cannot remember being hit at all. On the contrary, he says, his father spoilt him. 'He give me anything I want – money for the pictures, new pair of football boots – it was ridiculous. I was really well looked after.'

The daughters were treated very differently from the boys. They were never hit, except Jess once, when he gave her a backhander for cheek when she refused to go on an errand. But generally, says Jess, 'Dad had the dealings more with the boys and Mum had the dealings with me.' Unlike the boys, she was never allowed to go dancing or to the cinema, and she received less pocket money, an unfairness which the boys themselves acknowledge. So, while Jess liked her father, 'I was more for me Mum than me Dad.' Mary, characteristically, puts it more strongly: 'He only wanted the boys. We women had to get on with the work.' He expected the women to look after him, and he never wanted Mary to leave home. Her courtship with Bert Cox after the war had to be conducted almost in secret, and Basil did not come to the wedding.

Yet even with the boys, he never took on the full range of concern and responsibility that Ellen might have wanted. 'In all the time I knew my Dad', says George, 'he never said "Look, this is what you want to do, son".' And Bunny, though one of his father's favourites, still comments on his lack of interest in him. 'I can never recollect him saying to me "How are you getting on? What are you doing of now?"' Lennie says much the same: 'He never put you right or wrong, sort of thing. The only thing he used to talk to me was pure sport.'

Basil rarely put himself out and he avoided unpleasantness. After a hard day's work he felt that he was entitled to peace and quiet. It was more restful having a drink and a game of darts with his mates at The Conqueror than having to be cooped up with the children in one or two rooms in Princes Court. And when he did stay at home he insisted on not being disturbed. 'He'd never let us argue, never,' says Mary: 'One thing he used to say to us as children,

"Keep silent. Silence is golden." That was his motto. "Silence is golden. Keep your place. I'm your father."' 'He didn't like arguing,' says Bunny. If, as they watched a football match together, Bunny 'jumped in' with his knowledge, 'he'd tell me not to interrupt the adults. "Keep quiet" and all that business.'

There was no stimulating controversy in the home, little scope for the development of the mind. Anything that was potentially disruptive was damped down. Even in 1948, when Eddie and Len had an argument, Basil told them to clear out: 'I don't want any of that there here.' But in many ways it was a sensible approach to the problem of living with such a large family in such cramped and crowded conditions, for there would have been no escape from bickering and argument. On the whole Basil achieved what he wanted, a calm, orderly home, with his meals on the table when he wanted them, the children quiet and respectful, and the freedom to go out to the pub or football match whenever he wanted. His proclaimed philosophy, of not doing any harm if you couldn't do any good, might have rested on a very limited assumption about the possibilities of human relationships, but at least those possibilities were realised.

He liked what was old and familiar. He was happy to wear the same clothes for years, and he never visited my parents at their new home in New Southgate, even when they offered to take him in the car. 'He had his way of life', says my father, 'and he wasn't really interested in any other.' He stayed in Princes Court throughout the blitz, and made no attempt to move away. Like many of them, says my father, 'He had a kind of fatalism. Whatever comes, if my name's on it, that's that.'

While Ellen was a warm-hearted, affectionate woman, who displayed her feelings openly, Basil, as far as we can tell, was not a man of strong feelings and rarely expressed what he felt. Humour, however, was important to him. 'Our Dad was always pulling your leg,' says Eddie: 'He had a typical Sanders expression. He looked miserable but he wasn't.' He 'loved to play a joke', says Len, and Jess says that 'He'd lead you up the garden.' It was not a witty or sophisticated humour, but a good-hearted way of provoking a bit of fun, especially with children. When my father was putting on weight he would ask him if the bed had fallen through; when Eddie was away during the war he wrote to tell him that his wife was doing very well and had just bought herself a lovely fur coat; and when his grandchildren came round he would tell them that he had no sweets for them today. 'He'd have hid them', says Len, 'and he'd make them find them. He'd get pleasure out of it.'

At Christmas-time, says George, he was 'quite a comedian'. He could sing very well, and he would come out with several of the old music-hall favourites, like 'When father painted the parlour', 'She was one of the early birds and I was one of the worms', and 'My wife's a cow – a cow-keeper's daughter'. 'Course, Mum would give him a dirty look.' Ellen also had a good voice, and would sing 'Terry, my blue-eyed Irish boy', or 'Just like the ivy'. We have compared these songs to signature tunes, and it was typical of Basil that he chose humorous songs that treated love and marriage as comic disasters and of Ellen that her songs were serious and sentimental and were centred on family devotion. Lal and Albert, her husband, would sing 'The old rugged cross'. 'Her and Albert', says Eddie, 'used to harmonise lovely.' Mary would recite a poem, and George would perform one of the latest numbers. My father would sing Harry Lauder's song, 'Keep right on to the end of the road', in which the great Christian virtue of perseverance was assured of its heavenly reward. Eddie, who thought more of the East End virtues of hospitality and good neighbourliness, sang 'Come round any old time and make yourself at home', Bunny sang 'McNamara's Band', while Lennie enjoyed the rollicking humour of Harry Champion's 'Any old iron'. Tom did not perform at all, and his silence was just as characteristic of him as their choice of songs was of the others.

For the neighbours, as one of them says, Ellen was a 'lovely woman'. She had much more to do with them than Basil, and this was not only because she was at home and took the rents. She was also a good neighbour in the Christian sense of the term. She made it her duty to look after the old ladies in the road. She would often send the children round to Mrs Fletcher to ask her if she needed anything, and if there were any treats at the Mission, like a trip to Southend, she made sure that Mrs Fletcher got a ticket. She also tried to keep an eye on Mrs Raines, the old woman who committed suicide. It was George, in fact, who found the body, since he had gone round to ask if she wanted anything. Young Alice Goldsmith, whose aunt and uncle were always fighting, says she was 'glad of Mrs Sanders many a time', since she was able to find a refuge at number 7 when the pots and pans were flying.

Basil, as we have seen, was uneasy about Ellen's work as the landlord's caretaker, since it meant that she knew whenever anyone was hard up, and 'no one likes you to know about their financial affairs'. He preferred to mind his own business. 'I wouldn't say he was *sociable*,' says Jess. 'Until he knew you he'd keep his distance. If he didn't like you he was very stand-offish, he didn't want to know you. It was only after we lost Mum that he really got to know people in the Court. Then he used to collect the bets.' Mary says that he was 'well respected' and 'he wouldn't interfere in any way with anybody', and according to Bunny he was 'very well liked' though 'he kept himself to himself'.[2] He did not drink with his neighbours in the local pubs, but went some distance to drink with his old mates at The Conqueror, some of them friends from his footballing days. After his retirement from Jackson's his old workmate, Mr Hermon, came to see him every week, and he remained close friends with Mr Taylor in Black Notley, who used to come and visit him once a year.

Towards the end of his life he rarely left the house, and he could only move slowly because of his bad leg. His longest journey was to a shop in the Bethnal Green Road to get the accumulator for his wireless recharged. He always wore a shirt without a collar, and in winter, like his Uncle Alf in Black Notley, he tied a red choker round his neck. He smoked Players Woodbines at five for 2d., and like most printers he regularly took snuff. 'He'd blow his bloody head off,' says Len, and the snuff would always be spilt down his shirt front. He was as quiet as ever and on occasion at least he seems to have been aware of the impression he made on others. Two days before he died he wrote a letter to Tom and his wife, Sally, to thank them for their Christmas present. 'What do you think Sal', he wrote, 'Bunny Brings a girl home Now Wonders Will never Cease She seems a descent Sort very found of Nobby [his dog] I have not had much to Say to her She Looks at me and I suppose She thinks hes a right Old Sort.' It is a warm, affectionate letter, full of his little jokes. He fancies West Bromwich Albion for the Cup, calls his grand-daughter Marjorie Margarine, guesses at Sally's weight ('abt. 14 st. my guess') and finishes with three kisses 'And May God Bless you All'.

As a boy I was taken to visit him about once every two or three months, usually on a Saturday morning. I remember him as a kindly, slow-speaking man, who always used to talk to me about sport, and who gave me some of the most prized possessions of my childhood, a collection of cigarette cards of footballers and football teams. I once made him laugh by asking him how to spell Hamilton Academicals. He got his own back by asking me to spell a made-up word, which he said came from the language of the gypsies. I wonder now if I was hearing a last faint echo of his grandmother, Jessamy Gray.

Every birthday he sent me a shilling and a card with a short note. When I was eleven, and had just passed the eleven-plus exam, he wrote:

Dear Pete.
    just a Card to Wish you all the Best on your Birthday And to Congratulate you on Winning the Cup I am sorry Pete I mean the Scholarship as I was very pleased to hear it and always remember Pete Silience is Golden
      From Grandad.

Every card he sent me included those words: 'Always remember Pete Silience is Golden.'

50. My grandfather with his dog, Nobby, in the back garden of 7 Princes Court, *c*. 1950.

51. Lal and Albert. According to Mary, they met at the Wednesday night Bible classes which were run at the Mildmay Mission Hospital. Albert was a carpenter who worked for his father. His parents disapproved of the marriage, and his father sacked him on the morning of the wedding.

52. Mary and her son, Ron.

53. My parents and myself, 1938.

54. Tom and his wife, Sally, at their wedding in 1935. They met in Manchester, where Sally was a Salvation Army nurse, For Tom, as a Salvation Army officer, there were strict rules about marriage. His wife, who had to work with him, could not be more than five years older, and he had to get permission for 'correspondence with a view to courtship', then for getting engaged and finally for getting married.

55. George, Cath and their son, Ken in 1932. Cath had come to London from Wales to work in service, and George met her in Hyde Park. He had gone to meet a friend, but the friend did not turn up and he 'banged into Cath' instead.

56. Jess, her husband, Fred, and their son, Derek, 1942. In Fred's words, 'It was Lal who brought us together. I did a milkman's round and used to call on her. . . . She showed me a picture of Jess, and I said I'd like to meet her. So one evening I went round and Jess was there, and we sort of mucked in together straightaway, didn't we, Jess?'

57. Eddie and his wife, Em. He met her at the Mission. 'She used to go to the GLB [Girls' Life Brigade]. One evening I said, "See you home?" And she said, "If you like". And after I'd taken her home a few times I said, "How about you and me going out regular?" And she said, "All right". But there were one or two other chaps hanging about, and so I had to tell them to lay off. And that was how it started.' On the day after they married Eddie had to leave for the army, and they did not see each other for the next six years.

58. Len, his wife, Anne, and their son, Roy, 1944. For how they met, see page 160.

25

The Cockrells: the Shadow of the Workhouse

My father met my mother at the Nichol Street Mission, and they started going out together in 1929. Ellen Cockrell was then living in a four-roomed flat in Marlow Buildings, part of the Boundary Street Estate, with her father, Charlie Cockrell, and five of her six brothers and sisters. Her mother was dead, and one of her sisters had left home.

In some ways her background was very similar to my father's. Charlie Cockrell, like Basil Sanders, came from a family of East Anglian labourers and craftsmen and, again like Basil, he was illegitimate and had been given his mother's surname. He had been born in the workhouse at Stanway, near Colchester, and he had an elder sister, Carrie, who was also illegitimate, and who had been born in Dedham a few miles away. No one now knows who their father was. On their birth certificates the space for his name was left blank, and none of Charlie's children asked any questions.

In 1877 Charlie's mother married James Wishart, a Scottish soldier, and a few years later they set up home in Dedham, where James became a farm labourer. The Wisharts had eight children, step-brothers and -sisters to Carrie and Charlie. James Wishart, the father, died in 1902, and Mary Ann, the mother, outlived him by thirty years. Most of their children stayed in Dedham or Colchester, but Carrie and Charlie Cockrell came to London, where Charlie was employed as an ostler, an occupation often taken by boys from the country. In later years his children would visit Dedham in much the same way as the Sanders visited Braintree, and they remembered it as a kind of country idyll. Granny Wishart, as they called her, lived with her sons at the bottom of Coopers Lane in a tiny cottage next to a meadow with a well in the garden and

TABLE 4:
ELLEN COCKRELL'S FAMILY

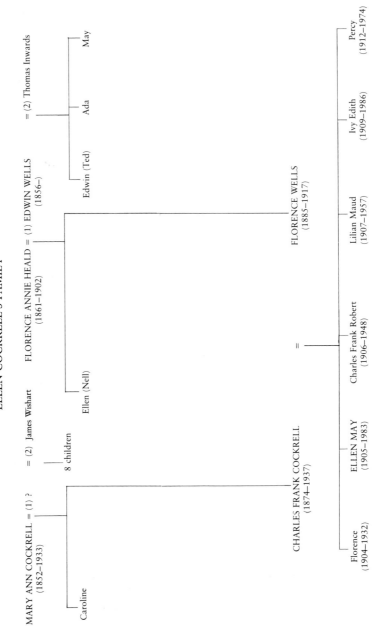

chickens and rabbits and a pig in a sty. She gleaned so much corn that she had enough for the whole year. She baked her own bread, brewed beer for the labourers at harvest time, and made wine from sloes and elderberries. She dispensed country medicines and remedies to people who came to her because they could not afford a doctor, and with the help of a 'dream-book' she interpreted their dreams. She made a fuss of the children and fed them well, with suet pudding as the first course for every dinner and rabbits for breakfast which their uncles had ferreted out at the crack of dawn.

In 1903, when he was twenty-eight, Charlie Cockrell married Florence or 'Flo' Wells, who was nine years younger than him and whose family came mainly from the area of Clerkenwell. Her father, who had died of consumption when he was thirty-one, had been a printer, and her mother had taken in washing. She and her elder sister, Nell, were the only two of the Wells' children who survived – two others at least died young – and they both worked as boxmakers for a jewellery firm. After her father's death her mother married again, and she had three half-sisters and -brothers, Ted, Ada and Mary.

When her mother died at the age of forty-one Nell, her elder sister, became the family's main support. She had married a printer, Harry Hunt, and although they were never well off they were always at hand when Flo needed help.

Flo was weak and sickly from birth. She had poor eyesight and suffered from asthma, and her half-sister May remembers her with such distress that she can hardly bring herself to talk about her. She was very 'kind-hearted', 'whatever she had she'd share it with anybody', but she was wracked by ill health and dragged down still more when she and Charlie had six children in the space of eight years – Florence (1904), Ellen, my mother (1905), Bob (1906), Lil (1907), Ivy (1909) and Percy (1912). She also had a child who was stillborn.

Charlie drank heavily. For a while he worked for Truman's Brewery in Brick Lane, but he was unable to hold down a job for long and he brought home very little each week. Before the war, my mother remembers, he was earning only 24s. a week, and when he joined the army in 1915 he gave his occupation as a labourer. They inevitably fell behind with the rent from time to time, and when things became too bad they were evicted. In the space of ten years they had at least six homes in Islington, Finsbury and Hoxton.

Charlie 'thought the world' of Flo, but that did not stop him, when he was drunk, from giving her 'the occasional knock', though my mother is quick to add that he 'never punched her about', 'not like many others at the time'. She did not think you could say he was 'a violent man', but he became 'aggressive' and 'he'd throw things about'. He was free with his use of the belt on the children. 'To tell you the truth I was a bit frightened of him.'

He was 'always going off drinking' on what my mother describes as his 'sprees'. When she was four he disappeared for several weeks. Flo, who was nearly eight months pregnant, was left destitute, and the whole family was taken into the Islington Workhouse in St John's Road. My mother remembers that she was ill at the time and that she was sent to the workhouse's infirmary. After a few days Nell got them out and for a while, until Charlie reappeared, she looked after them all at her home in Dufferin Street.

My mother never mentioned this episode until the last years of her life, and even then she insisted at first that it should not be told to anyone outside the family. It was the darkest of all the shadows that fell across her childhood, and it came to symbolise the shame of the poverty that she was determined to put behind her. 'I was very frightened', she said. 'It was such a great shock to me. We always felt it was a disgrace, you see. That's why I've always kept quiet about it, but it's always been there at the back of my mind.' The workhouse records bear out her memory completely – the admission of the family on 4 October 1909; my mother's being sent to the infirmary on Highgate Hill; and the discharge of the whole family on 9 October.[1]

A month later Ivy was born at Aunt Nell's home in Dufferin Street. We do not know where the family moved to after that, but by 1913 they were living in Hoxton Place, and by 1914 in Georges Square, off Hoxton Street. My mother believes that after this her father 'came to his senses' a little, though Ivy remembers a 'spree' to Scotland. At any rate, they were able to stay put in Georges Square.

It was no great advantage, however, for a young family to be brought up in Hoxton. Its reputation was as bad as Bethnal Green's, and its criminal quarter was one of the worst in the country.[2] Georges Square lay outside the roughest area, but it was still a place of terrible poverty. My mother remembers the whole family being together in one room, and the walls covered with bugs.

The eldest daughter, Florence, was an added worry for Flo, for she was a difficult, uncontrollable child and suffered from epileptic fits. If any of the other children annoyed her she would attack them physically, and the younger ones were terrified of her. 'She was a horrible person,' says Ivy: 'I don't know how she came to be like that in our family.'

In 1915 Charlie joined the Army Service Corps, though at forty he was well over age, and he served three years in France. He was not especially patriotic, but as a soldier he was paid 36s. a week which he was able to send back to Flo. 'He thought it might give my Mum some more money to live on,' says my mother. 'It did a bit, but she couldn't manage. She was a poor manager.' She was now in so much pain from her chest that she rarely left the house, and since Florence, the eldest sister, would not help, a lot of the work fell to my mother. 'Every day', she says, 'I had to go round to the moneylender in Georges Square. My Mum would borrow 5s. a time, 5s. a day that is. And on every shilling she had to pay a penny a week. Then on Monday she got my Dad's pay from the Army, and she'd pay it to the moneylender.' Every Monday too my mother had to take the family's clean washing to the pawnshop in the Hoxton Road and redeem it with interest on Friday: 'I used to hate having to go there, having to beg people to lend you money on clothing.' She was already aware that her mother could have arranged things better: 'I was always saying to her, "Why can't you make the money last out a bit more, and then we wouldn't have to pay the interest?" But she could never manage.'

Flo 'tried to earn a copper or two by doing mangling for the neighbours', and my mother used to turn the handle for her. She also went on with her trade of box-making, and my mother helped her in this as well. They collected the cardboard from a nearby factory; my mother cut out and folded the boxes, while Flo heated the glue and spread it on strips of paper which were then fastened round the boxes to hold them together. 'It was quite nice to do' when you got used to it, my mother says. Towards the end of the war she went out on her own in the evenings and earned a few pence by making boxes for ammunition.

They could not afford to buy food in any quantity, and bought items like sugar and condensed milk in tiny, uneconomic amounts of penn'orths and halfpenn'orths. So my mother 'was always going down to the shops'. School dinners during the war were a help, but they never ate well. The children 'often went to Burtt's Ragged School in Hoxton Square,' says my mother. 'There we lined up and walked to the Leysian Mission in City Road for a free meal. That was a real treat as we were often hungry.' And twice a week 'we used to buy a large jug of soup for 2d. from the soup kitchen in Hoxton Place.' Sometimes, when there was no food in the house at all, my mother would be sent to get stale bread from some friends in Islington. It was a long walk, and she was 'glad to chew a crust' on the way home. They were poorly dressed. Before the war Charlie used to patch their shoes with scraps of leather bought at the market, and Flo, like many other women at the time, used to wear her husband's cloth cap when she went out because she was too poor to have a hat of her own. Once she angered her sister Nell by going to see her with a great hole in her stocking. 'I think she was more ashamed of us than anything, we were so poor,' my mother says. There were no presents for the children at

Christmas, except the usual new penny and an orange. My mother once asked Flo for a scooter and was told that she could have it 'when my ship comes home'.

The children's health was inevitably undermined. When she was five my mother spent a month in the Mildmay Hospital and another fortnight convalescing, being looked after by a couple in a London suburban home. 'There was nothing particularly wrong with me,' she says: 'I was wasting away, they said.' In other words, she was suffering from malnutrition. When she was eight she had pleurisy and spent four months at St Bartholomew's Hospital and another month convalescing in the country. 'But I was all right after I had pleurisy.' Florence, the eldest sister, died when she was twenty-eight; Bob when he was forty-two ('he never enjoyed good health, poor old Bob'); and Lil, who had rickets as a child, when she was fifty. 'Percy lasted till he was sixty-two.' My mother died at the age of seventy-eight, while this book was being written. Ivy was seventy-five when she died in 1986.

My mother's school was Hoxton House, and she did very well there in spite of her illnesses. She was particularly good at English and arithmetic, and she was 'always easily top of the class'. She passed the examination at the age of eleven and 'would have loved to have gone to the grammar school', but, she says, 'I had to take all the papers home to be signed, and of course my mother was there by herself – my father was abroad – and she just had to sign everything "no, no, no", because I would have had to have stayed at school until I was sixteen and she couldn't see her way clear to keep me at school. It was just rubbed out.' She was not upset at the time, because 'education wasn't anything in the family in those days', though 'the headmistress felt I was missing my chances and she was really angry about it.' But, looking back, she says that her 'greatest ambition would have been to have had a good education.' She left Hoxton House as soon as she was thirteen.

Apart from school, my mother believes that the greatest influence on her at that time was the Hoxton Academy and its Girls' Life Brigade. Neither of her parents was religious – 'far from it', says my mother, in the case of Charlie, though he did tell Ivy that she must not sew on Sundays, since if she did she would be piercing our Lord's side every time she put the needle through the cloth. 'We weren't even allowed to cut our fingernails on Sundays.' But the children were all sent to the Hoxton Academy Sunday School, which was run by the Browns.[3] It was very different from the Nichol Street Mission, for the Browns were not narrow fundamentalists: 'they taught you to think for yourselves,' says my mother. They were Socialists and conscientious objectors, though in this my mother was not influenced at all. Their daughter ran the

Girls' Life Brigade, and she and her helpers taught the girls infant care and first aid, gym and dancing. More than that, says my mother, 'They taught you to lead a Christian life. You had to sign the pledge and attend Sunday School regularly, and they told you not to smoke. I never looked back.'

When my mother was about ten Flo had a stillborn child and was very ill for some time. She recovered, but not for long. On 30 March 1917, when she was thirty-two, she died of broncho-pneumonia. My mother remembers every detail. It was Friday, and the children had been allowed to stay at home because a scripture examination was being held at school. Flo was sleeping, and my mother, who was doing some washing, noticed froth round her mouth. She called in a neighbour, Mrs Duffy, who held a mirror in front of Flo's face to see if she was breathing. 'The mirror stayed clear, so Mrs Duffy thought she was dead and advised me to go and tell my Aunt Nell. I hurried round there and she came back with me. Then she sent me to ask Dr O'Dwyer to call straight away, but he said that there was no point in hurrying to a dead woman.' (My mother never forgot the inhumanity of this.) 'Aunt Nell really took over then. . . .' Later that day Charlie arrived home on leave from France. 'He didn't know anything about it. He broke down completely.'

Flo's brief existence had been afflicted by pain and weighed down by poverty. She had 'a terrible life', says my mother, and Ivy's only memory of her is lying in bed. Had she and Charlie been happy together? They were 'devoted' to each other, says my mother, but 'I don't think they could have been happy, they were so poor'. As for the children, 'I suppose we were happy. After all, it was our life. We didn't know any other.'

In the week before the funeral there was talk of sending the six children to an orphanage until Charlie could come home permanently. 'We were terribly worried', my mother says, 'wondering what was going to happen to us.' But then Nell agreed to look after them. At first they stayed in Georges Square, and went for their meals during the day to Nell's flat in Sonning Buildings, part of the Boundary Street Estate. Then Nell managed to get a two-roomed flat for them on the floor beneath her own. When Charlie was discharged from the army in July 1918 he joined them there, and in 1920 they were allocated a three-roomed flat in the same block on the ground floor.

Nell and Harry and their two boys shared their flat with Nell's half-brother and -sisters, whom the children knew as Uncle Ted, Aunt Ada and Aunt May. With several incomes they were much better off than the Cockrells, and Nell was a good housekeeper too. There was none of Flo's talk of ships coming home or visits to the moneylender and the pawnbroker. ' "Neither a borrower nor a lender be": she was always saying that.' All their aunts and uncles were very kind to the children. They gave them their first 'afters' after dinner, jelly and custard: 'we thought that was marvellous.' And in the Christmas of 1917, the first Christmas they had spent without their mother, the four girls were given their 'first decent Christmas present', a doll's set consisting of four cups and saucers, one for each of them. Nell was particularly fond of my mother, who helped her to run the two flats, and she taught her dressmaking and had her taught the piano.

The rent was 3s. a room, and so the Cockrells' three rooms on the ground floor cost them 9s. a week. The flats in Sonning Buildings were a great improvement on the slums in Georges Square – they were 'really very nice', says Ivy – but they provided very few comforts. Financial constraints had cut back the whole of the Boundary Street Estate to standards which the LCC itself described as barely reasonable.[4] There were four flats on each of the five floors, and the rooms were small and overcrowded. Water was not piped to the flats themselves, but there was a long sink on each landing with a tap at either end. Most of the families did their weekly washing in the sink – 'you got to know your neighbours, washing at that sink' – but for drinking, cooking, washing up and baths they carried jugs and bowls of water into their flats and brought out and emptied the dirty water when they had finished. The toilets were on the landing too, one for each flat.

The Cockrells did most of their cooking on a coal range, which the girls had to black lead every week, and there was also a gas ring for heating the kettle. Their furniture was simple: they had six wooden chairs, a table and a large armchair which the children could only sit in if Charlie was not there. In the living room there were two big pictures of angels on the walls and the mantelpiece was decorated by a runner of white macrama cotton crocheted by the girls.

Their neighbours were mainly quiet, self-respecting Jewish families, and there was none of the violence that disturbed the peace in Princes Court and Hoxton. 'There was a big Jewish population,' says my mother. 'Friendly. It was better than where we came from.'

In 1924 they moved to a four-roomed flat at the top of Marlow Buildings, which was also part of the Boundary Street Estate. The four eldest children were at work by this time, and they could afford a three-piece suite and a piano. Their days of penury were over.

Charlie had been discharged from the army because he had an illness of the kidney which, according to his character certificate, had been 'aggravated by Active Service'. He had been awarded a full army pension. My mother and Ivy cannot remember how much this was, 'but it wasn't much, about £1 a week.'

When he came home he was 'very poorly' for some time, and he was not strong enough to take up his old work as an ostler. He was often in pain, and was always taking pills and under hospital treatment. After a while, however, he joined Beck and Pollitzer in the City and worked for them as a packer and then a liftman. Every night he and Aunt Nell and Uncle Harry went out to one of the local pubs, but he no longer went off on his 'sprees'. The Army had described him as 'An honest sober and reliable man', and according to my mother he seemed 'cowed down' by his war experiences. But he still 'got mad' and belted the children at times: 'he wouldn't think twice about giving you a bashing,' says Ivy.

Florence, the eldest, worked as a bookbinder for Waterlows, while my mother stayed at home to look after the flat. When she was sixteen, however, my mother determined to go out to work, and it was agreed that it could be managed if everyone helped in the flat. She began as a presser for Stuteley's in Great Chapel Street, near Oxford Street, who made curtains, cushions and runners. She found it exhausting, standing and ironing from 8.30 a.m. to 5.30 p.m. on weekdays and from 8.30 a.m. to 1 p.m. on Saturdays. The firm were very strict on timekeeping. 'If we lost more than fifteen minutes a quarter we lost our holiday money for either Easter, Whitsun, August Bank holiday or Christmas. If we lost more than sixty minutes in the year, we lost our week's holiday money. It wasn't compulsory to pay for holidays, so we thought we were lucky.' If there was any overtime they had to do it: they could not pick and choose. There was no trade union, and she was paid 12s. a week. After she had been there for two months she was taught how to operate a Cornely machine, working embroidery with wools onto curtains which had been marked with a pattern beforehand. By the time she got married in 1932 she was earning £2 5s. a week. Apart from a period during the Second World War, when she took over my father's insurance round, she was a Cornely machinist for the rest of her working life.

Bob, her brother, went into the print, and he and my mother were always arguing. 'We used to flare up over nothing really. I don't know why. I suppose we were very similar, you see.' Bob argued with his father too. He was conscious of his own ability and intelligence, and bitter that he had had to leave school so early. While the rest of the family were Liberals, Bob turned to the Labour Party. He had 'a violent temper,' says my father, and 'he used to read *The Daily Herald*.'

The other three children, Lil, Ivy and Percy, were much quieter, and were very close to each other. When the rest of the family was out in the evening 'we little ones', says Ivy, 'used to have games in the kitchen – skipping and leapfrog and things like that. We used to have a real good time.' Lil joined my mother at Stuteley's, Percy became a milkman, and Ivy, when she left school, took over the running of the house. 'I had to do as I was told,' she says. 'Dad told me to stay, and what your mother said went as well.'

Soon after they had gone to Marlow Buildings Florence, the eldest sister, left home, taking all my mother's clothes with her. 'She made a set for a man called Thomson,' says my mother, 'who was living with a woman he wasn't married to.' At first she slept rough on the streets for a few weeks, but then Thomson married her and 'all three of them lived together. It was a funny set-up.' The younger ones in particular were relieved that she was gone. 'I was so pleased when she went away,' says Ivy: 'I was terrified of her. And whenever there was a knock on the door after that I was afraid it was her coming back.' They saw her around the shops occasionally and heard rumours that her husband was treating her badly. But she never returned. She died in May 1932, two months before my parents' wedding.

My mother was twenty-seven when she married, a year and a half older than my father. She had joined the Nichol Street Mission soon after the Cockrells' move to Sonning Buildings, and she had started up a branch of the Girls' Life Brigade there. She went to evening classes on the subjects that she herself had been taught at Hoxton – infant care, first aid, gymnastics and dancing. Apart from the weekly meetings, she organised the GLB's displays, for which the Mission hall was always 'packed out'. They had first aid sketches, club swinging and gymnastic exhibitions, folk dancing, sword dancing and 'fancy marching', when they marched in patterns while my mother shouted out the orders.

She felt her lack of education very keenly, but she had no good advice on how to make up for it. 'I went round all the secondhand bookstalls', she says, 'buying up secondhand books. Books that I didn't even understand, trigonometry and things like that, and I didn't know the first thing about them.' In later years her bookshelves were lined with compendiums of knowledge, like *Blackie's Complete Self-Educator*, and guides to the correct use of English and good letter-writing. She wrote in a neat, controlled hand, and though she did not go to elocution lessons she cultivated a carefully enunciated diction with very little trace of a Cockney accent. At one time she wanted to be a nurse, at another time a teacher. But she would have needed qualifications, and she 'never really had time to study'. 'I think I'd have made a good teacher,' she says. 'She would have been a headmistress,' says Ivy.

In her early twenties she kept a commonplace book in which she noted elevated or instructive sentiments that she found in her reading or heard from the pulpit. She recorded the grim warning that 'Where ignorance predominates, Vulgarity invariably asserts itself.' And although she comforted herself with Disraeli's observation that 'To be conscious you are ignorant is a great step to knowledge', she knew that the intellectual adventure was full of pitfalls:

> A little learning is a dangerous thing.
> Drink deep, or taste not the Pierian Spring.

She was on safer and more familiar ground with the moral virtues, like duty:

> Never to tire, never to grow cold,
> To be patient, sympathetic, tender,
> To hope always, like God to love always,
>   This is Duty.

And she tried hard to see her life of toil as sanctified by God:

> Lord of all pots and pans and things, since I've no time to be
> A saint by doing lovely things, or watching late for Thee,
> Or dreaming in the dawnlight or storming Heaven's gates,
> Make me a saint by getting meals and washing up the plates.

As well as being able and ambitious, she had a powerful strain of romanticism, but she was never strong enough to break through completely the harsh limitations of upbringing and circumstance. She tapped her foot to the popular musical classics and was 'gripped' by the stories of Charles Dickens, particularly those of Oliver Twist and Little Nell, with whom she could easily identify. But in the end, frustrated of spiritual and intellectual fulfilment, she threw all her energy and hard work into getting on, bettering herself financially and acquiring a decent home.

There were many other women with the same aspirations, particularly those, like herself, hoping to move out from the East End to homes of their own, but worried that what their parents had taught them would not be good enough for the more refined and demanding standards of suburbia. The women's magazines of the period offered them endless advice, and in the winter of 1929/30 my mother attended a course on homemaking run by the Polytechnic Education Department in Regent Street. She purchased a hard-back notebook from the Department, wrote 'E.M. Cockrell' neatly on the front, and made careful and in part verbatim notes on what she was taught. Homemaking, she was told, was much more than mere housekeeping. She had to be careful in her choice of house, having regard to soil, aspect, foundations, walls and windows. She had to plan her time carefully so as not to turn herself into an overworked drudge, 'as interesting to her husband as an old newspaper'. She was responsible for 'the judicial outlay of her housekeeping allowance', and she was to avoid 'unnecessary extravagance such as the buying of cleaning materials, which with little trouble could be made at home' – for example, '*Scouring Mixture*: ½lb. silver sand, ½lb. whitning, ½lb. soap powder (Hudsons). Method: Pass all through a sieve and mix thoroughly. Store in a tin or jar.' She had to wage a constant war with dust, 'which is the greatest enemy a housewife has to fight'. She was advised of the benefits of electric lighting, which 'all most sceptically minded people will agree . . . has amply proved itself to be superior to any other method of illumination'; she was given 'hints on the buying of lamps'; she was counselled on the choice of carpets and rugs and on how to protect them against moths; she was told how to remove stains caused by tar, paint, ink, tea, wine, soot, paraffin and blacklead. And so the course and her notes went on, through diet, hygiene and the choice of linen to the overall economy of running a home.

It was at her insistence, as we have seen, that my father left his job as a shop assistant and went on to become an insurance agent. They were courting for three years, a sedate, unadventurous courtship, going regularly to religious services and scout concerts together and twice to the theatre, which they thought was very daring, to see *Mr Cinders* and *Lilac Time*.

They were married at the Nichol Street Mission, spent a few days' honeymoon at Windlesham in Surrey, and then went to live in a rented flat at 62 Pyrland Road, Highbury. This, they thought, was 'a lift-up' in the world, since Highbury was 'a very select area in those days'; and of course it was the home of the Mission's patrons. They had three rooms and shared a toilet, and after they had been there a year a bathroom was installed on the ground floor. They paid 18s. 6d. a week rent, which was more than either of their families was paying in Princes Court or Marlow Buildings. My mother continued to work at Stuteley's, while my father went out on his insurance round, and at the Mission they ran the evening Sunday School, showing lantern slides of Biblical stories and of the lives of men and women like Livingstone and Florence Nightingale.

At the end of five years, in 1937, they had saved enough money to put down a £50 deposit on a three-bedroomed semi-detached house in New Southgate. The total cost was £800. Charlie Cockrell came to visit them soon after they had moved in, and amused himself by crawling through the hatch between the dining room and the kitchen. He died a few months later, at the age of sixty-two. He had lasted almost twice as long as Flo.

I was born in June 1938, and I was dedicated at the Nichol Street Mission.

59. 'Granny Wishart' at her cottage in Dedham. Probably in the late 1920s.

60. Flo and Charlie Cockrell, c. 1910.

61. Flo Cockrell.

Islington Workhouse.

62. The Islington Workhouse, where Flo Cockrell and her children were taken for a few days in 1909 while Charlie Cockrell went off on one of his 'sprees'.

63.   My mother's class at Hoxton House School, *c.* 1910. My mother is fifth from the right in the front row.

64.   The Hoxton Academy Sunday School, 1920.

65 (above). Ellen and Henry Hunt ('Aunt Nell and Uncle Harry'), *c.* 1910.
66 (left). Charlie Cockrell in the Army Service Corps, *c.* 1916.

67. The Cockrell children shortly after the death of their mother in 1917. In the back row, from left to right: my mother, Bob, Florence. In the front row: Ivy, Percy, Len Hunt (their cousin), Lil.

68. Hoxton Place, where the Cockrells were living in 1913. This photograph was taken in 1923.

69. Sonning Buildings, part of the Boundary Street Estate, a photograph taken in 1902. The Hunts lived in the top flat, just below the arch. The Cockrells moved to the ground floor flat which is to the left of the doorway on the right.

70.   My mother as a young woman.

71.   My parents on their wedding day at
the Nichol Street Mission, 1932.

New Southgate: from 1937

26

The Suburban Dream

Number 77 Pymmes Green Road – a semi-detached, pebble-dashed, bow-fronted house with designs of coloured glass in the frosted upper windows. Downstairs, a dining room, living room and kitchen. Upstairs, three bedrooms and a bathroom. None of these rooms was larger than twelve feet square. The woodwork inside was brown-varnished, shiny and grained, and the wallpaper pale brown or pale green. Later my mother painted the woodwork cream and hung new wallpaper, bright with patterns. In the dining room, as well as the dining table, chairs and sideboard, were my mother's sewing machine in a small cabinet, the bookcase-bureau at which my father sat every evening to enter figures into his insurance book, and three armchairs, since this was where we spent most of our time. We only used the living room at the front of the house when visitors came, or later when I did my homework there. Usually it stood cold and silent, like the parlour in Princes Court, with a three-piece suite and a glass-fronted bookcase. On the walls, in their heavily framed wedding photographs, my parents stood stiff and smiling with their best man, page boy and bridesmaids. In later years these photographs were replaced by large pictures from Boots, one of a dark-haired woman with bare shoulders embracing a tree against a background of a dark green forest, and another of eighteenth-century prelates and aristocrats in rich brocades and silks laughing genteelly over a glass of sherry and a game of chess. The back garden was laid out according to a plan purchased through a women's magazine, with flower beds surrounding a carefully shaped lawn and arched trelliswork dividing off the vegetable garden and the fruit trees at the back.

My mother's pride was invested in this little property. She had embroidered all the quilts and the cushions, and she came to do all the decorating herself, outside as well as in. She was constantly making changes and improvements, and visitors were always taken on a tour of the house to see the latest decorations and to have pointed out to them, for example, how the green leaf in the wallpaper picked out the green in the curtains. Later she went to woodwork classes and made an oak linen chest, and she even bought her own set of brushes and swept the chimney herself. She was an anxious and terrifying perfectionist. My cousins knew when they came to visit that they had to be on their best behaviour. Any crumbs that they dropped on the floor were swept up with a brush and pan as soon as they got down from the table. She was worried that the cream painted knob on the banisters would get dirty, and so it was protected by a polythene bag. And she once came back from visiting Mr Hart in the end house, who had just painted his kitchen, and announced in disgust that he had not painted behind his cupboard because he did not think that anyone would look there.

Beyond the back fence of the garden was a sports field belonging to John Dale, a local engineering firm, where my father and I used to watch football and cricket at weekends, and beyond the field we could see Alexandra Palace on the horizon. Pymmes Green Road formed two sides of a square of roads surrounding the field, all of them lined with ornamental bushes and flowering cherries and almonds. There was a solid Victorian farmhouse with broad overhanging eaves at the bottom of our part of the road. Apart from a footpath opposite the farmhouse, leading across Pymmes Brook into Hampden Way and ultimately, as far as I was concerned, to Osidge Primary School, the only way out of this respectable enclave was Ryhope Road, which linked one corner of the square with Waterfall Road, the boundary between Hertfordshire on our side and Middlesex on the other. Very little traffic came into this square, just the occasional tradesman, like the baker and the grocer in their vans and the milkman with his horse and cart. (I had to dash out with a bucket and shovel to gather up any manure that fell, and tried not to scoop up too many little stones at the same time.) The only man in the road to run a car was Mr Turner, who had built the houses on the other side, and he owned a black Ford 8. We were five minutes walk from Arnos Park, and ten minutes from Arnos Grove tube station and the Piccadilly line, which had been extended to this area in the 1930s. On most of our journeys we set out from there. When our East End relations came to visit us they would jokingly complain of how far they had had to walk, especially if it was a cold day. 'You've dragged us out to the blinkin' country,' they would say.

When my parents moved into the area it was still being developed. Round the corner John Dale were still building houses for their employees, and by the war they had not quite reached the corner. Afterwards they sold off the remaining land to the East Barnet Council, who built a dozen houses there. Some of the residents were alarmed, but according to my mother the Council assured them they would 'put in only a suitable type of person' and in the end the character of the area was not changed.

With so little traffic the children could play safe and undisturbed in the road. On the whole, I think, we were well behaved, though some of the neighbours complained of the noise at times. We often went down to Pymmes Brook, building camps in the elderberries and willows on the banks or splashing in and out in our Wellington boots, racing sticks against each other between the waterfall and the bridge.

It was a quiet, staid neighbourhood, and the only intrusive noise came from the electric trains going by on the viaduct through Arnos Park and by the brook. We regarded ourselves as lower middle-class, and most people in the road would have said the same. Several of them came from the East End, but most from areas like Islington and Wood Green. The occupations of the men ranged from a porter in Smithfield Market to the manager of the printing firm, De La Roux, a dapper little man whom my mother always referred to as Burlington Bertie. At least two men were in the print and two were butchers; a few were skilled craftsmen and three were policemen. Several worked for Ever-Ready Batteries in Wood Green or the Standard Telephone Company, which was the largest local employer. Some had white collar jobs with public authorities, like London Transport and the LCC. There were two insurance agents, including my father, a commercial traveller, and the chief clerk of Barclay's Bank in Wood Green. The corner house on the other side was occupied by the builder, Mr Turner. Those on our side had been built by Mr Cox, whose daughter lived in one of them for several years.

Nearly half of the women went out to work. One was a nurse, another a milliner, and several had jobs at the Standard. Some of them preferred not to work but had to during the war. One or two, it is said, had children at that time since this released them from the obligation to be employed.

The neighbours were mainly young couples, like my parents, who were moving in to a new development. The most notable exception were the Roffeys, who lived next door to us at number 75 and were a full generation older. They were the only family with more than two children, and even they by that time had only one son living with them. Apart from them, on our side of the road I can remember two families with two children, ten with one child, and two with none. Contraception, of course, was now in common use, but my mother added another explanation: 'We could not afford to have more than you. The big thing was to be sensible. In the old days poverty was the normal thing. People accepted it.'

Most people in the road had risen socially, and most voted Conservative. There were a few Labour supporters, like Jack Wright next door, the Briarleys, who came from Bethnal Green, and the Vardys, who painted their house a bright red. My father remained Liberal, but my mother swung over to the Conservatives, if only for negative reasons: 'We always thought if you voted Liberal, the Labour stood a good chance of getting in, and I never wanted the Labour to get in.' My father's old scouting friend, Frank Blanchard, became a Conservative councillor in Enfield, and invited them to several Conservative events which they were pleased and interested to attend. In the 1945 landslide the Barnet constituency returned the Labour candidate, Stephen Taylor, but in 1950 the seat was won by Reginald Maudling for the Conservatives and has remained Conservative ever since. My parents admired Maudling's brilliance, but did not like it when he came round to canvass them 'half-cut' and 'reeking of drink'.

Most people in the road were 'good' neighbours, which meant on the one hand that they did not give themselves airs and that they would greet you with a friendly word if they met you in the street, and on the other that they did not lower the tone of the neighbourhood by allowing their paintwork to peel off, for example, or by working in their front gardens in a vest. We were all very private, and for the most part we knew very little about each other. Every house, as far as I can remember, had net curtains at all the front windows. My mother, however, was friendly with Mrs Smith who lived opposite and had two young children of her own, and with old Mrs Roffey, who lived next door.

Most children in the road were sent to Sunday School, but I was the only one who was sent to the school at Bowes Park Methodist Church, which was in Palmers Green nearly two miles away. The old Nichol Street Mission had been closed down in 1939 under a Dangerous Structures Order (though it is still standing today as a community centre), and my father decided to go to Bowes instead. It was a huge, brick-built church, put up at the turn of the century, rich with woodwork and stained glass windows, with choir stalls behind an elevated pulpit and continuous curved galleries on the other three sides. About 400 people went to the Sunday evening service and about 1,000 children to the Sunday School. My father was a teacher there for twenty years and still attends the Sunday service. My mother gradually drifted away from organised religion, although she went occasionally to the City Temple, where she enjoyed the sermons of Leslie Weatherhead and joined the Literary Society. 'They had some good speakers there,' she said, 'and of course, a lot of these others, they're not well up, are they? They're not what you'd call first class speakers. And I really enjoyed a good sermon.' Weatherhead was also my father's favourite. 'He could stir you up,' he said, and he had all of Weatherhead's books on his shelves, like *The Transforming Friendship*, *Jesus and Ourselves*, and *Christianity and Sex* (though this last was concealed in a brown paper cover).

My father kept in touch with his old employer, Mr Pugh, who had come to live in Palmers Green, and we visited him occasionally on Sunday afternoons after Sunday School. He lived alone with his housekeeper, and I remember him as a tired, baggy-eyed old man, who had lost a foot through gangrene and who talked endlessly of the Mission in days long past. My mother remained friends with Dorothy Erlebach from the Mission, who had also come to live in Palmers Green. Every Christmas, when I was a boy, she sent me a copy of *Uncle Arthur's Bedtime Stories*, which were described as 'simple gospel and moral-lesson stories', teaching 'unselfishness, promptness, obedience, persistence, truthfulness, loyalty, forgiveness, faith in God, respect for parents, Sabbath observance, and many other virtues.' They had titles like 'Trouble at Prayer Time', 'Honest Tommy', 'Thinking of Others' and 'God's Plans for You'. My father used to read them at bedtime to me, and they left me feeling guilty and ill at ease.

In 1939 my mother's brother and sister, Percy and Ivy, came to live with us, since Ivy, who had started work just before her father died, had become ill with the worry of running the flat and doing a job at the same time. Percy never settled in Pymmes Green Road. After the liveliness and bustle of Bethnal Green he found the quietness unnerving, and in 1940 he left to get married. Ivy stayed on until her death in 1986. She went to work at the Standard, and was employed there until she retired thirty-five years later.

In November 1940 my father was called up to join the War Department Constabulary and was posted to the security force at the armaments factory at Waltham Abbey. He was mainly on night shifts, and every evening he set out on his bike in an outsized police raincoat which he pulled up in great bundles over his belt. He had been earning £5 a week as an insurance agent, and my mother took on his round instead.

During the blitz we could see the red glow on the horizon as the London docks went up in flames. The Standard was bombed, with more than 200 people losing their lives, and nearer to home the houses opposite were hit. Nobody was killed, but six houses had to be pulled down. In our own house there were just a few cracks in the ceilings. 'It stood up to it very well, really,' my mother said. Buried in our back garden we had an Anderson shelter, where several of the neighbours would join us when the bombing was particularly bad. Later we had a Morrison shelter as well, a cast iron table with wire mesh at the sides. When I slept there I felt completely safe, since I could not imagine anything that could break through that iron protection. Some neighbours paid very little attention to the bombing, like old Mrs Roffey, who would insist on making her husband's dinner before she came down to our Anderson shelter. And at nights she would not go down there at all, saying that she would rather die in her bed than in a hole in the ground. Others spent every night at Bounds Green underground station.

My parents always looked back on these days as a time when there was 'a wonderful spirit' and people really pulled together. It was 'terrifying', they said, when France surrendered and England stood completely alone, and there were constant rumours of German landings on the coast. And when the docks went up, said my father, 'we really didn't know what was going to happen. But I think that, being British, we always had that faith in our army that we'd win through in the end. Especially after Churchill's speeches.' 'He was wonderful really', my mother said, 'when he spoke to the people. Everybody sort of thought we were going to win, you know, the bulldog spirit, and everything was going to be all right.'

Towards the end of 1944 my mother had to give up the insurance round because she overstrained herself riding the bike and began coughing up blood. My father was allowed to resign from the Constabulary on compassionate grounds and went back on the round himself. She had done well for him. She had not only maintained the existing book, pushing and carrying her bike through the rubble during the blitz, but she had bought a new book and paid off the loan on it. 'So we doubled our income,' my father said, and my mother was naturally very proud of what she had done. 'He was in clover when he came back,' she said.

After the war she taught Cornely machining for a year at a college in Barrett Street, behind Selfridges, and then she went back to the factory floor at Tealedown's, in Bounds Green. She was still full of restless energy and ambition. At home she had an odd habit of scampering upstairs on all fours, and when she was out with my father she complained that he walked so slowly that she always had one leg up in the air waiting to come down again. She was sometimes angry that she did all the decorating herself, but she was such a perfectionist that she would not let anyone help. At one time she wanted to buy a small shop, but my father would have nothing to do with it. She called him an 'old stick-in-the-mud', but at least in 1946 she was able to persuade him to buy Mr. Turner's old Ford 8 for £275. 'He'd bought it for £110 before the war, my father says, 'but it was difficult to get hold of cars after the war, and he'd not used it much.' After that his insurance round was much easier for him and he was able to extend it.

At every stage of their life together my mother had taken the major initiatives. When they had begun courting, 'to tell you the truth', she said, 'I had to chase him a little bit,' and it was she who had made him change his job. She also claimed that but for her they would never have bought the house. 'He was content with the flat. He just needed a little push.' He was always generous and free of pride in acknowledging the leads she had given. 'Your mother had the brains and the go,' he told me. But how did he feel when she showed off her handiwork round the house? 'Another man might have objected,' he said, 'but I let it pass.'

He had his strengths too, and he was well aware that they were precisely those strengths that my mother lacked. The Cockrells, he said, were not 'good mixers', and it was only with his help and encouragement, he believed, that my mother 'came out' with people who were not members of the family or old friends. She was always anxious that they should put their best foot forward and not show themselves up with others who had been better educated or had come from a more refined background. When my father said 'we come' instead of 'we came' she would correct him, even when other people were there. He did not worry. He was a self-assured, cheerful, easy-going man, who made friends quickly and kept them. He had a certain natural authority, and with his experience of preaching at the Mission he spoke freely and confidently in public.

He could have gone on and become a superintendent in the Royal London, but he found after the war that he could earn more as an agent, and later he decided, with the encouragement of his friends, to seek office in the Royal London Staff Association. In 1952 he was elected as the Association's Treasurer, and in the following year as General Secretary. There were only about 2,000 members, and at that stage it was only a part-time job. But in 1966 it was made full-time, and he spent the rest of his working life as a trade union official. In the meantime, in 1959, the Association had become the Royal London Section of the National Union of Insurance Workers, but he had retained the title of General Secretary.

He was happy in the job, just as he had been happy as an insurance agent. As the only full-time official of the Section he acquired an expertise and held a status that no other member could match. He enjoyed the challenge of negotiating, he enjoyed travelling round the country and attending meetings, and above all he enjoyed the annual conference, which was usually held at a seaside town like Eastbourne or Blackpool. He also attended the TUC's annual conference. My mother, with her wartime experience as an agent, was able to share a great deal with him and give him valuable support. She took him off to dancing lessons so that they should not let themselves down at social functions, and she made her own dresses for the conferences' balls and receptions. We may argue today that, instead of being a factory girl at Tealedown's and supporting my father as General Secretary, she should have had a fulfilling career of her own. But she herself no longer thought about that, and she was not bitter or resentful.

My father would not have risen to the top in a union committed to the politics of the Left. But most members of his Section had Conservative sympathies, and there was little call for confrontation and struggle. There were inevitably contentious issues and hard individual cases, but relations between management and the staff side were very good on the whole. When my father retired in 1972 the company magazine recorded of him that he could 'smile his way through any crisis' and paid tribute to his 'constructive' negotiating: 'A kindly man, he represents all that is best in British trade unionism.' His farewell dinner was attended by several company directors, and the guest speaker was Len Murray, himself a Methodist, who placed him in that tradition of the union movement which 'owes more to Wesley than to Marx'.

My mother was determined that I should enjoy and exploit to the full that education of which she herself had been deprived. She taught me to read before I went to school and trained up my memory with games of Pelmanism, which depended on remembering pairs of cards turned up by alternate players. I spent hours spelling words with wooden letters, and I was encouraged to listen to general knowledge quizes on the wireless. I was sent to piano lessons with Miss Elsie Piper and elocution lessons with Miss Lydia Heale. ('Why do I need elocution?' I asked. 'Because you say "siook" instead of "silk".' I was told.) My primary school, Osidge, in Southgate, strained every nerve to get as many children through the scholarship as possible. Its catchment area was largely middle class, and its results were much better than the national average. In my year there were between 110 and 120 children, and from the age of seven or eight we were divided into three streams according to ability. The awesome responsibility of teaching 4A, the top class in the scholarship year, was alternated between Mr Fraser and Mrs Jackson, and the parents watched them like hawks to see which of them would get the most children through the exam. We had the impression that there was a deadly rivalry between them and that in history they waged a coded war with each other. According to Mrs Jackson Queen Elizabeth was the most splendid monarch ever to sit on the throne of England. According to Mr Fraser she was much over-rated. In my year 4A was taken by Mr Fraser, and about forty of the forty-five passed the scholarship.

I could then have gone, and would have wanted to go, to East Barnet Grammar School, which was co-educational, which did not matter to me, and played football, which mattered a great deal. Instead, on my mother's insistence, since she believed that it was better academically, I was sent to Queen Elizabeth's Grammar School in Barnet, which was single sex and played rugby. My mother was fearful of the standards she admired: on my way to the scholarship interview with the headmaster she had warned me not to mention that she worked in a factory.

Queen Elizabeth's had 360 boys, 60 in each year. It had been founded in 1573 and had been a public school until shortly after the war. Its motto was *Dieu et Mon Droit*. Its badge was the crown with Tudor roses. It had four houses: Leicester, after the Earl of Leicester, who had asked the queen to grant the school's charter; Broughton, after an old boy who had become Bishop of Australia; Underne, after the rector of Barnet at the time of the school's foundation; and Stapylton, after a former chairman of the Governors. We had Speech Day, with speeches from the headmaster and a visiting dignitary, speeches from selected boys in English, French, German, Greek or Latin, and the awarding of prizes, like the Bishop Broughton Prize for Divinity and the John Bond Lee Prize for Classics. We had Founder's Day, with a service in Barnet Church, a roll call, when every boy's name was called out and we had to reply 'Adsum', the school chronicle, which was read by the headmaster from a scroll in antiquated prose which he had written himself ('Be it known unto all men', it began), and the annual cricket match between Past and Present, watched by a great gathering of masters, parents, boys and old boys, known as Old Elizabethans. Lessons were held on Saturday mornings and games were played on Saturday afternoons ('And don't come to us with the excuse that you've got to visit your auntie'). The playing fields were spacious and well tended. Whenever we went out we had to wear our school cap and tie. We boys called each other by our surnames and we gave the masters nicknames like Frosty and Poker. The headmaster referred to us as gentlemen, and told us in our history lessons that 'Napoleon was a poisonous little upstart' and that 'Byron, gentlemen, Byron was a blister.' Most of the masters were Oxford graduates, and each year about fifteen boys were duly despatched to university, about six of them to Oxbridge.

I went on to Oxford to read Greats and my mother was overwhelmed with pride. Even my father, when he introduced me to friends, invariably announced that I was studying at Oxford. 'I never thought that one of mine would ever go there,' he told me. They took pleasure in visiting me, in being shown round the colleges and punted up the Cherwell. But there was one consequence of my education that my mother had not foreseen. Having been devoted to her as a boy, I had grown slowly away from her. There was no break, but a quiet distancing. I remained committed to her, but when she was asked at my wedding how it felt to lose a son, she replied that she had lost me some while ago.

In my religious belief I had remained firmly in my father's and grandmother's tradition. After going to Sunday School I had joined the church at Bowes, and had found Christianity so compelling that the only career that I could contemplate was the Methodist Church. I did not touch alcohol until I was twenty, not because of principle, but inclination, and I became a local preacher and an accepted candidate for the ministry. But at Oxford I lost my faith. That long, early period of Christian experience and teaching had marked me, but the formal continuity with the past was broken.

My grandfather's love of sport remained. My father first took me to see the Spurs when I was five, and I have been going ever since, not regularly, but three or four times each season. Until recently my father, Bunny, Eddie and Len used to attend every home match, and a visit to the Spurs was always a family as well as a sporting occasion.

Other links with the wider family remained intact. Almost every weekend during my childhood there had been visits to or from aunts and uncles and cousins. Children were indulged and were the centre of attention. Aunts hugged them and uncles made them laugh. Christmas above all was a time of wild excitement. The house was crowded with relatives, and in the evenings we had games and the old party turns, with my father singing 'Keep right on to the end of the road' and Albert, the best entertainer of them all, singing 'Oh it's a windy night tonight'. When he came to the lines 'The wind's a blowing round the 'ouses, and I can feel it blowing up me trousers', he used to hitch up his trousers above his knees and reveal a skinny, glistening white shin under a sock suspender, and my mother and her sisters would shriek with laughter and take off their spectacles to wipe away their tears. Then he sang 'My wife's a luxury, too big a luxury for me', and when Lal looked suitably offended he made it up to her with 'My Old Dutch'. We did not serve alcohol at Christmas, but Albert and Alf, Lil's husband, used to slip off to the bathroom to share a hip-flask of whisky together. We children could never understand why two grown men should want to go to the bathroom together, or why they looked so conspiratorially happy when they came out. Albert enjoyed every family occasion. At my wedding he had too much to drink and fell asleep in the middle of Wadham's front quad. My father explained to my enquiring mother-in-law that he got very tired nowadays.

The Simple Annals

There were naturally some members of the family whom I continued to see quite often, and others whom I saw only at occasions like marriages and, increasingly, funerals. But I never lost touch completely with any, and the writing of this book has been a fusion of two aspects of my experience which for a long time had been very separate, the world which is part of the history of the book, of East End relations and a suburban home, and the world which I had to enter in order to write it, of historical research and creativity.

My parents, aunts and uncles have all talked freely about their lives in Bethnal Green. Several of them have gone out of their way to get information for me, and some have now visited Stansted and been shown the sites of the family's history, like Guiver's and Mary's house in the old Newmarket Road and their grave in St Mary's churchyard. 'That's been very interesting,' said Mary: 'I hope you finish this book before I conk out.'*

My mother in particular became caught up with it all, and towards the end she came with me to help with the research at the Essex Record Office. Her legs were too short to reach the floor. The chair squeaked as she wound it down, and she apologised to the assistants for making a noise. She read through Stansted's Poor Law Records, and the story of Samuel Sanders, who died in the workhouse in 1804, is recorded in her meticulous hand. She was now reconciled with her past. When I came back from the Greater London Record Office and showed her a copy of her own admission to the Islington Workhouse in 1909 – 'Nellie Cockrell, age 4' – she was no longer worried that anyone else should know, but pleased that her memory had been so amply confirmed. Having read Robert Roberts' *The Classic Slum*, she wrote four pages of her recollections of her early years in Hoxton. She was happy to share in the work that gave her a fragment at least of that cultural fulfilment that she had missed throughout her life. My father, as always, was more independent, and his interest in the work was quieter and less intense.

My mother died on the last day of 1983. I wish that I could have shared this book with her.

---

* In fact she died in 1988, before the book went to print. But at least she was able to read it – and to enjoy it – in manuscript.

72.   Number 77 Pymmes Green Road in the 1940s.

73.   My mother (second from left at the front) with 'the girls at work' at Tealedown's, Bounds Green, about 1950.

74. My father (on the left) with fellow delegates of the National Union of Insurance Workers at a T.U.C. conference at Blackpool in the 1960s.

75. My father on his retirement as General Secretary of the Royal London Section of the National Union of Insurance Workers, 1971.

76. Going to see the Spurs. Eddie and myself, August 1950. Boys at Queen Elizabeth's were required to wear their school cap and tie whenever they went out – which I dutifully did, even when watching the Spurs. The woman looking out from the doorway would take in bikes for a few pence each and look after them during the game.

77. The headmaster, prefects and sub-prefects at Queen Elizabeth's Grammar School, 1955. I am second from the right in the back row.

78 and 79. My parents in their garden: my mother in 1980, my father in 1987.

Epilogue

We have been accustomed to think of ordinary individuals as being on the receiving end of history – either under the control of their rulers and employers or swept along by the great currents of social and economic change. In the words of William Harrison, the Essex pastor, writing in 1577 and referring to everyone below the rank of yeoman, they had 'neither power nor authoritie in the common wealthe, but are to be ruled and not to rule other'. There are strong arguments to support this view. They had to live within a framework of constraints erected and held in place by others, and they were inevitably influenced, even conditioned, by the prevailing modes of thought and behaviour. They were drawn by contemporary pulls, driven by contemporary pushes.

But this view of ordinary individuals fails to do justice to the great variety of their experience, and to the validity of their opportunities and the energy with which they pursued them. Obviously there were many, like the farm labourers and the factory workers of the nineteenth century, whose power over their own lives was wretchedly limited. But there were many others who were not merely the helpless victims of change, or even its lucky beneficiaries. They were able to make decisions for themselves and to take command of their own destiny.

In Stansted, after the uncertain experience of Thomas and Sarah, the Sanders were literally their own masters in their carpenters' workshops. As substantial householders they could, and did, hold parish office. And the elder Guiver and Mary were very much at home in the culture of Dissent, which provided an alternative to the powerbase of the Anglican vicars and gentry – and even, in the New Meeting of Josiah Redford, an alternative to the mainstream respectability of the Independent establishment. In Braintree the younger Guiver, running his own public house, had considerable control over his own fortunes, and even Charlie, after starting as a labourer, became his own master as a calf-dealer. He was a self-made man, no doubt with all that is implied by that term. Such individuals were not uncommon among the ordinary people. Indeed they were there in considerable force: independent-minded, self-reliant, not necessarily ambitious or successful, but owing nothing to anyone. They make up a powerful tradition in English national life.

Of course they did not enjoy the same kind of choice as the gentry. They could not set out on the Grand Tour; they could not acquire large estates or build up a library or an art collection. They were not free to spend their days hunting, shooting and fishing. In order to make a decent living in Stansted the Sanders had to stick to their carpenter's trade. But within the small world of the parish – and that was the world that mattered to them – they were people of some substance and account.

It is only with Aunt Galley in the silk mills and Basil Sanders in the print that we come to the 'wage-slaves' of the capitalist economy. In their factories and at their machines they were tightly controlled. They had to do what they were told. But they had freedom of belief and the practice of their own customs, and the choice of their pleasures was their own. It is belittling to regard their working-class culture, with its sport, the pub and popular religion, as a 'retreat' from the wider world, as the only place where they could win the esteem and self-respect that were denied them by their 'betters'. It was a source of great satisfaction and fulfilment to them, and they had a proper sense of its value.

My parents enjoyed a wider freedom. True, my mother, as one of 'the girls at work', had a job which was far below her ability. But at least she chose to go out to work – several of her neighbours chose not to – and she did so mainly because she wanted the extra money for the home and family that were so important to her. And my father took great pleasure and pride in his work, both as an insurance agent and as a trade union official. Now eighty-two, he often comments that he has had 'a good run', meaning not only a long life but a happy and rewarding life as well.

Of course ordinary individuals do not 'make history' in the same way as royalty, statesmen or generals – the 'Ambition' and 'Grandeur' of Thomas Gray's *Elegy*. They are powerless to change the course of events on any but the smallest scale – though we are now more aware of the complexity of change and more questioning of the extent to which it can be effected by any particular individuals at all. But the activities of ordinary individuals are essential to change. The boom in speculative building at the end of the eighteenth century, for example, was made by men like the elder Guiver. The drift in population to London consisted of people like the Galleys and my grandfather. And it was people like Aunt Galley (in spite of her initial lapse) who enforced what became known as Victorian morality. They were not entirely at the mercy of the powerful and the great. They were not blown around by every wind that blew. For long periods, it is true, they had to be content with carrying out the donkeywork of the world. But they were never the ciphers of history: they were its active agents.

References

Introduction

1 The name comes originally from Alexander, and the French, Alésaundre, explains why there are two forms, Sanders and Saunders. The family name was clearly Sanders, but the form Saunders was sometimes used.

Chapter 1 The family in Stansted

1 There are several reasons for believing this. He named his first son John, and first sons were commonly named after their grandfathers. And it seems that the Thomas Sanders who was born in Ware did not stay there, for his name does not appear in the town's register of burials. The dates fit, because most men in that period married in their late twenties, and the fourteen miles from Ware to Ugley were just about as far as a man would normally migrate. (See D.E.C. Eversley, 'Population History and Local History', in E.A. Wrigley (ed.), *An Introduction to English Historical Demography from the Sixteenth to the Nineteenth Century* (1966), p. 22.) However, the registers of several parishes around Stansted do not go back to this period, and it is possible that Thomas Sanders was born in one of them. The registers in Takeley only date from 1662, and we know from other sources that there were Sanders living in Takeley at this time and that they were connected with families in Ugley. Another candidate is the Thomas Sanders whose parents' names are not given, who was born at Great Hallingbury in December 1617, but this seems a little early.
2 On average there were two or three marriages recorded each year in Ugley's parish registers. In the ten years between 1644 and 1653 only seven were recorded in all.
3 E.A. Wrigley and R.S. Schofield, *The Population History of England 1541–1871: a Reconstruction* (1981), p. 424.
4 Wrigley and Schofield, op. cit., p. 234. See also R.W. Malcolmson, *Life and Labour in England 1700–1780* (1981), p. 60.
5 Malcolmson, op. cit., p. 71.
6 Malcolmson, op. cit., p. 70.
7 Keith Wrightson, *English Society 1580–1680* (1982), p. 105; Malcolmson, op. cit., p. 60;

References

Peter Laslett, *The World We Have Lost – Further Explored* (1983), p. 112.

8   Malcolmson, op. cit., p. 61; Laslett, op. cit., pp. 119–20; Linda A. Pollock, *Forgotten Children* (1983); Alan MacFarlane, *Marriage and Love in England, 1300–1840* (1986) pp. 52–3.

9   Essex Record Office (hereafter ERO) D/P 109/12/1, entry for 2 May 1749.

10 Laslett, op. cit., pp. 91–4. See also Alan MacFarlane, *The Family Life of Ralph Josselin, A Seventeenth Century Clergyman* (1970), p. 159.

11 ERO, D/P 109/12/4.

12 ERO, D/P 109/12/18

13 E.J. Hobsbawm and George Rudé, *Captain Swing* (1969), p. 62.

14 ERO, D/P 109/13/3: removal order, 4 September 1771.

15 ERO, D/P 109/12/6–9.

16 See, e.g., Laslett, op. cit., pp. 74–7.

17 Of the first hundred males to be baptized in St Mary's Church in the eighteenth century, if we discount those who died in infancy, fewer than half were buried there. For the origins of newcomers in the parish, see the examination of twenty-nine men in 1791 to discover 'the place of their last legal settlement'. Nearly all of them came from Bishop's Stortford or the neighbouring villages. See ERO, D/P 109/8/5.

18 Wrightson, op. cit., pp. 41–4; Malcolmson, op. cit., pp. 71–4.

Chapter 2 The parish of Stansted Mountfitchet

The economy of the parish

1   For the early history of this road, see F.H. Maud, *The Hockerill Highway: the story of the origin and growth of a stretch of the Norwich road* (1957). The quotation from Woodforde is taken from the Bishop's Stortford and District Local History Society, *Bishop's Stortford: a Short History* (2nd edition 1973), p. 56.

2   P. Muilman, 'A Gentleman', *People's History of Essex* (1772), Vol. III, p. 17.

3   A.F.J. Brown, *Essex at Work 1700–1815* (1969), p. 71.

4   Muilman, op. cit., p. 17.

5   Thomas Wright, *The History and Topography of the County of Essex* (1836), Vol. II, p. 155.

6   Muilman, op. cit., p. 17.

7   ERO, Q/RTh series.

8   D.E.C. Eversley, op. cit., p. 78; Peter Laslett, 'The Study of Social Structure from Listings of Inhabitants', in E.A. Wrigley (ed.), *An Introduction to English Historical Demography from the Sixteenth to the Nineteenth Century* (1966), p. 78.

9   These changes broadly reflect what was happening in the country as a whole. Between 1700 and 1800 the population of England is estimated to have risen from about five million to more than eight and a half million, with nearly all the increase coming after 1750. See Wrigley and Schofield, op. cit., p. 210.

10 For Hearth Tax analysis, see Margaret Spufford, *Contrasting Communities: English Villagers in the Sixteenth and Seventeenth Centuries* (1974), pp. 37–45; Malcolmson, op. cit., pp. 18–9.

11 The last remnants of the open fields were enclosed in 1848: ERO, Q/RDc 36A.

12 ERO, C/CT 328.

13 Arthur Young, *General View of the Agriculture of the County of Essex* (1807), Vol. II, pp. 380–1; A.F.J. Brown, op. cit., p. 28. Chapman and André's map, however, shows that by 1777 this process was largely completed.

14 Census returns, 1831. To take one crude indicator of the change, in 1710 forty-seven men exercised their right to vote in an election, a right that was based on the tenure of freehold property; in 1768, twenty-seven; and in 1830, nineteen.

15 ERO, Q/RJ 1/2 and D/P 109/3/4. See also Young, op. cit., Vol. I, Chapter 4.

16 Stansted's response to question 49 in The Report of the Commission on the Poor Laws, 1834.

17 For the Essex woollen industry, see A.F.J. Brown, op. cit., pp. 1–27.

18 ERO, Q/SPb 20.

19 *The Chelmsford Chronicle*, 24 October 1834.

20 Wrigley and Schofield, op. cit., pp. 638–40.

21 The two maps are those by Chapman and André of 1777 and the tithe commutation map of 1843 in the ERO.

The government of the parish.

22 Note in the parish register, ERO, D/P 109/1/1.

23 For the Myddletons, see articles in the *Dictionary of National Biography*; Philip Morant, *History and Antiquities of the County of Essex* (1760–8), Vol. II, pp. 578–9; David Stephenson, 'The Myddletons of Stansted Mountfitchet. A Seventeenth Century Gentry Family', *Transactions of the Essex Archaeological Society*, Vol. 8, 1976, pp. 282–7.

24 For the Heaths, see Morant, op. cit., p. 579.

25 For the Houblons, see Lady Alice Archer Houblon, *The Houblon Family: Its Story and Times* (1907).

26 ERO, Poll Book 1710.

27 ERO, Q/SR 1019.

28 ERO, D/DTu 235.

29 For the vestry minutes, see ERO, D/P 109/8/4–5.

30 ERO, D/P 109/8/4.

31 ERO, D/P 109/8/4–5.

32 Stansted's response to question 22 in the Report of the Commission on the Poor Laws, 1834.

33 Saffron Walden Museum, Papers of J.J. Green, List of Overseers of the Poor of Stansted Mountfitchet in the handwriting of Thomas Heath.

34 Though in the seventeenth century Sir Thomas Myddleton, like several of the squires around, attached so much importance to the roads that he became one of the surveyors himself. See ERO, D/P 109/8/4 and F.H. Maud, op. cit., pp. viii, 77, 129.

Organised religion and education in the parish

35 T.W. Davids, *Annals of Evangelical Nonconformity in the County of Essex* (1863), pp. 473–4.

36 ERO, D/P 109/1/2.

37 Guildhall Library, Churchwardens' Presentments, Ms 9,583 series.

38 ERO, D/P 109/1/2.

39 Guildhall Library, Ms 9,583/14.

40 The Independents were the leading Nonconformists in Essex as a whole. In 1829, out of 57,984 Dissenters, 30,919 were Independents.

41 Davids, op. cit., p. 474. For the early history of the church in Stansted, see ERO, D/NC 2/1/1.

42 Guildhall Library, Ms 9,583/11 and Ms 9,583/14.
43 For a discussion of this, see Jeffrey Weeks, *Sex, Politics and Society* (1981), pp. 61–4.
44 Wendy Walker, *Essex Markets and Fairs* (1981). See also R.W. Malcolmson, *Popular Recreations in English Society 1700–1850* (1973), p. 149.
45 R. Burls, *A brief review of the plan and operations of the Essex Congregational Union* (1848), pp. 12, 32.
46 Guildhall Library, Gibson Papers, Ms 25,751, Episcopal Visitation, 1727.
47 ERO, D/NC 2/13.
48 See, e.g., *Pigot's Directory* 1839.
49 Peter Laslett, *The World We Have Lost – Further Explored* (1983), pp. 232–33.

Chapter 3 Poverty and prosperity

1 See, e.g., the accounts presented by Thomas Stock in 1718: ERO, D/P 109/5/2.
2 Cecil Deedes and E.J. Wells, 'The Church Bells of Essex', *Essex Review*, IV, 1895, p. 184.
3 ERO, D/P 109/8/4.
4 Mr Robert Buck, a draper from Ugley, had left land in his will in 1620 from which the proceeds were to pay for the gift, every year, of cloth for six suits of clothes, together with hats, shoes and stockings, to three poor men and three poor women, who had to be 'of honest name and fame'. Three villages were to benefit, Stansted, Manuden and Ugley, each every third year, and in Stansted, when 'Mr Buck's gift' was not made, Sir Thomas Myddleton made a gift himself. See *The Reports of the Commissioners appointed . . . to enquire concerning Charities . . . relating to the County of Essex*, 1819–1837, pp. 695–6. See also the notice-board in Manuden Church.
5 ERO, D/P 109/25/1.
6 ERO, D/ABR/15/120, Will of Matthias Palmer. See also ERO, D/DWv M30.
7 ERO, D/P 109/3/1–2.
8 ERO, D/ABR 21/189.
9 ERO, D/ABR 23/88, Will of Ann Peacock. See also ERO, D/DHt T207/2.
10 It is possible that the John Sanders who was an elector in 1722 was the first John Sanders and not the second. It seems unlikely, however, since the first John does not appear in any previous list of electors and the second John was certainly qualified by as early as 1734.
11 Morant, op. cit., Vol. II, p. 579.
12 ERO, D/P 109/3/2.
13 ERO, D/ABR 25/95, Will of Richard Piggott.
14 ERO, D/P 109/12/4–5.
15 ERO, D/P 109/12/3.
16 Guiver was the maiden name of Margaret Piggott, his maternal grandmother, and he was probably named after one of her family.
17 ERO, D/ABR 35/566.
18 ERO, D/P 272/25/2. John Clarke was one of 'Twenty poor persons' in Manuden who received 'Mr Gardiner's Gift'.
19 ERO, D/DGl M10A, p. 146, D/NC 2/7.
20 ERO, Q/RJ 1/12.
21 Hertfordshire Record Office, Land Tax Assessments for Bishop's Stortford, 1815–31. See

also W.J. Hardy, (ed.), *Hertford County Records: Sessions Books* (1931), Vol. IX, p. 557.

22 For Guiver's property, see ERO, D/DGl M10–10A, 12, court rolls of Bentfieldbury manor; ERO, D/DBb T63; ERO, D/DMd 179; ERO, D/NC 2/7; ERO, D/ABR 35/566; deeds in the possession of Dr and Mrs Robinson of the Old Manse and Mr and Mrs Peck of Roycot.

23 The particulars of sale, which are incomplete, are in the possession of Irving Sanders' family. See also the advertisement in *The Chelmsford Chronicle*, 15 May 1835.

24 For the use of coal, now more available because of the Stort Navigation, see Arthur Young, *General View of the Agriculture of Essex* (1807), Vol. II, pp. 380–1.

25 'An Account of the Population of the Parish of Stanstead Mountfitchet in the County of Essex. Taken on Monday, May 27, 1811, and following days'. Photostat in possession of Irving Sanders' family.

26 ERO, D/P 109/3/4, Q/RPl 922.

27 Arthur Sanders, the builder referred to on p. 49, was born in Braintree c. 1837 but returned to Stansted as a boy. I have been unable to find any record of his birth. Mary Gentry, who is referred to on p. 000, was the daughter of Thomas Sanders, the oldest son of Guiver and Elizabeth, and was born and brought up in Stansted.

28 This pattern was not unusual. Cp. the history of the Brands, who were blacksmiths in the Essex village of Elmdon, in Jean Robin, *Elmdon: Continuity and Change in a North-West Essex Village 1861–1964* (1980), pp. 174–79.

29 These details are taken from the court records of Bentfieldbury and Thremhall Priory manors in the ERO, both of which are indexed. See also George Sanders' will, ERO, D/ABR 25.

30 ERO, Q/SPb 9 and Q/SR 666.

31 ERO, D/P 109/12/1B–5, *passim* for payments to George Sanders' wife and children.

32 ERO, Q/RTg 1, Register of Gamekeepers. We can be fairly sure that the John Sanders referred to in the Register is Guiver's elder brother because of the reference to John Sanders, aged 72, 'formerly Gamekeeper and Tithe Collector to the Lord of the said Manor' in ERO, D/DGl M32, 'A Perambulation of the Boundary of the Manor of Bentfield Bury', 1814. John's signature on that document is almost identical with that on his carpenter's bill, ERO, D/P 109/21/1.

33 ERO, D/P 109/3/4.

34 ERO, D/P 109/15, bond dated 3 August 1777.

35 ERO, Q/SPb 18 and Q/SR 962.

36 ERO, Q/SMc 2.

37 ERO, Q/SPb 18, Q/SR 962, Q/RSc 1/2.

38 ERO, Q/RLv series.

39 ERO, D/ABR 34/234, Will of Joseph Sanders.

Chapter 4 The carpenter's shop

1 ERO, D/P 109/3/2.

2 ERO, D/P 109/3/2.

3 ERO, D/P 109/5/1 and D/P 109/21/1 and 22/1.

4 Walter Rose, *The Village Carpenter* (1937, republished 1973).

5 Rose, op. cit., pp. 35–6.

6 A tax was levied on apprentices between 1710 and 1808. The records relating to it are in the

References

Public Record Office. Two indices of apprentices have been made, one covering 1710–62 and the other 1762–74, and the first of these covers masters as well as apprentices. These are in the Library of the Society of Genealogists.

7   ERO, D/P 109/3/2. For a 'ringe', see James Britten, *Old Country and Farming Words*, p. 107: 'The farmer cuts and lays the growth [of wood] indiscriminately as it arises in rows, called *ringes*, and sells them at so much a *ringe*, or so much a rod.'

8   ERO, D/P 109/12/11.

9   *Chelmsford Chronicle*, 2 October 1807.

10 Rose, op. cit., p. 37.

11 A.H. Byng and S.M. Stephens, (eds.), *John Wilkins: The Autobiography of an English Gamekeeper* (1892), p. 96.

12 J.G. Geare, *Farnham Past and Present*, p. 108.

13 ERO, D/P 109/12 series and references in fn. 3 above.

14 ERO, D/P 109/12/1.

15 ERO, D/DMd 205.

16 Rose, op. cit., p. 38.

Chapter 5 Status and belief

1   ERO, D/ABR 25/95, Will of Richard Piggott.

2   Deeds in the possession of Dr and Mrs Robinson.

3   ERO, D/P 109/8/4.

4   ERO, D/P 109/9.

5   See, e.g., Dr Williams's Library, L 52/4/43, John Sanders to Revd John Blackburn, 22 April 1822.

6   ERO, D/ABR 21/189.

7   ERO, Poll Books for 1722, 1734, 1763 and 1768.

8   ERO, Q/RPe 1.

9   ERO, Q/RPe 2.

10 Anon.: *Essex County Election. Report of the Speeches delivered at the Hustings, and of the interesting proceedings during the contest of fifteen days, for the representation of the county of Essex, Commencing on Friday, the 6th of August, 1830, and terminating on Monday, the 23rd* (1830).

11 ERO, Q/RPe 5.

Chapter 6 The Independent Church

1   ERO, D/NC 2/2/1, Church Book of the New Meeting. Except where otherwise indicated, this chapter is based on the Church Books of the Old and New Meetings, D/NC 2/1/1 and D/NC 2/2/1.

2   Dr Williams's Library, New College MSS L 52/4/44, W. Chaplin to J. Blackburn, 14 May 1822.

3   See, e.g., ERO, D/NC 2/7.

4   William Sanders, son of Edward and Mary Sanders, was born in Finchingfield in 1802. He was clearly connected with the Sanders of Stansted. As a boy he took part in the perambulation of Bentfieldbury manor in 1814 and gave his occupation as a carpenter, and as a man he rented property from Guiver and witnessed his will. It seems most likely that his father, Edward, was one of the sons of Guiver's elder brother, John. None of John's children was baptized in the Anglican Church, and they were probably baptized in the Independent Church, whose register for this period no longer survives.

5   Mark Rutherford (pen-name of William Hale White), *Autobiography* and *Deliverance*, (2nd ed. 1888), pp. 5–8.

6   In the Church Book Redford says that William Sanders made this protest. In a contemporary letter (Dr Williams's Library, New College MSS, L 52/4/22, Redford to Blackburn, 11 Feb. 1822), he gives Blackaby's name, and this must be right since Blackaby was a member and William Sanders was not.

7   Dr Williams's Library, MS 201.41(h), 118, W. Chaplin to T. Wilson, 25 April 1822, gives a third account, making no mention of the trust deed. Chaplin writes 'that the final resignation was universally understood to be occasioned by your and Mr Clayton's presence, with a determination to make some public communication if he did not give way.' Chaplin may well be right in saying that the fear of wider disgrace was a factor, but he does not seem to have been present at the meeting and Redford's account is probably the more reliable.

8   Dr Williams's Library, MS 201.41(h), 118, W. Chaplin to T. Wilson, 25 April 1822.

9   Dr Williams's Library, MS 201.41(h), 120, R. May to T. Wilson, 28 November 1825 and New College MSS, 299/49, R. May to T. Wilson, 30 November 1831.

10 ERO, Q/CR 3/2/99.

11 Dr Williams's Library, MS 201.41(h), 120, R. May to T. Wilson, 28 November 1825.

12 John Clyde Goodfellow Binfield, 'Nonconformity in the Eastern Counties 1840–1885, With References to Its Social Background' (Ph.D. thesis, Cambridge, 1965), p. 248.

13 Will of John Sanders, 1842, in possession of Irving Sanders' family.

14 The plaque is no longer there, but is remembered by older people in Stansted who went to Sunday School in the building. See also the reference to it in ERO, T/P 68/37/1, notes by J.J. Green.

Chapter 8 A leather purse and twelve gold sovereigns

1   For the details of this case, see ERO, Q/SBd 11/6/7, and Q/SMc 6; *Chelmsford Chronicle*, 10 and 17 June, 8 July 1836.

2   ERO, P/HM 2, entries for 15 and 28 December 1836, and J. Cunnington's letter to C.G. Parker, 30 December 1836, Q/SMc 6.

Chapter 9 The Falcon and the town of Braintree

1   T. Wright, *The History and Topography of the County of Essex* (1836), Vol. II, p. 16.

2   It is now a shop, Halford's, but apparently the old inn was pulled down before the shop was built.

References

3   At the time of the 1841 census, when the Cooks were running the house, there were no lodgers, and they had only one living-in servant.
4   For the brewing industry at this time, see Sidney and Beatrice Webb, *The History of Liquor Licensing in England, principally from 1700 to 1830* (1903), pp. 118–31, and Peter Clark, *The English Alehouse: a social history 1200–1830* (1983), pp. 263–6.
5   ERO, Q/RLv series.
6   ERO, D/P 264/11/42.
7   Except where otherwise indicated, this account of Braintree is based on Michael Baker, *The Book of Braintree and Bocking* (1981) and W.F. Quin, *A History of Braintree and Bocking* (1981).
8   ERO, Accessions 5052: John Cunnington, 'A History of the Ancient Town of Braintree' (1833), Vol. II, p. 137.
9   *The Braintree and Bocking Advertiser*, 13 December 1871.
10 Cunnington, op. cit., Vol. II, pp. 137–8.
11 Cunnington, op. cit., Vol. II, pp. 134–5.
12 W.F. Quin, op. cit., p. 229. This appears to have been better than the national average: see Geoffrey Best, *Mid-Victorian Britain* (1971, new ed. 1973), pp. 115–7.
13 For the silk industry, in addition to Baker and Quin, see John Booker, *Essex and the Industrial Revolution* (1974) pp. 54–61; Alec B. Hunter, *A History of Warner & Sons Limited* (1949) and Hester Bury, *A Choice of Design, 1850–1950* (1981).
14 *The Braintree and Bocking Advertiser*, 2 September 1874.
15 Quoted in Baker, op. cit., p. 130.
16 *The Braintree and Bocking Advertiser*, 10 November 1880.
17 For the quotations, see *The Braintree and Bocking Advertiser*, 29 July 1868, 18 August 1869 and 9 July 1890, and Hunter, op. cit., p. 9.
18 *The Braintree and Bocking Advertiser*, 2 September 1874.
19 *The Braintree and Bocking Adveriser*, 11 October 1893.
20 For this correspondence, see *The Braintree and Bocking Advertiser*, 24 November, 1 and 8 December 1869.
21 *The Braintree and Bocking Advertiser*, 10 November 1880.
22 For a general discussion of these issues, see Peter Laslett, *Family Life and Illicit Love in Earlier Generations* (1977), pp. 106–7; Jeffrey Weeks, *Sex, Politics and Society* (1981), pp. 57–76; John Burnett (ed.), *Destiny Obscure: Autobiographies of childhood, education and family from the 1820s to the 1920s* (1983; paperback 1984), p. 256.
23 ERO, Q/RSc 1/2.
24 *Chelmsford Chronicle*, 29 August and 5 September 1834.
25 ERO, P/HM 21.
26 ERO, P/HM 24.
27 Information from Mr John Corley.

Chapter 10 The dealer and the gypsy: a family of poor repute

1   There are many references to the Grays in the *Journal of the Gypsy Lore Society (JGLS)*: see, e.g., the articles by Thomas William Thompson, 'Borrow's Gypsies', *JGLS*, New Series, Vol. III, 1909–10, p. 167; 'The Gypsy Grays as Tale Tellers', *JGLS*, Third Series, Vol. I,

1922, pp. 118–21; 'Gleanings from Constables' Accounts and Other Sources', *JGLS*, Third Series, Vol. VII, 1928, pp. 40–1. See also Sydney Jones Library, Liverpool University, Scott Macfie Collection, Notes, including a folder on the Grays, by Revd George Hall; and William A. Dutt, 'With the East Anglian Gypsies', *Good Words*, Jan. 1896, pp. 120–6.

2 Thompson, 'Borrow's Gypsies', op. cit.

3 Cambridgeshire Record Office, Q/S 06, p. 121.

4 See, e.g., Cambridgeshire Record Office, Q/S 014, p. 207, a case involving Ambrose Gray, a tinker, in 1824.

5 ERO, D/P 264/1/36, marriage of Jacob Andrews and Sarah Clark, 25 December 1839.

6 ERO, Q/RSc 1/6.

7 ERO, D/P 264/11 series: Overseers' Rates.

8 In the census of 1881 they are recorded as living on Hoppit Hill, which was later renamed as the Notley Road, with their son Fred and his family living a few doors away. We know from the electoral registers that from 1889 at least the two families were living in this way on Rifle Hill. Rifle Hill is not listed in the 1881 census, and since side roads were sometimes not named under the main roads, it seems probable that Rifle Hill was included under Hoppit Hill. Charles Sanders first appears in the Black Notley Highway Rate Book in 1878. He is recorded as having cottages and a garden to the annual value of £4 5s.: ERO, D/P 150/20/3.

9 *The Braintree and Bocking Advertiser*, 2 May 1894. 'SUDDEN DEATH. Mr Coroner Harrison was informed on Saturday of the sudden death of a widow named Saunders, of Rifle-hill, Black Notley. Death was due to natural causes; and no inquest will therefore be held.'

10 Unless Emily Sanders was the same person, which perhaps she was, as the 'refractory pauper' of that name in the Union Workhouse who was sentenced to fourteen days hard labour for refusing to do some washing in 1870: *The Braintree and Bocking Advertiser*, 9 February 1870.

11 *The Braintree and Bocking Advertiser*, 4 May 1892.

12 For these cases, see *The Braintree and Bocking Advertiser*, 6 March 1872, 21 October 1874, 19 September 1877, 12 December 1883, 1 September 1886, 23 May 1888. There was another family of Sanders at Stisted, two or three miles east of Braintree, including a Charles Sanders born in 1852, and several of them were poachers too. It is not always clear which family is being referred to, and the text is confined to those cases in which it is clear that the Sanders of Black Notley were involved.

13 *The Braintree and Bocking Advertiser*, 14 September and 26 October 1870.

14 ERO, P/HR 5.

15 ERO, P/HM 14.

16 On two other documents on which his father's details were needed, on the admissions register of the Manor Street school in 1887 (ERO, E/MA 67/1) and his marriage certificate in 1899, his grandfather's details were given instead – Charles Sanders, calf dealer of Rifle Hill, Black Notley.

17 Weeks, op. cit., pp. 75–6.

18 Charlotte Cook had been present at the death of Charles Sanders, the two-year-old son of Charlie and Jessamy: see his death certificate, 29 November 1850.

19 *The Braintree and Bocking Advertiser*, 10 November 1880. For Mary Gentry, see chapter 3, fn. 27.

20 ERO, E/MA 67/1, Register of Admissions to Manor Street Junior Mixed School, in which 'Russel' is clearly a mistake for Basil.
21 *The Braintree and Bocking Advertiser*, 4 May 1892; ERO, P/HM 17 and P/HR 2.

Chapter 12 The Galleys in Stratford

1 These arrangements were not always the same. For a time one of the rooms upstairs was used as the living room.

Chapter 13 The borough of Bethnal Green

1 Raphael Samuel, (ed.), *East End Underworld: Chapters in the Life of Arthur Harding* (1981), p. vii. Harding, who was born in the Nichol, sometimes talks of the Mount as if it were part of it, and sometimes as if it were close to it: see Samuel, op. cit., pp. 1, 7 and 222.
2 More precisely, that part of it which was then called Tyssen Street.
3 Mrs Basil Holmes, *The London Burial Grounds* (1896), p. 295.
4 Hector Gavin, *Sanitary Ramblings* (1848), p. 42.
5 Gareth Stedman Jones, *Outcast London* (1971; paperback 1984), pp. 219–20.
6 John Reeves, *Recollections of a School Attendance Officer* (1913), p. 31.
7 Report of the Medical Officer of Health for St Matthew, Bethnal Green, November 1883.
8 Housing of the Working Class in London (London County Council, 1913), p. 30.
9 John Henry Mackay, *The Anarchists* (1891), pp. 169–71.
10 A. Fried and R. Elman, (eds.), *Charles Booth's London* (1969, paperback edition 1971), pp. 54–5.
11 See, e.g., Arthur Morrison, *A Child of the Jago* (1896; paperback edition 1982), p. 165.
12 On employment in the East End during this period, see in particular Charles Booth, (ed.), *Life and Labour of the People in London* (1896); P.G. Hall, *The Industries of London since 1861* (1962); Stedman Jones, op. cit.; Colm Kerrigan, *A History of Tower Hamlets* (1982), pp. 24–37.
13 Peter Laslett, *The World We Have Lost – Further Explored* (1983), p. 246.
14 See, e.g., Reeves, op. cit., p. 32.
15 Quoted in P.J. Keating, introduction to Arthur Morrison, op. cit., p. 25.
16 Morrison, op. cit., pp. 45, 113.
17 Keating, op. cit., p. 32.
18 Samuel, op. cit., pp. 1, 222.
19 Peter Keating, (ed.), *Into Unknown England 1866–1913* (1976), pp. 11–32; Stedman Jones, op. cit., pp. 281–314.
20 Henry Walker, *East London: Sketches of Christian Work and Workers* (1896), p. 79.
21 Samuel, op. cit., p. 2.
22 On the churches and missions in this area, see Walker, op. cit., pp. 71–100; 'F.W.M.' (F.W. McPherson), *'The Nichol' 1836–1936* (1936?).
23 Samuel, op. cit., p. 26.
24 Walker, op. cit., pp. 84–9.

25 Walker, op. cit., pp. 89–92; Phyllis Thompson, *No Bronze Statue: a Living Documentary of the Mildmay Mission Hospital in the East End of London* (1972).

26 K.S. Inglis, *Churches and the Working Classes in Victorian England* (1963), pp. 143–74; Anon., *The Oxford House in Bethnal Green 1884–1948*; Mandy Ashworth, *The Oxford House in Bethnal Green* (1984?), pp. 7–9.

27 'The "Missionary", A Review of Twelve Years' Work in the Nichol Street District, Shoreditch', *The London City Magazine*, September 1894, p. 226.

28 Anon., *The Oxford House in Bethnal Green 1884–1948*, p. 34.

29 For a general discussion on the churches and the working classes, see Inglis, op. cit. The quotation from Walsham How is on p. 323; from Keir Hardie on p. 229.

30 Kerrigan, op. cit., p. 54.

31 Inglis, op. cit., pp. 173–4.

32 Inglis, op. cit., p. 225.

33 'The "Missionary"', op. cit., p. 225.

34 Stedman Jones, op. cit., pp. xvi, 337–49.

35 Inglis, op. cit., p. 336.

36 Gareth Stedman Jones, 'Working-Class Culture and Working-Class Politics in London, 1870–1900: Notes on the Remaking of a Working Class', in *Languages of Class* (1983), pp. 179–238.

37 See, e.g., James H. Robb, *Working-Class Anti-Semite* (1954), p. 193; Ruth Glass and Maureen Frenkel, 'How They Live in Bethnal Green', in A.G. Weidenfeld and H. de C. Hastings, *Britain between East and West* (1946), p. 40.

38 John Stevenson, *British Society 1914–45* (1984), pp. 203–5; Bethnal Green Sanitary Condition Reports in Tower Hamlets Local History Library; Sir Hubert Llewellyn Smith (ed.), *The New Survey of London Life and Labour*, Vol. III (1932), p. 345.

39 Glass and Frenkel, op. cit., pp. 39, 43; Robb, op. cit., pp. 47–9; Smith, op. cit., Vol. III, p. 345.

40 *The Oxford House Magazine*, May 1928, pp. 10–11; Stevenson, op. cit., pp. 192–3.

41 Samuel, op. cit., p. 236.

42 Stevenson, op. cit., pp. 118–9, 271.

43 Stevenson, op. cit., p. 163.

44 Stevenson, op. cit., pp. 125–7.

45 Glass and Frenkel, op. cit., p. 40.

46 Smith, op. cit., Vol. III, pp. 345–6.

47 Samuel, op. cit., p. 344.

48 *The Oxford House Magazine*, May 1933, p. 7.

49 Quoted in Stevenson, op. cit., p. 50.

50 *The Oxford House Magazine*, May 1933, p. 7.

51 Robert Skidelsky, *Oswald Mosley* (1981), p. 393.

52 Robb, op. cit., pp. 92, 98–100.

53 See the club's annual reports and other documents kept by The New Cambridge Boys' Club, Bethnal Green.

54 Stevenson, op. cit., pp. 382–3.

References

Chapter 14 The family in Bethnal Green

1   Fried and Elman, op. cit., p. 250.

Chapter 15 Princes Court

1   Samuel, op. cit., pp. 180–2.
2   On violence between husbands and wives at this time, see Jerry White, *The Worst Street in North London: Campbell Bunk, Islington, between the Wars* (1986), pp. 139–47.
3   Samuel, op. cit., p. 279.

Chapter 17 Earning a living

1   For information about the Cropper machine, I am indebted to Nigel Roach of the St Bride Printing Library. On terms and conditions, see John Child, *Industrial Relations in the British Printing Industry* (1967).
2   It was common for wives not to know how much their husbands earned. See, e.g., Peter Townsend, *The Family Life of Old People* (1957; paperback 1963), p. 82.
3   In 1911 only 40 per cent of printers were trade unionists: John Burnett, *Useful Toil* (1973; paperback 1983), p. 330.
4   Gail Braybon, *Women Workers in the First World War* (1981), pp. 46, 62, 114, 160.
5   See p. 129 below. The Sanders remember this as being at the age of sixteen. But see also Jerry White, op. cit., p. 163: 'The circulation of labour within it [i.e. the labour market for boys] was broken at two points – at sixteen and eighteen years. Until 1934, sixteen was the age employers had to begin paying National Insurance contributions; and eighteen was the age most youths sought an adult wage and employers sought cheaper labour.'

Chapter 20 The Nichol Street Mission

1   It may well be the Gibraltar Walk Mission that is so vividly described by George Acorn, *One of the Multitude* (1911), pp. 140–54.
2   F.W. McPherson, *The Stock Exchange – a market for enterprise* (1948).
3   This is not a Biblical text, and my father cannot now say where it came from.

Chapter 22 On and off the streets

1   *The Oxford House Magazine* (OHM), November 1929, p. 24.
2   *OHM*, November 1931, pp. 12–13.
3   *The Oxford House in Bethnal Green: Report*, 1934, p. 17.

4   *OHM*, May 1928, p. 7.
5   *OHM*, May 1933, p. 7.
6   *OHM*, November 1936, pp. 7, 13–15. See also Mandy Ashworth, *The Oxford House in Bethnal Green* (1984?), pp. 37–8.
7   *OHM*, November 1927, p. 19.
8   The last quotation is from Ashworth, op. cit., p. 35.
9   *OHM*, May 1931, p. 22.
10 *OHM*, May 1928, p. 11.
11 *Ibid.*
12 Ashworth, op. cit., pp. 30, 35.
13 Apart from the club's annual reports and magazine, see Sidney Blunt, *Jewish Youth Work in Britain: Past Present and Future* (1975), pp. 125–31.
14 *The Blue Anchor* (the club's magazine), March 1938, p. 7.
15 News sheet, 25 October 1938.
16 *The Blue Anchor*, June 1938, p. 3.
17 *The Blue Anchor*, November 1938, p. 4.

Chapter 24 Husband and father, wife and mother

1   This was clearly a common working class pattern. See, e.g., Bill Williamson, *Class, Culture and Community: A Biographical Study of Social Change in Mining* (1982), p. 136.
2   For a 'good neighbour' in Bethnal Green, see Townsend, op. cit., p. 140. He, or she, is 'someone who did not expect to spend time in your house or pry into your life, who exchanged a civil word in the street or over the backyard fence, who did not make a great deal of noise, who could supply a drop of vinegar or a pinch of salt if you ran short, and who fetched your relatives or the doctor in emergencies.'

Chapter 25 The Cockrells: the shadow of the workhouse

1   Greater London Record Office, Is.B.G./286/29, 310/4 and 277/8.
2   George R. Sims, *Off the Track in London* (1911), pp. 197–212.
3   It was Hoxton Academy which had trained ministers for Independent churches, including the church at Stansted. Thomas Wilson, the treasurer, who played a large part in the scandal of Josiah Redford, had purchased the land on the main street of Hoxton where the Academy's Sunday School was built.
4   Greater London Record Office, HSG/Gen/2/16: Owen Fleming, 'Working-Class Dwellings – the Rebuilding of the Boundary Street Estate', p. 7.

Select Bibliography

Place of publication given only if outside London.

PART I: ESSEX

1. Manuscript Sources

A. Public record repositories

Cambridgeshire Record Office
Isleham parish registers (transcript).

Dr Williams's Library, London
MS 201. 41(h) series. Letters from churches in Essex preserved in the Congregational Library.
New College MSS. See references in index to William Chaplin, R.E. May, Josiah Redford, Stansted and Stansted congregation.

Essex Record Office
Deeds, in particular:
   D/DBb T62 (deeds relating to The Three Colts public house, Stansted);
   D/DHt T207/2 (indenture, 13 August 1743, relating to property of John Sanders);
   D/DMd series (deeds relating to Bardfield, Stebbing and Stansted, 1544–1908).

Educational records:
   E/MA 67/1 (admissions register of Manor Street School, Braintree).

Manorial records:
   D/DGl M series (Bentfieldbury manor);
   D/DWv M series (Thremhall Priory manor).

Marriage licences:
for family references, see R.H. Browne's Index, D/AZ 3/1–3.

Nonconformist records:
D/NC 2 series (relating to Independent Church in Stansted).

Parish records, in particular:
D/P 109 series (Stansted Mountfitchet);
D/P 150 series (Black Notley);
D/P 264 series (Braintree).

Petty Sessions records:
P/HM and P/HR series, relating to South Hinckford Division.

Quaker records, in particular:
T/A 285, relating to the Stansted Preparative Meeting.

Quarter Sessions records, in particular:
Q/CR 2/5–12 (census returns);
Q/CR 3/2/99 (calendar of Nonconformist chapels, Stansted, 1829);
Q/RDc 36A (Stansted Mountfitchet enclosure award, 1848);
Q/RJ 1 series (Essex books of freeholders);
Q/RLv series (records of licensed victuallers, 1769–1832);
Q/RPe 1–10 (poll books);
Q/RPl series (Land Tax assessments);
Q/RSc series (conviction books, 1791–1915);
Q/SBd 11/6, 7 (including papers on prosecution of Charles Sanders, 1836);
Q/SMc and Q/SMr series (calendars of prisoners and recognizance books);
Q/SPb series (process books of indictments);
Q/SR (sessions rolls);
Q/RTh series (Hearth Tax returns, 1662–73, supplemented by T/A 169, microfilm
of Hearth Tax returns in Public Record Office);
Q/RTg 1–3 (Game Duty registers, 1784–1806).

Tithe commutation map and schedule for Stansted, 1843:
D/CT 328.

Wills:
D/ABR series. For family references, see index in F.G. Emmison (ed.), *Wills at Chelmsford*, 3 vols. (1958, 1961 and 1969).

John Cunnington's unpublished manuscript, 'A History of the Ancient Town of Braintree' (1833). Accessions 5052.

Select Bibliography

Guildhall Library
Churchwardens' presentments: Ms 9,583 series.
Diocese book, 1770–1812: Ms 9,557.
Episcopal visitations, 1723–47: Gibson Papers, Ms 25,750–55.

Hertfordshire Record Office
Land Tax assessments for Bishop's Stortford, 1815–31.

Public Record Office
Census records relating to Black Notley, Braintree and Stansted Mountfitchet.
Stansted Independents: Old Meeting: Register of Baptisms: R.G. 4 1077.
Stansted Independents: New Meeting: Register of Baptisms: R.G. 4 2541.

Registrar of Births, Marriages and Deaths, London
Certificates of births, marriages and deaths from 1837 onwards.

Saffron Walden Museum
Papers of J.J. Green relating to the history of Stansted.

Society of Genealogists' Library, London
Indices to apprenticeship records in Public Record Office, 1710–62 and 1762–74.

Sydney Jones Library, Liverpool University
Scott Macfie Collection: Notes, including a folder on the Gray Family, by Revd George
  Hall.

B. Private Papers

Mr Aubrey Levey (of Chapel Hill, Stansted):
  carpenter's notebook, 1802 onwards.
Mr and Mrs Peck:
  deeds relating to 'Roycot', Silver Street, Stansted.
Dr and Mrs Robinson:
  deeds relating to 'The Old Manse', Silver Street, Stansted.
Family of Mr Irving Sanders (of the Recreation Ground, Stansted):
  many papers, but in particular:
    'An Account of the Population of Stanstead Mountfitchet in the County of Essex
    Taken on Monday, May 27, 1811, and following days': a photostat;
    particulars of sale of property of Guiver Sanders, 1835;
    will of John Sanders, 1842.

2. *Printed Sources*

A. *Primary Sources: Books and Articles*

Andrews, C. Bruyn (ed.), *The Torrington Diaries: a selection from the tours of the Hon. John Byng (later Fifth Viscount Torrington) between the years 1781 and 1794* (1954).

Anon. *Essex County Election. Report of the Speeches delivered at the Hustings, and of the interesting proceedings during the contest of fifteen days, for the representation of the county of Essex, Commencing on Friday, the 6th of August, 1830, and terminating on Monday, the 23rd* (Chelmsford, 1830).

Anon., 'Essex Elections', *Essex Review*, Vol. 2 (1893), pp. 224–30 and Vol. 3 (1894), pp. 86–92.

Brown, A.F.J. (ed.), *English History from Essex Sources, 1750–1900* (Chelmsford, 1952).

Burls, Robert, *A Brief Review of the Plan and Operations of the Essex Congregational Union* (Maldon, 1848).

Burnett, John (ed.), *Destiny Obscure: Autobiographies of Childhood, Education and Family from the 1820s to the 1920s* (1983; paperback 1984).

Burnett, John (ed.), *Useful Toil: Autobiographies of Working People from the 1820s to the 1920s* (1974; paperback 1984).

Byng, Arthur H., and Stephens, Stephen M. (eds). *The Autobiography of an English Gamekeeper, by John Wilkins* (1892; reprinted, Chesham, 1976).

Charity Commissioners, *The Reports of the Commissioners appointed . . . to enquire concerning Charities . . . relating to the County of Essex* (1819–1937).

Christian, Garth, (ed.), *James Hawker's Journal: a Victorian Poacher* (Oxford, 1961; paperback 1978).

Cobbett, William, *Cottage Economy* (1822: Oxford, 1979).

Dutt, A., 'With the East Anglian Gypsies', *Good Words*, January 1896, pp. 120–6.

Select Bibliography

Electoral Registers

Emmison, F.G. (ed.), *Essex Freeholders Book 1734* (Chelmsford, 1982).

The Essex Congregational Remembrancer (Bocking, 1827 onwards).

Forster, J. (ed.), *Selections from the Letters and Other Papers of William Grover, preceded by a biographical notice of his life* (London, 1828).

Kelly's Directory.

Morant, Philip, *History and Antiquities of the County of Essex* (2 vols., London, 1768).

Muilman, Peter, ('A Gentleman'), *People's History of Essex* (1772).

Pigot's Directory.

Poll Books 1694, 1702, 1710, 1715, 1722, 1734, 1763, 1768, 1774, 1810, 1812, 1830, 1830.

Poor Law Enquiry Commissioners, *Report of H.M. Commissioners on Poor Law*, no. 44 (1834).

Post Office Directory

Rose, Walter, *The Village Carpenter* (Cambridge, 1937).

Rutherford, Mark, *Autobiography* and *Deliverance* (2nd ed. 1888; reprinted Leicester, 1969).

Salmon, William, *The Country Builder's Estimator . . .* (Colchester, 1727?; many later editions, both by William Salmon himself and William Salmon the younger, with varying titles).

Vancouver, Charles, *General View of the Agriculture in the County of Essex* (1795).

Thompson, T.W., 'Borrow's Gypsies', *Journal of the Gypsy Lore Society*, New Series, Vol. III, 1909–10: 'The Gypsy Grays as Tale Tellers', *JGLS*, Third Series, Vol. I, 1922, pp. 118–21.

White's Directory

Wright, Thomas, *The History and Topography of the County of Essex* (2 vols., 1836).

Young, Arthur, *General View of the Agriculture of the County of Essex* (2 vols., 1807).

B. *Primary Sources: Newspapers*

Braintree and Bocking Advertiser
Braintree and Witham Times
Chelmsford Chronicle
Essex Herald

C. *Secondary Sources*

Baker, Michael, *The Book of Braintree and Bocking* (Chesham, 1981).

Bishop's Stortford and District Local History Society, *Bishop's Stortford: a Short History* (Bishop's Stortford, 2nd edition, 1973).

Brown, A.F.J., *Essex at Work 1700–1815* (Chelmsford, 1969).

Brown, A.F.J., *Chartism in Essex and Suffolk* (Chelmsford and Ipswich, 1982).

Bury, Hester, *A Choice of Design 1850–1980: Fabrics by Warner & Sons Limited* (1981).

Clark, Peter, *The English Alehouse, a Social History 1200–1830* (1983).

Crowther, M.A., *The Workhouse System 1834–1929: The History of an English Social Institution* (1981; paperback, 1983).

Davids, T.W., *Annals of Evangelical Nonconformity in the County of Essex from the time of Wycliffe to the Restoration* (1983).

Deedes, Cecil, and Wells, E.J., 'The Church Bells of Essex', *Essex Review*, Vol. 4 (1895), p. 184.

Dickin, E.P., 'Provision for Guests and Horses in Essex in 1686 and later', *Essex Review*, Vol. 53 (1944).

Duffy, Maureen, *Inherit the Earth: a Social History* (1980).

Fleming, Patricia Harvey, *Villagers and Strangers: An English Proletarian Village over Four Centuries* (Schenkman, Massachusetts, 1979).

Geare, J.G., *Farnham, Essex: Past and Present* (1909).

Select Bibliography

Hampson, E.M., *The Treatment of Poverty in Cambridgeshire, 1597–1834* (Cambridge, 1934).

Hey, David, *Family History and Local History in England* (1987).

Horn, Pamela, *The Rural World 1780–1850: Social Change in the English Countryside* (1980).

Houblon, Lady Alice Archer, *The Houblon Family: Its Story and Times* (1907).

Hunter, Alec B., *A History of Warner and Sons Limited* (Leigh-on-Sea, 1949).

Laslett, Peter, *Family life and illicit love in earlier generations* (Cambridge, 1977).

Laslett, Peter, *The World We Have Lost – Further Explored* (3rd edition, London, 1983).

Laslett, Peter, and Wall, Richard, (eds.), *Household and family in past time* (Cambridge, 1972).

Macfarlane, Alan, *The Family Life of Ralph Josselin, a Seventeenth Century Clergyman* (Cambridge, 1970).

Macfarlane, Alan, *Marriage and Love in England, 1300–1840* (Oxford, 1986).

Malcolmson, R.W., *Popular Recreations in English Society 1700–1850* (Cambridge, 1973).

Malcolmson, R.W., *Life and Labour in England 1700–1780* (1981).

Marshall, Dorothy, *The English Poor in the Eighteenth Century* (1926).

Maud, F.H., *The Hockerill Highway: the story of the origin and growth of a stretch of the Norwich road* (Colchester, 1957).

Mingay, G.E., *Rural Life in Victorian England* (1977).

Munsche, P.B., *Gentlemen and Poachers: The English Game Laws 1671–1831* (Cambridge, 1981).

Namier, Sir Lewis, and Brooke, John, *The History of Parliament: The House of Commons 1754–1790* (1964; reprinted with corrections 1985).

Orton, Ian, *The Book of Bishop's Stortford and Sawbridgeworth* (Chesham, 1976).

Oxley, Geoffrey W., *Poor Relief in England and Wales 1601–1834* (1974).

Pollock, Linda A., *Forgotten Children* (1983).

Pond, C.C., 'Eighteenth Century Migration and Mobility in Rural Essex', *Essex Journal*, Spring 1982, Vol. 17, No. 1.

Porter, Roy, *English Society in the Eighteenth Century* (1982).

Quin, W.F., *A History of Braintree and Bocking* (Braintree?, 1981).

Robin, Jean, *Elmdon: Continuity and change in a north-west Essex village, 1861–1964* (Cambridge, 1980).

Smith, J.R., *The Speckled Monster: Smallpox in England, 1670–1970, with particular reference to Essex* (Chelmsford, 1987).

Spufford, Margaret, *Contrasting Communities: English Villagers in the Sixteenth and Seventeenth Centuries* (Cambridge, 1974).

Stephenson, David, 'The Myddletons of Stansted Mountfitchet. A Seventeenth Century Gentry Family', *Transactions of the Essex Archaeological Society*, Vol. 8 (1976), pp. 282–7.

Stone, Lawrence, *The Family, Sex and Marriage in England 1500–1800* (1977; abridged and revised edition, 1979).

Walker, Wendy, *Essex Markets and Fairs* (Chelmsford, 1981).

Waugh, Alec, *Merchants of Wine: Being a Centenary Account of the Fortunes of the House of Gilbey* (1957).

Webb, Sidney and Beatrice, *The History of Liquor Licensing in England, principally from 1700 to 1830* (1903; reprinted 1963).

Weeks, Jeffrey, *Sex, Politics and Society: the regulation of sexuality since 1800* (1981).

Wrightson, Keith, *English Society 1580–1680* (1982).

Wrightson, Keith, and Levine, David, *Poverty and Piety in an English Village: Terling, 1525–1700* (1979).

Select Bibliography

Wrigley, E.A. (ed.), *An Introduction to English Historical Demography from the Sixteenth to the Nineteenth Century* (Cambridge, 1966).

Wrigley, E.A. and Schofield, R.S., *The Population History of England 1541–1871: a Reconstruction* (1981).

D. Unpublished Theses

Binfield, J.C.G., 'Nonconformity in the Eastern Counties, 1840–1885, with reference to its social background' (Ph.D. thesis, Cambridge, 1965).

Gyford, Janet, 'Men of Bad Character: Property Crime in Essex in the 1820s' (MA in Social History, University of Essex, 1982).

Thomas, E.G., 'The Parish Overseer in Essex, 1598–1834' (MA thesis, London University, 1956).

PART II: LONDON

1. Manuscript Sources

A. Public record repositories

Greater London Record Office and History Library

HSG/2/16. Fleming, Owen, 'Working-Class Dwellings – the Rebuilding of the Boundary Street Estate' (1900).

Is.B.G. 231/31; 277/8; 286/29; 310/4. Documents relating to the workhouse in St John's Road, Islington, and the infirmary on Highgate Hill, covering the year 1909 when the Cockrells were admitted.

Tower Hamlets Local History Library

Bethnal Green Sanitary Condition Reports, 1883–1898.

Bate, George Paddock, 'The Metropolitan Borough of Bethnal Green: Report on the Sanitary Condition and Vital Statistics during the Year 1909' (1910).

Valuation Returns for Bethnal Green, West Ward, 1905 onwards.

B. Private papers

Cambridge and Bethnal Green Boys' Club. Committee minutes, news sheets, magazines, members' records, etc.

Private papers in the author's possession. Notes and transcripts of interviews with members of the family, and numerous family papers.

2. Printed Sources

A. Primary Sources

Acorn, George, *One of the Multitude* (1911).

Booth, Charles, *Life and Labour of the People of London* (1892–7).

Gavin, Hector, *Sanitary Ramblings: Being Sketches and Illustrations of Bethnal Green* (1848).

Glass, Ruth, and Frenkel, Maureen, 'How They Live at Bethnal Green', in Weidenfeld, A.G., and Hastings, H. de C. (eds.), *Britain between East and West* (1946).

Jasper, A.S., *A Hoxton Childhood* (1969).

Jay, Revd A. Osborne, *Life in Darkest London* (1891).

Jay, Revd A. Osborne, *A Story of Shoreditch* (1896).

London County Council, *Housing of the Working Class in London* (1913).

Mackay, John Henry, *The Anarchists: a Picture of Civilization at the Close of the Nineteenth Century* (Boston, Massachusetts, 1891).

'The Missionary', 'A Review of Twelve Years' Work in the Nichol Street District, Shoreditch', *London City Magazine*, September 1894.

Morrison, Arthur, *A Child of the Jago* (1896; reprinted 1982).

The Oxford House Magazine

Redwood, Hugh, *God in the Slums* (undated).

Reeves, John, *Recollections of a School Attendance Officer* (1913).

Reeves, Maud Pember, *Round About a Pound a Week* (1913; reprinted 1979).

Select Bibliography

Robb, James H., *Working-Class Anti-Semite* (1954).

Samuel, Raphael, *East End Underworld. Chapters in the Life of Arthur Harding* (1981).

Sims, George R., *Off the Track in London* (1911).

Smith, Sir Hubert Llewellyn, *The New Survey of London Life and Labour* (nine volumes, 1930–35).

Townsend, Peter, *The Family Life of Old People* (1957; abridged edition, 1963).

Walker, Henry, *East London. Sketches of Christian Work and Workers* (1896).

White, Jerry, *Rothschild Buildings: Life in an East End tenement block 1887–1920* (1980).

White, Jerry, *The Worst Street in North London. Campbell Bunk, Islington, between the Wars* (1986).

Williamson, Bill, *Class, Culture and Community. A Biographical Study of Social Change in Mining* (1982).

Young, Michael, and Willmott, Peter, *Family and Kinship in East London* (1957).

B. Secondary Sources

Anon., *The Oxford House in Bethnal Green 1884–1948* (1948).

Ashworth, Mandy, *The Oxford House in Bethnal Green* (1984?).

Blunt, Sidney, *Jewish Youth Work in Britain: Past, Present and Future* (1975).

Braybon, Gail, *Women Workers in the First World War* (1981).

Briggs, Asa, and Macartney, Anne, *Toynbee Hall: the First Hundred Years* (1984).

Bush, Julia, *Behind the Lines. East London Labour 1914–1919* (1984).

Child, John, *Industrial Relations in the British Printing Industry* (1967).

Dictionary of National Biography. Sir Percy Alfred Harris (1876–1952).

Fried, Albert, and Elman, Richard (eds.), *Charles Booth's London* (1969; paperback edition, 1971).

Grant, Betty, *The Story of Joe Vaughan. First Labour Mayor of Bethnal Green* (1954).

Hall, P.G., *The Industries of London since 1861* (1962).

Holmes, Mrs Basil, *The London Burial Grounds. Notes on their history from the earliest times to the present day* (1896).

Inglis, K.S., *Churches and the Working Classes in Victorian England* (1963).

Jones, Gareth Stedman, *Outcast London* (Oxford, 1971).

Jones, Gareth Stedman, 'Working-Class Culture and Working-Class Politics in London, 1870–1900: Notes on the Remaking of a Working Class', in *Languages of Class* (Cambridge, 1983), pp. 179–238.

Keating, Peter (ed.), *Into Unknown England 1866–1913* (Manchester, 1976).

Kerrigan, Colm, *A History of Tower Hamlets* (1982).

Leslie, R.F., 'The Background of Jewish Immigration', *East London Papers*, Vol. 6, No. 2 (1963), pp. 69–78.

Lonsdale, Gillian 'The Changing Nature of East London Industry', *East London Papers*, Vol. 5, No. 2 (1962), pp. 91–102.

Marwick, Arthur, *British Society since 1945* (1982).

McPherson, F.W., 'The Nichol' *1836–1936* (1936?).

McPherson, F.W., *The Stock Exchange – a market for enterprise* (Leyton, 1948)

Oliver, J. Leonard, 'The East London Furniture Industry', *East London Papers*, Vol. 4, No. 2 (1961), pp. 88–101.

Skidelsky, Robert, *Oswald Mosley* (1975; revised edition 1981).

Smith, T. Harper, 'Re-Readings: 2 A Child of the Jago', *East London Papers*, Vol. 2, No. 1 (1959), pp. 39–47.

Steffel, R. Vladimir, 'The Evolution of a Slum Control Policy in the East End, 1889–1907', *East London Papers*, Vol. 13, No. 1 (1970), pp. 25–35.

Stevenson, John, *British Society 1914–45* (1984).

Thompson, Phyllis, *No Bronze Statue. A Living Documentary of the Mildmay Mission Hospital, in the East End of London* (1972).

Index

Index

Index

Index